Strengthening the Canadian Armed Forces through Diversity and Inclusion

The Canadian Armed Forces has not always embraced diversity and inclusion, but its future depends on it. As the country's demographic make-up changes, its military must adapt to a new multicultural reality and diminishing pools of people from which it can recruit. Canada's population is increasingly urbanized, immigrant, and not necessarily Christian, white, or bilingual. To attract and retain CAF personnel, the military will have to embrace and champion diversity while demonstrating that it is inclusive.

Using a number of cases to highlight both challenges and opportunities, *Strengthening the Canadian Armed Forces through Diversity and Inclusion* provides a timely look at an established Canadian institution in a rapidly changing world. The authors explore how Canadian Muslim youth, LGBTQ+ individuals, women, racialized minorities, Indigenous communities, and people of non-Christian faiths see their experiences in the CAF. While diversity is a reality, inclusion is still a work in progress for the Canadian Armed Forces, as it is for society at large.

(UTP Insights)

ALISTAIR EDGAR is the associate dean of the School of International Policy and Governance and associate professor in the Department of Political Science in the Balsillie School of International Affairs at Wilfrid Laurier University.

RUPINDER MANGAT has recently completed her PhD in Global Governance from the Balsillie School of International Affairs at Wilfrid Laurier University.

BESSMA MOMANI is a professor in the Department of Political Science at the University of Waterloo and the Balsillie School of International Affairs and Senior Fellow at the Centre for International Governance and Innovation and the Stimson Center.

T0339173

UTP insights

UTP Insights is an innovative collection of brief books offering accessible introductions to the ideas that shape our world. Each volume in the series focuses on a contemporary issue, offering a fresh perspective anchored in scholarship. Spanning a broad range of disciplines in the social sciences and humanities, the books in the UTP Insights series contribute to public discourse and debate and provide a valuable resource for instructors and students.

Books in the Series

- Alistair Edgar, Rupinder Mangat, and Bessma Momani (eds.), *Strengthening the Canadian Armed Forces through Diversity and Inclusion*
- David B. MacDonald, *The Sleeping Giant Awakens: Genocide, Indian Residential Schools, and the Challenge of Conciliation*
- Paul W. Gooch, *Course Correction: A Map for the Distracted University*
- Paul T. Phillips, *Truth, Morality, and Meaning in History*
- Stanley R. Barrett, *The Lamb and the Tiger: From Peacekeepers to Peacewarriors in Canada*
- Peter MacKinnon, *University Commons Divided: Exploring Debate and Dissent on Campus*
- Raisa B. Deber, *Treating Health Care: How the System Works and How It Could Work Better*
- Jim Freedman, *A Conviction in Question: The First Trial at the International Criminal Court*
- Christina D. Rosan and Hamil Pearsall, *Growing a Sustainable City? The Question of Urban Agriculture*
- John Joe Schlichtman, Jason Patch, and Marc Lamont Hill, *Gentrifier*
- Robert Chernomas and Ian Hudson, *Economics in the Twenty-First Century: A Critical Perspective*
- Stephen M. Saideman, *Adapting in the Dust: Lessons Learned from Canada's War in Afghanistan*
- Michael R. Marrus, *Lessons of the Holocaust*
- Roland Paris and Taylor Owen (eds.), *The World Won't Wait: Why Canada Needs to Rethink Its International Policies*
- Bessma Momani, *Arab Dawn: Arab Youth and the Demographic Dividend They Will Bring*
- William Watson, *The Inequality Trap: Fighting Capitalism Instead of Poverty*
- Phil Ryan, *After the New Atheist Debate*
- Paul Evans, *Engaging China: Myth, Aspiration, and Strategy in Canadian Policy from Trudeau to Harper*

STRENGTHENING THE CANADIAN ARMED FORCES THROUGH DIVERSITY AND INCLUSION

Edited by Alistair Edgar, Rupinder Mangat, and Bessma Momani

UNIVERSITY OF TORONTO PRESS
Toronto Buffalo London

© University of Toronto Press 2020
Toronto Buffalo London
utorontopress.com

Chapter 3 (Negotiating Gender Inclusion) is subject to Crown copyright and
may not be reproduced without written authorization.

ISBN 978-1-4875-0355-0 (cloth)   ISBN 978-1-4875-1822-6 (EPUB)
ISBN 978-1-4875-2273-5 (paper)   ISBN 978-1-4875-1821-9 (PDF)

Publication cataloguing information is available from Library and Archives
Canada.

University of Toronto Press acknowledges the financial assistance to its
publishing program of the Canada Council for the Arts and the Ontario Arts
Council, an agency of the Government of Ontario.

Canada Council
for the Arts
Conseil des Arts
du Canada

ONTARIO ARTS COUNCIL
CONSEIL DES ARTS DE L'ONTARIO
an Ontario government agency
un organisme du gouvernement de l'Ontario

Funded by the
Government
of Canada
Financé par le
gouvernement
du Canada

Canadä

Contents

Strengthening the Canadian Armed Forces through Diversity and Inclusion

chapter one

Unpacking Diversity and Inclusion

RUPINDER MANGAT, BESSMA MOMANI, AND ALISTAIR EDGAR

Diversity has become a management buzzword for national and international organizations today. Business magazines and newspapers extol the pursuit of diversity of personnel as being both necessary and valuable for these organizations, yet we rarely read any serious analyses about how it works in practice, and about the challenges that are involved. For most organizations and institutions, "diversity" entails demographics – race, gender, religion, ethnicity, sexuality, and/or disability. Adopting an active approach to diversity usually means promoting a policy of accepting those who are different, while inclusion means welcoming the contributions of diverse personnel to the operations and activities of an organization. Substantial academic research supports the potential importance of diversity to enhance organizational productivity, but the challenges in accomplishing such diversity are less explored. This book makes the case for diversity and inclusion in the Canadian Armed Forces (CAF) while examining and reflecting upon the inherent opportunities and obstacles to understanding and implementing diversity and inclusion.

In the Canadian Armed Forces Diversity Strategy, *diversity* is defined as "respect for and appreciation of differences in ethnicity, language, gender, age, national origin, disabilities, sexual orientation, education, and religion. It is about understanding each other and moving beyond simple tolerance to embracing, celebrating, and integrating the rich dimensions of diversity within each individual."[1] In moving to the "diversity within each individual" approach, the CAF opens up space for demographic diversity, and also for diversity of identity in more complex ways. This latter concept takes diversity to an individual level, considering the place and importance of invisible differences and intersectional identities. Moving towards individual diversity also tackles the resistance of some critics to the idea of "special treatment" accorded to those who are demographically different.[2]

Demographic diversity, in the more commonly used sense, still is a valuable goal because the basic, visible representation within the ranks of the CAF of different demographic groups in contemporary society allows all Canadians to picture themselves as part of the military. Counting "diverse" personnel in this more direct or "simple" manner has been the preferred way to measure organizational diversity, and it should continue to be implemented, even as more complex ways of measuring diversity are introduced. This demographic perspective, however, has its limitations. Most importantly, it differentiates some people on the basis of a particular version of "standard" or "normal." This is a concern for all organizations that seek to become more diverse and inclusive, including the Canadian military. Okros argues for a more personalized perspective on diversity: "Diversity is more about elements such as world views, belief systems, ethical frameworks, role obligations and other personal perspectives that reveal how individuals see themselves and perceive others and, more importantly, how they exercise independent reasoning and judgement."[3]

The move to a more complex consideration of individual diversity is an important break from the concept of demographic diversity because it acknowledges an often unstated or implicit assumption – the supposed sameness of the "straight white Christian male soldier" – which is a falsehood. Even the personalities of monozygotic (identical rather than fraternal) twins can be quite distinct, despite their sharing 100 per cent of their genetic material.[4] By taking an individual diversity approach, the CAF rejects the simple and simplistic notion of a typical soldier, against which all differences then are measured. Often differences are presumed to be inferior to the norm, problematic to the functioning of the military unit, and therefore, primarily a challenge to be overcome by training.

Why Diversity and Inclusion Are Valuable

Often the addition of diverse groups to a (presumably) homogeneous organization or institution has been driven by necessity or legal imperative. Clark lists three broad motivations for a military organization to change: first, external direction that overcomes military conservatism; second, internal direction that emanates from a visionary leader; or third, an institutional reaction to an external shock.[5] For the CAF, the initial forays into diversity were responses to the external shock of a paucity of personnel during the world wars, and external directions such as the Canadian Human Rights Tribunal rulings and the Canadian Charter of Rights and Freedoms' requirements to open military ranks to different demographic groups. In recent years, the CAF has leaped forward in promoting diversity and inclusion. As early as 1991, Chief of the Defence Staff General John de Chastelain had advised the government to lift the ban on gay and lesbian personnel serving in the Canadian military, but the federal government did not support the suggested policy change until the courts ruled that the ban encroached on the Charter rights of CAF personnel. At times the Canadian military has been ahead of the government and public opinion on diversity and inclusion, but equally or more often, it has been a laggard in embracing such change.

The military's incentives to encourage diversity and inclusion have increased in the past few years. For example, as Davis has argued, "Recent operational experiences (and in Afghanistan in particular) have highlighted the need for today's military leaders to adapt to new cultural settings and to effectively engage in a complexity of multicultural interactions within a dynamic landscape of potential belligerents and allies."[6] The CAF's engagement in Afghanistan brought home the importance of having – and also being able to make appropriate use of – diversity among its personnel. For example, in the Canadian Army documentary *Desert Lions: Canadian Forces Mentors in Kandahar*, Lieutenant-Colonel Mike Vernon notes that some members of the Canadian Operational Mentoring and Liaison Team struggled with the language barriers and cultural differences between themselves and the Afghan

National Army (ANA) personnel whom they were mentoring.[7] Corporal Kashif Dar's experience, however, was different. As a Pakistan-born, Urdu- and Punjabi-speaking Canadian soldier, the corporal brought these language and cultural capabilities into play as the Afghan National Army soldiers often came to Corporal Dar with their questions or concerns.[8] Dar's ethnicity and language skills made it much easier and more efficient for the Afghan soldiers or trainees to communicate with him, and in turn to learn to trust him and perhaps by extension the Canadian team. Diversity – demographic and otherwise – can play an important and even critical role in improving operational efficiency and effectiveness. Greater diversity can be a very real and practical asset for operational success in what can be highly challenging international (and possibly also domestic) missions.

The chapters presented in this volume point to five related, and practically grounded, arguments for why the Canadian Armed Forces should embrace diversity and inclusion:[9]

1. The **rise of identity politics** has empowered groups more actively to argue – and even to demand – that they should be considered for service in the military. This demand for diversity and inclusion can take the form of legal action by individuals from different identity groups. The military had advised that the ban against lesbian and gay people serving in the military be lifted, for example, but it would do well to remain proactive instead of waiting for cases to go to the courts. Chouinard, in this volume, notes that the disenfranchisement and frustration of French Canadians during and after the Second World War contributed to the Quiet Revolution, which culminated in the 1975 October Crisis. Failure to acknowledge the francophone identity, and the occasional deliberate dismissal of it, created a national crisis. The military had a role in the resolution of the crisis, and, as Chouinard notes, it remains a national symbol of the diverse identities of Canadians.

2. Including diverse groups from existing or evolving national demographics can help the military improve, or at least

reinforce and maintain, its **public legitimacy**. When Canadians see that their community members have been accepted into a national institution and are succeeding and thriving within it, their sense of belonging within the institution and the country is strengthened. George, in this volume, notes that CAF's limited racial representation amongst its top brass can dishearten personnel. If members of the lower ranks cannot see others like themselves rising to senior positions in an organization, they may give up trying to work hard and pursue leadership. This also can have a more immediate and negative impact on new personnel recruitment as well as retention and overall morale.

3. With recruitment becoming increasingly difficult, the military can benefit from opening up to a broader range of people for potential new volunteers. Canada's **demographics are shifting**, and to continue or to increase the levels of recruiting into CAF, diversification of personnel is vital. The traditional recruiting pools of the military are shrinking. According to Statistics Canada, "Nearly one in two Canadians could be an immigrant or the child of an immigrant by 2036."[10] Against this changing social and demographic context, making the case for diversity is imperative to the long-term viability of CAF. Leuprecht shows how Canadian demographics are changing, while Finn and Momani look at Muslim youth as one of the fastest-growing subsets of those demographics. Both chapters propose how to improve CAF recruitment and retention of diverse demographic groups.

4. Diversification can help improve CAF mission planning at higher institutional levels, and assist individual units' operational effectiveness, by building intercultural awareness and improving communication skills. As Hajjar notes, "Cross-cultural competence provides strategists with necessary insights to develop sound military policy and operational plans."[11] The **cultural competency** that comes from engaging with diverse personnel can help CAF "better predict, comprehend, and influence the behaviour of diverse people in foreign lands (including populations, adversaries, and nongovernmental

organizations)."[12] It can help protect soldiers' lives. Consider that many U.S. military and government officials attribute at least some of their difficulties during the American occupation of Iraq to cultural incompetence and a dearth of local knowledge about Iraqi society.[13]

5. A diverse CAF prepares personnel to work with a variety of partners on international missions. A diverse Canadian military can enjoy a comparative advantage when **participating in, or leading, international coalitions and multinational operations**. As part of Operation REASSURANCE in Latvia, the CAF has led a multinational battlegroup, and managing international missions requires intercultural awareness and competency.[14] By celebrating diversity, the CAF can mitigate frictions or misunderstandings that inevitably result from working with military, government, non-government, or other partners in multicultural settings.

While we agree these five arguments for diversity are valuable to the CAF, diversity alone cannot create a cohesive and effective organization. Inclusion is a necessary part of ensuring that diversity works.

From Demographic Diversity to Inclusion

Inclusion means that organizations must strike a balance between providing personnel with a sense of belonging while also appreciating (and making the best use of) their uniqueness.[15] Mor Barak defines *inclusion* as "the individual's sense of being a part of the organizational system in both the formal processes, such as access to information and decision-making channels, and the informal processes, such as 'water cooler' and lunch meetings where informal information and decisions take place."[16] If individuals are not included, and especially if they are excluded, they may spend time and energy suppressing their differences in order to blend in, or even give up on the organization and merely do the minimum of what is asked of them until they can leave.[17] In both cases, the organization suffers by losing out on the immediate and potential contributions individuals can make when they feel that they are a valued part of the organization. While recruiting new demographic groups to CAF can be driven by law or circumstance, inclusion cannot. Inclusion can be built only over time through education, interaction, and dialogue. Achieving inclusion will require that the organization, public, state, and society at large improve and evolve.

Inclusion encourages acknowledging and embracing differences, and incorporating these differences into the organization in ways that improve mission outcomes. As Hajjar notes, "The military's ability to build a cohesive and effective force from a diverse constituency hinges on cultural understanding, appropriate attitudes, relevant skills, appropriate policy, and organizational commitment."[18]

Diversity and inclusion should also be considered when recruiting into the military. As Leuprecht notes in this volume, the military is aware of the demographic shifts that will necessitate recruitment from a diverse array of groups within the Canadian population. However, arrangements born of necessity do not foster inclusion. Recruiting from diverse groups merely to fulfil basic organizational needs in the short term fails to meet the needs of those who serve.

One issue that is underdeveloped in the discussion of organizational diversity is the role of intersectionality. A co-author of this chapter, Rupinder Mangat, is a woman, a Sikh, a person of colour, and a person of South Asian Indian descent. All these demographic attributes are embodied within her at all times. Her experiences as a woman are affected by her religious and cultural heritage, and her experiences as a brown woman are influenced by her gender and upbringing in India and Canada. Race, gender, ethnicity, religion, and other characteristics must be considered concurrently in a conversation on diversity, because people are a complex mix of demographic identities. As Hill Collins notes, intersectionality is the "critical insight that race, class, gender, sexuality, ethnicity, nation, ability, and age operate not as unitary, mutually exclusive entities, but as reciprocally constructing phenomena that in turn shape complex social inequalities."[19] Those who belong to more than one identity group can feel further marginalized when only one of their sources of identity is accounted for; and an organization may fail to use those dimensions as assets in pursuit of its own mandate or functions.

What is it like to be a black Wiccan gay woman in the Canadian military? Most reports on diversity will count her in the gender and race categories of diversity, but the combined impact of those groupings is rarely studied. Relying on categories of analyses that are easy to define, such as visible demographic factors, can make it easier to count and report, but it also can create a skewed perspective on the complexity of people's experiences. Encouraging diversity without tackling the intersectional effects that some personnel experience may put them in the precarious position of trying to adhere to the "right demographic category," while possibly depriving the organization of valuable potential assets to its own operations.

Celebrating individual differences must consider respect for CAF personnel's intersectional identities. This becomes particularly relevant when differences are not as visibly apparent as race or gender, as in the cases of religious faith or sexual orientation. A Catholic white male soldier may appear to fit in with the dominant demographic of the Canadian military, but if that soldier is gay, then it would challenge our assumption of how he represents the organization's "typical" soldier. The challenges that this soldier might experience as a gay man who is part of the Catholic faith, for instance, could harm his performance as a soldier and therefore the effectiveness of his unit and the organization.

Taking the idea of individual diversity from concept to practice, however, will involve changing the military's organizational culture. According to Jeffery, "Organizational culture can be considered the personality of the organization, made up of the values, beliefs and behaviours of the organization's members. It is, in short, 'how we do things' and develops as a consequence of the other organizational elements."[20] Changing organizational culture takes time and can face deliberate or unintended resistance, or both, but it can be done and it can have positive practical results for the organization.

Inducing Organizational Change

While organizational culture can resist change, it can also help propel it. Heffron defines *organizational culture* as "the shared beliefs, attitudes, and values of members that determine organizational norms of behaviour."[21] One way to induce change in organizational culture is through re-education. The military has a system of education for its personnel from the day they join to the day they leave the organization. CAF education is a powerful tool that helps personnel adapt to a new organizational culture, in venues such as the Royal Military College and the Canadian Forces College. Diversity can be emphasized in these learning spaces. CAF can benefit when diversity and inclusion are integrated into its curriculum and when there is interaction between diverse students and instructors in a classroom.

Diversity may be understood rhetorically as a positive organizational goal, but critics of promoting diversity in the military often argue that it would harm group cohesion. Yet, as Irwin states, "Diversity can enhance group solidarity or cohesion because soldiers are valued for their differential contributions to mission success and to the social functioning of the unit."[22] Individual cultural differences can provide context for strengthening the *military culture* and *military identity* of personnel. After all, personnel may identify with a particular ethnic, cultural, religious, or geographical identity (such as region or city), but the Canadian Armed Forces identity is an equal part of their existence and indeed is meant to become their principal framework.

The military has powerful tools to "create and reinforce a 'tight culture' where in-groups undoubtedly develop."[23] However, as Pinch notes, this in-group identity is critical for military missions: "One unintended – often negative – result [of military socialization] is the emergence of norms, values, and stereotypes that exclude the 'not like us' groups. To some extent, the internal policy debates ... revolve around how militaries might maintain an intentional socialization regime – so as to optimize 'requisite' group characteristics – in a way that brings other social and cultural groups into the mainstream by incorporating essential aspects of them."[24] For an organization to benefit from diversity it must discover ways to socialize its personnel so that they will regard differences as opportunities and virtues. By focusing on individual diversity, an organization can encourage personnel to think of everyone as different, and eventually visible diversity will become normalized and included in the same way as invisible diversity.

Leadership can also drive change in organizational culture. The CAF have made visible progress on increasing diversity in its leaders. In 2011, Lieutenant-Colonel Harjit Sajjan became the first Sikh to command a Canadian Army reserve regiment.[25] In 2016, Major-General Jennie Carignan became Canada's first-ever woman combat arms General.[26] In 2017, Captain (Navy) Geneviève Bernatchez became Canada's first woman Judge Advocate General.[27] This diversity in leadership might inspire people from diverse groups to join the organization. Vocal support of diversity and inclusion from high-ranking and well-respected personnel can reinforce the organizational benefits of welcoming differences and can push for new norms and values that embrace diversity.

The civilian counterpart of the CAF, the Department of National Defence (DND), has lagged behind somewhat in placing diverse personnel in leadership. Kim Campbell was Canada's first woman Minister of National Defence in 1993, and she has been followed over two decades later, in 2015, by Harjit Sajjan, this time as Canada's first Sikh in the role of Minister of National Defence. Of course, the decisions to name ministers are political; however, observers within and outside of the CAF should be cognizant of the impact that the appointment of diverse people to leadership positions can have on the organization and the Canadian public.

When promoting a diverse and inclusive organization, a leader can help the organization to identify and deal with broader issues, to provide clear and consistent messaging to its personnel about the value of their service, and to maintain a sense of flexibility in making change happen.[28] Because militaries work through top-down command structures, the clarity of a commander's vision and consistency in messaging is especially important. Bennis describes four competencies of leadership: (1) management of attention, (2) management of meaning, (3) management of trust, and (4) management of self.[29] In the case of diversity, management of attention and meaning requires leaders to create a powerful vision of a diverse and inclusive organization and to communicate that vision to the members of the organization in a compelling manner. Without an engaging vision that has buy-in from an organization's personnel, any change in the organizational policy will likely fail. The third competency, management of trust, stems from the dedication and reliability of leaders, which in turn can be provided only if those leaders engage in critical self-management, involving reflection on diversity and an understanding of how they influence others in the organization.

When considering the role of leadership, it is important to emphasize that there are leaders at all levels of an organization. The military usually does well in preparing its personnel for leadership at all ranks. This training must now include the curriculum and tools to demonstrate how diversity creates opportunities, even though it can present challenges to achieving inclusion. In business, leaders may demand better sales numbers or improved productivity; military leaders may have to order their subordinates to put their lives at risk. The right to make such demands is accompanied by an immense duty for leaders in the military chain of command and the civilian government. Hence, the authority of military leaders can be used to propel organizational change effectively. As Wombacher and Felfe note, "What leaders can actually do to build community becomes central in the military environment."[30] For most Western militaries, a new normal stands apart from older perceptions of military masculinity. The CAF must be ready for these changes and plan for their effects. As Okros notes, "The fundamental shift required here is from conformity to creativity. ... There will also be a requirement for a shift from an emphasis on command through directive leadership to one of coordination through transformational leadership."[31] By shifting their focus to diversity at the individual level, the CAF have taken an important step towards recognizing that institutional policies must become responsive to the needs of the individuals who choose to serve.

In a highly hierarchical organization like the military, people in the ranks are also entrusted with leadership. Hence, leadership on diversity and inclusion is the responsibility not only of high-ranking officers, but also junior officers, non-commissioned officers, and non-commissioned members. Thinking about diversity and inclusiveness is as important for the Leading Seaman and the Second Lieutenant, for example, as it is for Warrant Officers and naval Captains. Learning diversity and implementing inclusion is a long-term endeavour for an organization and for personnel. Organizations are always in the midst of change. As Apelt et al. note, "Organizations are not only decided orders but are also constituted by ongoing decision-making processes."[32] Training personnel on diversity and inclusion at all stages of their military careers will ensure that as the diversity strategy ages and the organizational culture evolves, succession will become easier because more personnel will be adept with leading diverse teams.

Book Plan

This book brings together academic knowledge on diversity and inclusion in the Canadian military and examines the issue from multiple perspectives. The assembled contributions delve into the history of diversity integration in the CAF, analyse its present state, and offer recommendations for the future. The aim is to understand the tactical, normative, and national benefits – and challenges – of a more diverse CAF; to offer evidence on the recruitment and retention of diverse groups; and to recommend how the CAF can carry out diversification. The recently released Canadian Armed Forces Diversity Strategy is a move towards a holistic approach to diversity; contributors to this book provide research that informs CAF policy as it progresses.

Christian Leuprecht's chapter demonstrates how diversity within the CAF has grown and yet has failed to keep pace with the growth of diversity in the wider Canadian society. As CAF's recruitment rhetoric shows, the imperative for increased demographic diversity is clear to the military. But the recruitment of women, visible minorities, and Indigenous peoples still lags, and the military is struggling with diverse recruitment. From concerns about how diversity will interact with the military's functional imperative, to the lower salary and benefits offered by the military in comparison with private organizations, the organization will face uphill struggles – internal and external – to better reflect modern Canadian society. However, as Leuprecht and other contributors to this volume conclude, the effort will be worth it.

Understanding where we are now requires examining where we started. Women have been serving in the Canadian military for over 100 years, but their full integration did not begin until late in the twentieth century. Karen Davis reviews the history of gender integration in the CAF since the 1970s. She notes CAF's efforts to include women at all levels within the organization, as well as continuing resistance to women's presence in certain roles in the military. Davis has previously argued that taking a *gender-neutral* or *gender-blind* approach is not the best solution to gender inequity because it makes important issues such as differences in leadership styles and problem-solving invisible.[33] What is needed instead is a *gender-inclusive* approach that leverages the potential of all members, so that individuals and teams can react and adapt to the complexity of challenges that push beyond the guidance provided by sanctioned policy.

Nick Deshpande and Jacqueline Lopour discuss coming out as lesbian, gay, bisexual, transgender, and/or queer (LGBTQ+) in the Canadian Armed Forces. At one time, like other modern militaries, the Canadian military did not allow people who were even suspected of being LGBTQ+ to serve in the armed forces, and instead searched them out and dismissed them. The CAF have taken steps towards inclusion, as evidenced by Deshpande's personal narrative of coming out as well as the CAF's enthusiastic public participation in Pride Parades across Canada. As the authors note, however, many personnel still experience difficult working environments when they decide to come out. Lopour and Deshpande suggest how the CAF can improve inclusion of LGBTQ+ personnel.

Moving towards a more intersectional approach to diversity, P. Whitney Lackenbauer looks at the Canadian Rangers comprised largely of Inuit, First Nations, Métis, and non-Indigenous Canadians. This component of the Canadian Army Reserves is not organized in the same way as the CAF Regular Force or Primary Reserves. Lackenbauer emphasizes that the unique community-based structure and organization of the Rangers effectively promotes inclusivity and diversity, not only in Indigenous membership but also high rates of female participation. Providing an overview of the Rangers' history as well as the logic behind their terms of service, compensation, and current roles, Lackenbauer encourages a more nuanced approach to analysing their myriad contributions to addressing challenges in Canada's northern territories. Not only are the Rangers an integral "force multiplier" in CAF northern operations, Lackenbauer contends, their inclusivity serves core community interests. The alternative organizational structure of the Rangers highlights another kind of diversity, which may offer lessons to the CAF on how to better recruit and integrate diverse groups.

In a turn to the spiritual, Bianca Romagnoli offers a closer look at the CAF chaplaincy, which provides succour primarily to Christians. The CAF do not collect data on the religious make-up of the forces, even though this information is part of identification tags that personnel wear. Yet chaplains are trained largely in Christian doctrine and may not be as well equipped to provide moral and ethical guidance to those who follow a non-Christian religion. The notions of martial values in Western militaries also are predominantly informed by a Christian ethos, which might create problems for personnel of other faiths and beliefs who seek spiritual or religious guidance in the field, particularly after experiencing trauma. Romagnoli asks how the chaplaincy can better fulfil the diversity imperative.

Stéphanie Chouinard looks at the struggle of francophone Canadians to have their bilingual rights embraced by CAF. She argues that bilingualism policies remain relevant as a significant percentage of this country's population is made up of francophones. Maintaining a good mix of English, French, and bilingual personnel also allows the military to maintain a competitive edge during operations in French-speaking regions of Canada and the world. CAF personnel's French language skills have been useful during missions such as Operation LENTUS 17-01, when CAF assistance was requested after an ice storm in New Brunswick; and

Operation Hamlet, the Canadian contribution to the UN stabilization mission in Haiti. A formal recognition and ongoing inclusion of bilingualism in Canada signals acceptance not only to the francophones, but also to newcomers for whom the existence of two officially recognized national languages is the most visible sign that differences are welcome and celebrated.

Tammy George brings our attention to the experiences of racialized soldiers in the CAF. She looks at how race is understood in Canada, particularly how that interpretation has affected CAF policy on diversity. As importantly, she shares the personal experiences of personnel affected by diversity initiatives. Soldiers share their stories about not quite fitting into the pervasive Whiteness of the organizational and social life of the Canadian military. From the lack of racial diversity in leadership, to "not making a fuss" about dealing with racist experiences, the stories of these personnel suggest that work remains on racial equality and inclusion.

Melissa Finn and Bessma Momani look at Canadian Muslim youth, one of the fastest-growing demographic groups in Canada. They focus their study on the perceptions that Muslim youth have of the Canadian military and the youth's thoughts about joining the CAF. While they find that many Muslim youth are open to joining the Canadian military, many note that Western militaries can be forces of destruction for their brethren. Finn and Momani shine light on the complexity of individual identities, and how those identities may create different sets of priorities that affect people's decision to join the military.

Alan Okros concludes the book with an overview of where the CAF started in its demographic approach to diversity, and where it might be heading after the 2016 Diversity Strategy that is "designed to be an enduring feature of not only the composition of the CAF but how we operate."[34] He looks at how difference is constructed and perpetuated socially within CAF, and how "tradition" is used to resist change and inclusion. In a review of the preceding chapters, Okros explains how the CAF can progress in its journey towards becoming a more inclusive – and functionally effective – force.

This book presents an overview of CAF policies and their impact on personnel. Serving in the military requires sacrifices;

CAF personnel often spend months away from family, working in far-off places and sometimes in difficult or dangerous situations. It is unacceptable for soldiers to feel they must carry the additional burden of hiding their sexual orientation, working with others who may underestimate them because of their gender or race, or being unable to find spiritual succour in their time of need. There have been missteps on CAF's journey to diversity and inclusion – from the Airborne's Somalia legacy and the numerous cases of sexual misconduct to the interruption of an Indigenous ceremony in Halifax by CAF personnel who identified themselves as "Proud Boys, Maritime Chapter." There will be other missteps and obstacles, but the move to diversity and inclusion is long and arduous and requires fundamental changes. The organization will need not only to adapt to the needs of its new diverse and intersectional members, but also to take a closer look at its organizational culture as a whole.

Top-down policymaking and enforcement can go only so far. As Okros notes, personnel have to "out" themselves as being "different" to receive the same considerations as their colleagues from dominant groups. The onus to report mistreatment, to calculate the potential opportunity costs, and to deal with the fear of backlash persists for those experiencing improper conduct. Again, education has an important role to play in making personnel aware of what behaviours, language, etc., are unacceptable, but as part of that education, CAF must also empower personnel to defend their colleagues and fellow armed forces members. The adage "See something, say something" comes to mind.

The CAF is working hard to arrive at solutions. A workshop, and subsequently this book, was made possible by a Defence Engagement Program grant from the Canadian Armed Forces. The Canadian military personnel who attended the book workshop contributed their thoughts, ideas, and stories as well as support for the authors in accessing data or opportunities to speak with other personnel who could illuminate their topic. We thank them and hope our insights, research, and possible solutions serve to better the national treasure that is our armed forces.

chapter two

Demographic Imperatives for Diversity and Inclusion[1]

CHRISTIAN LEUPRECHT

Advanced industrialized democracies have been subject to a demographic transition bringing significant changes in population size as well as composition. The extent to which their populations are aging is without historical precedent. At the same time, Canadian society is diversifying more quickly than the Canadian Armed Forces (CAF). In the global context, the CAF actually fares better than most militaries, including among its democratic peers. But while the CAF is becoming more diverse in absolute numbers, the diversity gap in composition between the CAF on the one hand and on the other, the Canadian society from which it is drawn, continues to widen.

The armed forces previously struggled with accepting the idea and the practice of diversity in recruitment because of what critics of diversity argued would be the negative impact on its "functional imperative": an institution set apart from society for the particular purpose of effectively using military force when called upon by the government to defend Canada and its democratic values and the democratic way of life against external military threat. This chapter argues to the contrary that the compound effects of tightening labour markets, diminishing recruitment pools, declining recruit cohorts, and rapid rise in the salience of soft skills to mission success increasingly make diversity a complement – and even an important contributor – to that functional imperative.

The diffusion of diversity as a national and international societal norm is making institutional aberration from that norm ever more apparent and subject to scrutiny. International norms transfer is critical here, not only because they supersede jurisdictional sovereignty, which makes them difficult to dismiss, but also because their most fervent advocates are advanced industrialized democracies. Their legitimacy is closely tied to their practice by those who defend them: practise what you preach. Moreover, populations in democratic societies expect their state institutions to reflect their society and its values through their governments. Failure to diversify thus puts the armed forces at odds with the society they serve, which has the potential to hamper the institution's societal legitimacy and its ability to implement government policy. This can manifest itself in a legal-constitutional imperative. Greater diversity in the armed forces has often been the result of legal decisions, political decisions, or both. Aggrieved individuals challenge the status quo, with the result that other institutions impose solutions on the profession of arms. Since one hallmark of a profession is the autonomy it enjoys in regulating itself by setting its own standards and expectations, outside intervention calls into question the professional status the armed forces enjoy. An institution that regards itself as being set aside for a special purpose will want to relinquish as little latitude over its internal affairs to outsiders as possible. Legal and political decisions on how defence and security organizations are to deal with diversity curtail that autonomy; so, it is in the institution's interest to adapt proactively.

The compound effect of these demographic, economic, social, legal-constitutional, and political imperatives in support of the argument of seeing diversity as complementing the functional imperative can lead to a paradigm shift: diversity is not a "problem" that somehow needs to be "managed"; rather, as society becomes more diverse, the pressure for institutions to adapt will only increase. Instead of a management pattern with integrationist undertones, the CAF paradigm needs to shift to one of mutual accommodation. There must be some give and take on both sides. The defence and security sector has little choice but to be more accommodating: it has to identify which integrationist aspects of the institution are indispensable to its ability to carry out its mandate and mission, and which aspects are malleable and open to adaptation without compromising the functional imperative. Conversely, individuals who choose to join the CAF should not expect the institution to relinquish those aspects of its identity and culture that are integral to its raison d'être.

Diversity Naysayers

As noted in the editors' introduction, among the core objections commonly levelled against diversity in the armed forces is the argument that increased diversity undermines cohesion and thus the organization's functional imperative, and that minorities are not interested in joining the armed forces anyway. Both objections must be taken seriously. After all, members of the armed forces sign up for unlimited liability, including the possibility of loss of life; it is the only public institution in democracies that requires this level of commitment from its members. In a democracy, members of all other public and security institutions have the right to refuse to engage in situations that they feel might pose a threat to their personal safety. Not so with the armed forces. Members of the armed forces have signed up for a job where their lives are on the line; therefore it also is in the very nature of their work to minimize risk to their life and to optimize their chances of survival.

Work of the armed forces requires soldiers to act in groups of varying size and differing forms and levels of firepower. Groups face collective-action problems. One aspect of ensuring the functional imperative is thus to minimize collective-action problems through training and – as is apparent by the often-criticised institutional resistance to diversity, an issue to which I shall return below – recruitment. In essence, militaries do this by minimizing transaction costs. Such costs have different euphemisms, perhaps the most ubiquitous of which is "cohesion." As noted in the introductory chapter, cohesion of the CAF or any unit within it is a key to survival: the better the cohesion of a force, the lower its transaction costs and the better its capacity to fulfil the functional imperative. Survival is, of course, the ultimate key to the functional imperative; by definition, dead soldiers cannot complete their mission.

Given the compound effect of both human nature and their job, it should come as no surprise then that soldiers are apprehensive about anything and anyone that might possibly threaten cohesion.

The armed forces' organizational culture is resistant to change. The profession of arms also seeks to set itself apart through a greater emphasis on cohesion than almost any other profession. Diversity is perceived to threaten cohesion, thereby running the risk of undermining the military's ability to carry out its functional imperative, and consequently its relative autonomy. If the armed forces define themselves by their homogeneity, diversity is perceived to undermine cohesion.

This explains, at least partially, why institutional reluctance to accept or adopt significant (or any) change is pervasive across the armed forces. Change may lower transaction costs eventually, but in the short term it may actually raise them. Insofar as change is necessary, it should be organic and gradual. The fact that armed forces have been reluctant to recruit more diversely is thus part of their organizational culture in that diversity per se is equated with change. Rather than treating human beings as equals by their very nature, differences matter, whether perceived or real: phenotype, religion, gender, sexual orientation, disabilities, etc. Organizational behaviour theorists refer to this as the dialectic between "in-group" and "out-group." However, the evidence does not support the claim that diversity – as understood by the profession of arms – threatens cohesion. In the field, phenotype, religion, gender, sexual orientation, and so forth turn out to be irrelevant.[2] What counts is not different from what matters in any other job: whether someone "gets the job done," whether someone whines and complains, whether someone performs well, whether someone is risk averse, and so forth.

The other ubiquitous objection to diversity in the armed forces is that minorities do not want to join. The fact that minorities do join the military belies that claim. However, survey research shows a disproportionately lower rate of interest in the armed forces among non-traditional populations (women, after all, are not a minority!) than among Caucasian males.[3] But any number of reasons may account for this finding – such as those noted by Finn and Momani in this volume, and to a lesser extent by George – including new immigrants' possible negative perceptions and low standing of the armed forces in their country of origin. Although immigrants to Canada may readily distinguish between armed forces in their home country and the CAF, their interest or desire to join the CAF also may be limited by a wide range of influences, including competing notions of joining one of "the professions," and a failure to recognize the armed forces as being amongst them; parents' disproportionate influence over their children's choices; conservative family values that prize close geographical proximity of extended family; unfamiliarity with the organization and its variety of career paths; and the anticipated nature of expeditionary deployments.[4]

While the military as a whole consistently ranks among the most respected institutions in (mainly Western) democratic societies, the armed forces generally enjoy only moderate appreciation in those societies as a potential career path.[5] Insofar as respondents have expressed an interest in the armed forces, research nonetheless reveals a serious disconnect: the level of interest vastly surpasses minorities' actual representation as members in the armed forces. Far from inferring that non-traditional populations are disinterested in or opposed to the armed forces, the more appropriate question to ask is why some people are more apt to join, and others less so, when they may have similar levels of interest in the institution?

Answers to those questions are to be sought with the institution and its culture, recruitment, retention, promotion, and remuneration practices. These are difficult and complex questions, many of which warrant much greater attention in the literature than researchers have accorded them.[6] The pursuit of a military career has functional and instrumental determinants, and motivations vary by country. A study of prevailing attitudes among the officer corps identified service to the nation, general interest in the military, and propensity for leadership as key motivators for military service. Respondents also expected education and training, job security, and adventure.[7] Family and friends as well as an individual's social environment also influence their proclivity for pursuing a military career.[8] Lack of social recognition is an impediment for precisely the target group that the modern military needs the most: those individuals with a higher degree of education and skills. All-volunteer national military forces are notoriously short on technically skilled specialists, as Finn and Momani note in their chapter.[9] The higher one's level of education and the better one's technical or other skills, the lower one's chances of unemployment in the civilian economy and thus also the lower the incentive to look towards the armed forces for employment. This paradox leaves the armed forces with two options: either maintain high barriers of entry and run the risk of facing critical staffing impasses, or lower the level of quality required of new entrants, at the potential expense of institutional efficiency and effectiveness. Either way, the organization's prestige is likely to suffer. After all, who is keen to work for either an organization that is notoriously elitist, yet understaffed and overworked, or one that garners a reputation as an employer of last resort for the "worst of the desperate"?

The Normative Case for Diversity

The armed forces like to think of themselves as turning citizens into soldiers, but they play an equally important role in turning soldiers into citizens. Through their training, the armed forces have an unparalleled capacity to generate uniformity. The institution socializes people into its predominant norms, trains a high degree of uniformity in responding to specific situations, and teaches soldiers a common vernacular to ensure that they will understand commands as given, and act or respond accordingly. In light of the aforementioned labour market trends, the armed forces will also take on a greater role in facilitating social mobility. The bridging hypothesis initially posited the armed forces as a transition from adolescence to adult life.[10] It has since been refined to argue that minorities are particularly likely to benefit from military service as an opening to enhanced opportunities in life.[11] The armed forces have long been facilitating social mobility by promoting equality of opportunity.

Were the armed forces – and in this case, the CAF – to recruit more aggressively among the shrinking Caucasian cohort, the costs of doing so would climb exponentially. Both the cohort itself and its representation among the socio-economic strata from which the armed forces tend to draw disproportionately are on the wane. In its stead, it is being populated by racialized minorities. So the "business case" for recruiting more diversely is twofold. On the one hand, the proportion of racialized minorities among the recruitment cohort is growing; and on the other hand, so is their representation among the socio-economic strata from which the armed forces tend to recruit.

As the editors noted in the introductory chapter, greater involvement by minority groups in the armed forces will also help to legitimize the institution, its mission(s), and related government policy. As its engagements in international missions especially become more difficult and potentially controversial, the armed forces stand to benefit from having the broadest possible base of support among the electorate. The same holds true for a government (of whatever political party) in Ottawa that is looking to legitimize its policies. When a key institution of the government is unrepresentative of the population it serves, the chances are increased that the population will have an ambivalent relationship with that institution. Funding for the armed forces is one concrete example. Since the Department of Defence and the CAF have been concerned – even if not normally saying so in public fora – about the scarcity of funds allocated to the defence budget by successive governments, failure to ensure that the institution (usually one of the top three budget items in any democracy, and often the largest discretionary budget item) is representative of the population as a whole is unlikely to help the case for bolstering its resources.

Similarly, democratic governments like to portray themselves as representing the people. To this end, they enact both negative rights legislation to protect citizens from discrimination and positive rights legislation to rectify past wrongs and proactively increase the representation of underrepresented groups. Why, then, are governmental bureaucracies consistently among the least representative institutions in these same democratic societies? And among these national institutions, the armed forces usually are even less representative of the population as a whole than the rest of government. This is an inherent contradiction for all democratic governments: they claim to govern societies that allegedly prize equality of opportunity, yet they themselves trail the curve. This is not an abstract normative or moral claim: there is ample evidence that armed forces are not in tune with societal expectations on diversity. The courts and quasi-judicial human rights tribunals have been instrumental in opening or improving access to the armed forces.[12]

Gender has figured prominently in these decisions, but people who are LGBTQ+ and part of racial minorities have benefited as well[13] – a point further explored by Lopour and Deshpande's chapter. In other words, courts in democratic countries have clearly established a societal, legal, and constitutional imperative for promoting and achieving diversity in the armed forces. They have decided that this imperative supersedes any possible adverse effects that these injunctions might have on the armed forces' functional imperative. This leaves the armed forces with only two choices in the diversity debate: either be proactive, or learn to live with courts and other bodies telling the armed forces what to do about diversity.

As populations age, the proportion – and eventually the size – of the youth cohort shrinks. This development is not yet problematic, because the armed forces can compensate to some extent by substituting capital for labour. Of course, this is precisely what is happening in contemporary fourth- and fifth-generation warfare.[14] However, substituting capital for labour requires ever more highly qualified, trained, and skilled operators. Morris Janowitz anticipated this development in his observation that military organizations are becoming less distinct and looking increasingly like any other large, bureaucratic, technologically advanced organization.[15] This development is theorized further in Moskos's institutional/occupational thesis, which posits the military moving from an institutional to an occupational format that is driven by self-interest and a free market.[16] As a result, armed forces are now competing with civilian sectors for the same limited talent pool of highly qualified and technically or technologically skilled personnel. In the post-industrial economy, demand for this labour pool grows exponentially;[17] consequently, demand not only outstrips supply but the differential between demand and supply widens. The pressure on salaries rises as a result. To meet demand, the private sector enjoys greater latitude in adjusting – that is, increasing – salaries. Public-sector remuneration thus becomes less attractive. Under these conditions, armed forces must recruit as broadly as possible to harness the best return on scarce funds and to recruit the best talent available. The lower the quality of recruited personnel, the more the armed forces have to invest in "training up" and "educating up" that individual, thus imposing an unnecessary or unsustainable strain on scarce resources.

The question of resources becomes especially apparent during the new multinational missions of peace enforcement, stabilization, and counter-insurgency. Successful conduct and conclusion of such missions requires a high degree of civil-military cooperation in the form of civil affairs and psychology operations. The expansion of civil affairs and psychological operations units in recent years testifies to this claim. Under these conditions, soft skills such as linguistic competence, religious knowledge, and familiarity with local societal customs are proving indispensable to mission success.[18] Yet there is an even more straightforward argument for greater diversity among troops that are being deployed abroad. For the most part, they are being sent abroad to help diverse groups cohabit. If ethnic cleavages are a major source of conflict in the world, and one of the premises of intervention is to have competing ethnicities learn to cooperate, then the intervening countries and their armed forces (and their other civilian security-sector components such as policing) need to practise what they preach and model that. As noted in the introductory chapter, Canada's military is increasingly involved in multilateral missions and foreign operations that require high cultural competency. A diverse organization is a good way to model intercultural cooperation and to foster or acquire improved cultural competency skills. When deployed expeditionary forces look suspiciously homogeneous – and alien to the location of their deployment – then echoes of neocolonialism are likely to reverberate with locals.

Canada's Demographic Transition

Demographic cleavages are to the twenty-first century what class divisions were to the nineteenth century. Rarely can social scientists claim to be observing genuinely unprecedented phenomena. The world's contemporary demographic developments, however, are without historical precedent: women are consistently having fewer or no children than at any previous time, never have there been as many people on the planet, never has the world's population expanded as rapidly in as short a time (five billion people over the course of a century), never before have people lived longer and populations grown as old, never have there been more people of working age, and never have as many children lived in the developing world. For the first time in history, more people now live in cities than in rural areas.

Demographic trends allow us to anticipate developments in size and distribution of population groups. As such, demography is a harbinger of challenge and opportunity, a multiplier of conflict and progress, and a resource for power and prosperity.[19] In fact, fertility, mortality, and migration are the only set of variables in the social sciences that can be projected over the medium term with great accuracy: the population that will be growing old over the coming decades has already been born, and we also know the average number of children to which a woman in a given location is likely to give birth. Until quite recently, high birth rates had kept populations fairly young. As the result of wars and epidemics, such as the plague, few people grew old.[20] Innovations in public health and food security changed that. The result was a decline in death rates. Birth rates would initially remain high before levelling off. That change in birth and death rates, and the delta between them, is largely responsible for the phenomenon known as the demographic transition.

Canada and all NATO member states, with the exception of the United States, have been beset by aging populations. The scope of this aging is remarkable. By 2050, at least 20 per cent of the population in these countries will be over sixty-five. This demographic development, again, is without historical precedent. We know neither what to expect from a state with over one-third of its population over sixty years of age, nor how its economic growth and finances will be affected.[21] Canada's population is growing slowly in number, and aging rapidly. More Canadians are turning sixty-five every year than the compound effect of births and immigration. At 16 per cent of the population, the number of Canadians over sixty-five currently not only outnumbers those younger than fifteen years of age, but is projected to reach 25 per cent by 2025. Today, approximately four Canadians of working age support (through taxation and other contributions) those under fifteen and over sixty-five years of age; by 2031, that dependency ratio is projected to be 2:1.[22] Any growth in the labour pool is driven entirely by immigration, since the fertility rate of immigrants exceeds that of established Canadians. Even that fertility dividend levels off within a couple of generations after people have immigrated to Canada. Not only does this have obvious implications for the talent pool on which CAF recruitment can draw, but it also has implications for defence funding, because aging populations are thought to be a burden on economic growth, while expanded demand for health and social spending will impose systemic constraints on defence spending in the government budget. While recruitment for defence finds itself increasingly in direct competition with the private sector for the same high-priced talent, fiscal conditions impose additional constraints on the public sector's ability to compete on salary.

Volunteer professional armed forces, as opposed to those with mandatory military service, habitually over-recruit from rural areas and from lower socio-economic quintiles of society. Given Canada's high rate of urbanization, which stands at about 85 per cent, and the fact that urban populations have a younger age structure than rural ones, this dependence on rural recruits is another problem. Urban dwellers and racialized people remain relatively – and indeed, increasingly – underrepresented in the CAF. Moreover, Indigenous peoples have among the highest fertility rate in the country, followed by immigrants, and both remain relatively untapped sources of recruitment – how the Rangers are an exception, is further explored in Lackenbauer's chapter in this volume.

The aggregate recruiting challenge faced by the CAF is, therefore, compounded by (1) rapidly aging populations in the four Atlantic provinces whence the CAF had traditionally recruited disproportionately; (2) low population growth among francophones that, since 1981, has been only about half that of Canadian population growth as a whole;[23] (3) a decline in the proportion of francophones relative to anglophones; (4) a limited pool of potential bilingual recruits outside of Quebec relative to the CAF's needs; and (5) a francophone population that is increasingly allophone, with a predisposition to defecting to English universities and vernacular once they graduate from the secondary school system. Francophones have waned to 14 per cent of the Canadian population, and anglophones to 47 per cent. The proportion of the population that identifies as neither anglophone nor francophone has more than doubled since 2001. With the proportion of francophones on the wane due to low fertility, the fastest-growing French-speaking population is found among visible minorities. The CAF's bilingualism and diversity mandates are thus complementary: bilingualism becomes a function of diversity, as further pointed out by Chouinard in this volume. Maintaining and optimizing the armed forces' functional imperative suggests maximizing value for money and recruiting the best talent possible. Failure to recruit more diversely leads to suboptimal outcomes on both counts.

For the CAF, this presents a challenge: ensuring that it remains representative across all provinces, and maintaining its bilingual character, while becoming more representative of Designated Group Members (DGMs), as defined by the Employment Equity Act. This challenge especially relates to "visible" minorities and Indigenous peoples, with both groups over-represented among the lower quintiles of Canadian society, quintiles from which the CAF has traditionally recruited disproportionately. A comparison of the trajectory of the composition of Canadian society and the CAF over recent years finds that the rate at which the Canadian Armed Forces' composition will continue to diverge from the ethno-demographic composition of Canadian society is accelerating. At the same time, the opportunity cost of not recruiting more broadly is rising exponentially.

The impact on the CAF is already palpable: in 2016 the Auditor General identified a growing gap between the number of members needed and those who were fully trained. The Office of the Auditor General projected that the CAF would fall short of its 2018–19 recruiting targets. Among the eighty-five occupations for which the CAF recruits internally, as of 31 March 2016, twenty-one had been chronically stressed for at least three consecutive years, meaning that they were staffed with less than 90 per cent of the target because enrolments fell 10 per cent or more below the target that had already been adjusted down.[24] At the same time, in forty-four occupations more people left than joined, and twenty-three occupations experienced attrition rates in excess of 10 per cent. In light of these shortfalls, retention of current trained members becomes all the more important, especially in stressed occupations. Ensuring that all members feel treated equitably by the organization – especially DGMs – is critical. Twenty years ago, attrition of DGMs was statistically disproportionate to their non-DGM counterparts; but for the last fifteen years, that no longer appears to be the case. So the CAF appears to be making inroads in retaining the DGMs whom it does attract and recruit. Interest among visible minorities and Indigenous persons in joining CAF continues to rise, and both groups actually show an above-average interest in joining.[25] Yet the gap between the rate at which racialized minorities and Indigenous peoples are growing as a proportion of the Canadian population, and the CAF's ability to attract and retain them, continues to widen.

Current recruitment trends mean that the CAF is becoming less representative of Canadian society overall. Considering the inequitable distribution of DGMs across non-commissioned ranks versus officers, Reserve versus Regular Force, environments, occupations, and rank, and the challenge of recruiting and retaining DGMs (CAF Employment Equity Schedules 3–15, 2016),[26] the remedies for current shortcomings and shortfalls[27] become even more nuanced and variegated. For example, visible minorities show a much greater preference for becoming an officer rather than joining as a non-commissioned member, and a slightly greater interest in entering the support occupations.[28]

Table 2.1. Visible Minority Population Projection, by Selected Census Metropolitan Areas *Large Urban Areas*

	2006 (thousands)	2031 (thousands	2006 (% total population)	2031 (% total population)
Montreal	604	1,521	16.4	31.0
Toronto	2,281	5,572	42.9	62.8
Vancouver	910	2,061	41.7	59.2

Source: Data compiled from Statistics Canada, *Immigration and Diversity: Population Projections for Canada and Its Regions* (March 2010), https://www150.statcan.gc.ca/n1/pub/91-551-x/91-551-x2010001-eng.htm.

As has been indicated above (see table 2.1), shallower recruiting pools and tightening labour markets are precipitating an economic imperative where the costs associated with failing to recruit more broadly and diversely are rapidly outpacing any benefits from institutional homogeneity. The costs created by aging populations are bound to constrain spending on economic development and national defence. Population aging causes military personnel costs to rise. As demographic growth slows but economies continue to grow, the labour market tightens. Concomitantly, the nature of modern military organizations – as Janowitz observed decades ago – is less and less "an organization set apart" for a uniquely specific purpose, but is instead increasingly approximating any other private- or public-sector organization.[29] As a result, it competes for the same highly skilled and educated labour. The combination of a tightening labour market and growing competition for a small pool of highly qualified labour causes salaries to rise exponentially.[30] What accounts for the armed forces' inability to compete on the labour market against the private sector? How can the armed forces counter the higher private-sector salaries in Canada's strong economy? What options do the armed forces have when confronted with decreasing structural unemployment? How can the armed forces compensate for lagging in remuneration and non-material incentives? The economic dimension of CAF diversity matters.

Canada is aging rapidly, but as the result of a per capita legal immigration rate that is among the highest in the democratic world and higher fertility rates among recent immigration groups, Canada is actually aging less rapidly than similar countries and is among the few countries whose working-age population continues to grow. As a result, the pressures of eldercare over defence spending remain relatively favourable in Canada, and the increased substitution effect of labour for capital in defence budgets is bound to be smaller. Yet the entire growth in Canada's labour force is a function of immigration.

CAF's Future Recruitment Concerns

The broad objective of personnel policy is to ensure the timely and cost-effective supply of potential labour not only for current needs, but also with a view towards the organization's future strategic developments and requirements.[31] Recruitment may thus be defined as the process of searching out and finding qualified personnel in sufficient numbers to meet the organization's demand. In light of current demographic and labour market trends, this means that organizations in the future will have to rely increasingly on strong incentives, in tasks, working conditions, professional development, remuneration, and other benefits, both to retain their current workforce and to position themselves strategically for the future in an increasingly competitive labour market.

Personnel policy thus has internal and external ends. Internal personnel policy transpires within an organization. External personnel policy, by contrast, distinguishes further between a passive and an active approach. For the passive approach, the organization's familiarity plays a significant role in attracting unsolicited applications on which it can draw to meet potential personnel needs without having to devote resources to reaching out. These resources can then be redeployed elsewhere in the organization to bolster its familiarity further. The active approach, by contrast, requires resources to be invested in traditional media and other means of advertising, such as the internet, to target prospective applicants for a specific job. It also may involve recruiting agencies that seek out people with a desirable profile of skills. Rather than relying on external agencies, the armed forces usually devote a significant part of their budget to maintaining their own professional recruiting organizations. In a tight labour market with fierce competition for highly skilled personnel, this type of active personnel policy becomes increasingly important:[32] in contradistinction to materiel, people cannot just be procured at the organization's whim. Sustaining the organization's functional imperative in a tight labour market requires a sustained long-term strategy. Any shortcomings of that policy, or failures in it, will harm the organization's operational effectiveness.

As, or if, armed forces become less successful at recruiting quality personnel with existing and desirable skillsets, they will have to compensate by investing more in training and education. As they devote more time and money to education and training, retention will become even more important. With the investment per recruit on the rise, attrition will become even costlier to the organization, both financially and as a qualitative loss. Diversity challenges the organization on at least three levels: demography, function, and legitimacy. First, demographic projections show a sustained trajectory towards greater diversity. As a result of population aging, the overall pool of potential recruits relative to the population as a whole is growing shallower. The overall trend, however, is marked by considerable distortions: the Caucasian cohort is declining disproportionately while the cohort of racialized minorities, immigrant groups, and Indigenous people is expanding relatively rapidly as the result of both higher fertility rates and sustained immigration. Moreover, population aging is projected to precipitate a tightening labour market with growing competition for a contracting talent pool.

Second, if the armed forces do not step up recruitment from that cohort, they are bound to face increasingly suboptimal human resources outcomes with detrimental implications for their functional imperative. This challenge grows as both the locations where expeditionary forces are being deployed, and the nature of new missions for which civil affairs and psychological operations are integral, necessitate soft skills as a force multiplier.

Third, if a core purpose of armed forces in mature democracies is to defend the democratic way of life and the core values that underpin it, then should the civil security sector and armed forces not practise those same values? Whether in the United States of America under President Truman, the British Empire, or the French Republic of Jules Ferry, the armed forces have long been integral to nation-building. Conversely, how politically stable and economically prosperous countries are appears to correlate with how representative their armed forces are of the population they serve. The more homogeneous the composition of the armed forces, the less stable and prosperous the state. What prospect, then, does a widening gap between representation in the armed forces on the one hand, and demographic developments in society at large on the other hand, hold out for the future of democracy?

Far from being at odds, the functional imperative of the armed forces and the ideal of the citizen soldier are different sides of the same coin. Old sergeants claim that their job is to defend democracy, not to practise it. The evidence, however, leads to a different conclusion: the defence of democracy is inexorably linked to its practice.

Conclusion

In liberal democracies, if soldiers are citizens first, that implies that the armed forces as a whole should be representative of the society they serve: by modelling equality of opportunity. How representative they are is a matter of controversy, one that this chapter will not be able to resolve. However, from the premise of the citizen soldier one might normatively infer that, at a minimum, the armed forces at the least should be on a trajectory of becoming more representative of society. Diversity in the armed forces is the ultimate litmus test of just how free, equal, and fair a democratic society really is. If the armed forces have as their purpose to defend democratic values in the form of a free, equal, and just way of life, then all members of society have a stake in securing their defence.

chapter three

Negotiating Gender Inclusion

Karen D. Davis

In 1965, the number of women serving in Canada's military was restricted by the government to 1,500, representing just 1.6 per cent of all serving members.[1] By 2017, representation of women had grown to 9,700, well over 14 per cent of serving members of the Regular component of the Canadian Armed Forces,[2] including 400 women who serve in the land combat arms.[3] In tracing the increasing participation of women in the Canadian military, this chapter emphasizes strategies that leadership used to reinforce what they believed was an unequivocal relationship between the values of the masculine heterosexual warrior identity, a vocational orientation to military service, and operational effectiveness.

The military recognized that it needed the contribution of women in support roles, but until 1989 insisted on unique distinctions between women and men to protect all-male combat teams from the inclusion of women. In response to the direction of the 1989 Canadian Human Rights Tribunal to fully integrate women, Canadian military leaders adopted a gender-neutral posture that sought to satisfy the minimum requirements of that direction; based upon equitable opportunity and equal liability, gender integration was declared complete. Sex- and gender-based differences were minimized, though related challenges prevailed.

This chapter suggests that the persistent denial of women as women in the military, whether perceived as a gender-neutral or gender-blind perspective, raises important considerations regarding how sex and gender is constructed and understood, and as a result, limits the potential for gender-diverse contributions to the Canadian military.[4] The chapter begins with brief discussion of the theoretical context for the participation of women in the military, including an illustration of the insidious impact of unconscious, frequently well-intended impact of sex- and gender-based assumptions rooted in masculine organizational culture.

Sex, Gender, and the Military

A predominant theme that has consumed much of the debate about the participation of women in Western military organizations is the relationship between gender, sex, and the "warrior." Sociologist Helena Carreiras characterizes these discussions as the "rights versus readiness" perspectives – that is, the right of women to serve in the military versus the impact of female participation on the effectiveness or "readiness" of the military.[5] Carreiras notes that these debates have been intense, pervasive, and confrontational, and have had significant impact on government and military policy decisions on women's military service. In her analysis of gender integration in NATO military organizations, she notes that arguments presented to resist the expanded participation of women "have been produced *ad nauseam*."[6] Regardless of the actual questions presented, the enduring concerns in Canada and elsewhere have been about the maternity and maternal roles of women, the mental and physical suitability of women for military roles, the impact of women on group (male) cohesion and effectiveness, and public and personal attitudes towards women in the military.[7] In spite of the historical and cross-cultural evidence of women's ability to perform in a range of war roles, including combat,[8] opponents of women in combat continue to claim that women are not aggressive enough, do not possess the required physical strength, represent the risk of forced or consensual (heterosexual) sexual relationships, and compromise privacy between men and women. Finally, opponents have argued that the public will not tolerate women coming home as casualties of combat, being held as a prisoner of war, or in roles that require them to kill, even when those they kill are the enemy.[9] Importantly, such arguments are based upon assumptions about essential differences associated with the biological sex of soldiers. Alternatively, gender is socially constructed and recognizes that roles, experiences, attributes, and relationships among women and men are diverse and are not limited to biological and physiological characteristics.[10] Gender is most appropriately used to reflect individual experiences within society; however, reference to sex is used throughout this analysis when emphasizing dichotomous assumptions about females and males.

Dominant discourse in the Canadian military claims full gender integration, based largely on the fact that women are permitted to serve in all military roles and are serving in virtually all military occupations.[11] To illustrate, this chapter focuses on the struggle to expand military roles for women. However, the strategies to negotiate the inclusion of women also highlight the extent to which gender differences among males and females, including important intersections of gender such as ethnicity, age, ability, geography,[12] sexual orientation, and gender identity and expression,[13] are negotiated within military culture. A gender-neutral approach to policy strives to ensure equality for all members, yet that same policy, and the culture that it guides, can have varied impact. Alternatively, gender mainstreaming is a strategy to assess implications of any action, policy, program, etc. for both men and women, while recognizing differences between and among women and men.[14] Just as embedded gender-neutral cultural disposition can facilitate acceptance and career success for individual women and men, it also helps to sustain homogeneous cultural practices that shape member experience as well as response to operational challenges.

One such challenge took place on 17 May 2006, when Captain Nichola Goddard died on the battlefield in a firefight with Taliban insurgents in Afghanistan. Because she was the first female Canadian combat arms soldier to die in combat, the Canadian media response to Captain Goddard's death was extensive; this event and the media coverage had a significant impact on Canadian public discourse and signalled an important historical event in Canadian military history.[15] The formal Canadian military response to her death emphasized the importance of attributing equal value to the death of all soldiers, regardless of gender.[16] Canadians would expect nothing less than formal recognition by the military that all casualties were a significant loss to the military and the nation. In spite of the heightened coverage, analysis of Canadian media response further revealed equitable value attributed to both male and female casualties.[17] However, the responses of Goddard's colleagues, while intended to underscore her value as a soldier, persistently denied her gendered status. A male colleague, for example, emphasized that Captain Goddard was "more than just a female soldier" and insisted that she would want to be remembered as a Canadian soldier, rather than *just a female soldier* (emphasis added).[18] Still others placed sole emphasis on Captain Goddard's place in history as the first Canadian "FOO [Forward Observation Officer] to call in the bullets since Korea.... *Not the first woman* [emphasis added], the first FOO."[19] While it is important to recognize her contribution to military history, this recognition was premised on the insistence that she *not* be recognized as a woman or a female soldier, as if that would somehow diminish the value of her contributions.

The responses of Captain Goddard's peers were not consciously intended to undermine or minimize the importance of her contributions. In fact, Captain Goddard and many other women are held in high esteem by the institution and by their colleagues because they perform competently in their military roles, and they do so without asking to be recognized as women or in any other special way that sets them apart. It was very important to Captain Goddard's peers that she be recognized as a gender-*neutral* soldier. Even in the absence of overt resistance to women in traditionally masculine roles, such unconscious biases not only deny women, and some men, ready access to their foundational identity as socially gendered individuals, but also represent the potential suppression of diverse contributions to security challenges, including those sex- and gender-related challenges that are likely to be present before, during, and after conflict. Notwithstanding the increasing participation of women in the military, this discourse illustrates insistence that all women and men are the same, thus sustaining a homogeneous organizational culture based on traditional values, priorities, and processes established by a historically male-dominated institution.

Negotiating the *Participation of Women* in the Canadian Military

In 1970, the Royal Commission on the Status of Women in Canada (RCSW) presented 167 recommendations to the government of Canada in relation to the status of women. Five of these recommendations were concerned specifically with the participation of women in the military. The RCSW recommended that all occupations in the Canadian Forces be open to women; married women be permitted to join; the length of the initial engagement for which personnel were required to enlist be the same for women and men; a woman be permitted to continue to serve in the military after she had a child; and the Canadian Forces Superannuation Act be amended to include the same provisions for female as for male contributors.[20]

As a direct result of these recommendations, in July 1971 the Defence Council directed the removal of limitations on the employment of women, other than in primary combat, in remote locations, and in service at sea. "Womanpower" was acceptable when required, but under no circumstances would women be permitted to serve in combat occupations or in military units that might encounter combat on operational deployments. Regardless of the opportunities, there were challenges. Throughout the 1970s, the Director of Women Personnel (DWP), established in 1969 to advise senior leadership on matters affecting servicewomen in the Regular Force, was most often the only line of defence and advocacy for the status of women in the CF. In spite of the direction of Defence Council, the office of the DWP, and a small number of other influencers in National Defence Headquarters at the time, struggled "trade-by-trade" to convince senior leadership to open up greater opportunities for women.[21] They were largely successful.

By the time the Canadian Human Rights Act (CHRA) was proclaimed in 1978, women were employed in 81 of 127 non-commissioned trades and officer classifications.[22] However, despite the opening of numerous previously all-male occupations, most women continued to be employed in a small number of support occupations; those who were venturing into and facing the challenges of being a "first" in previously all-male domains were relatively few. The number of women serving in the Canadian military had nearly tripled, from 1,600 in 1968 to 4,786 in 1978 to represent 5.9 per cent of the Regular Force (see table 3.1),[23] yet a sex-based division of labour persisted. By 1980, 94 per cent of female officers and 71 per cent of female non-commissioned members were employed in medical and administrative occupations.[24]

In 1979, the Chief of the Defence Staff (CDS), Admiral Robert Falls, established the Servicewomen in Non-Traditional Environments and Roles (SWINTER) trials to negotiate the terms of the bona fide conditions of the CHRA. Given the many uncertainties, the SWINTER directive emphasized that "every effort must be made for the Canadian Forces to retain the initiative" in the employment of women to avoid potentially negative consequences, including "high-profile, counter-productive, media coverage," and tensions among unprepared men.[25] In spite of the need for "womanpower," the employment of women was considered risky and would have to be negotiated carefully. The SWINTER trials ran from 1979 to 1985, but they did not provide the bona fide evidence required by the CHRA to justify continued limitations to the employment of women. In fact, the SWINTER evaluations produced strong evidence that factors other than the actual abilities and performance of servicewomen influenced male attitudes towards women and ultimately the extent of integration achieved.[26] Consequently, by the mid-1980s, the military permitted women to serve in near-combat support roles but continued to restrict their participation in the combat arms and war-fighting platforms such as warships and fighter aircraft. By 1985, almost 7,500 women represented 8.9 per cent of the Regular Force (see table 3.1).

On the heels of the CHRA, the Canadian Charter of Rights and Freedoms was entrenched within the 1982 Canadian Constitution. Section 15 of the Charter was particularly relevant, as it provided equality for disadvantaged groups including legal protection against discrimination based on race, national or ethnic origin, colour, religion, sex, age, or mental or physical disability. This placed additional pressure on the CF to establish a strong case to limit the employment of women and also challenged military

Table 3.1. Increasing Representation of Women in the Regular Force
of the Canadian Armed Forces, 1965–2017

Year	Number of Women	Percentage of Women
1965	1,500	1.6
1971	1,600	1.8
1978	4,786	5.9
1985	7,467	8.9
1989	8,641	9.9
1999	6,664	10.8
2011	9,303	13.7
2017	9,716	14.7

Sources: For the years 1965, 1971, and 1978, Simpson, Toole, and Player, "Women in the Canadian Forces"; 1985, Canadian Forces, Assistance Deputy Minister (Personnel), *History of Women's Participation in the CF*, October 1995; 1989 and 1999, L. Tanner, *Gender Integration in the Canadian Forces: A Quantitative and Qualitative Analysis,* Department of National Defence, Director Military Gender Integration and Employment Equity, 1999; 2011 and 2017, Canadian Armed Forces Employment Equity Reports 2010–11 and 2016–17, respectively.

policy that excluded homosexuals from membership in the CF. The civilian Association for Women's Equity in the Canadian Forces provided testimony to the Parliamentary Justice Committee to challenge military claims to the requirement for male-only domains to preserve operational effectiveness. In response to the Charter and associated external pressure, in 1986, an internal CF Charter Task Force on Equality Issues (CTF) was struck to examine the impact of the employment of women and homosexuals on the CF. The CTF made a concerted effort to establish a warrior rationale for military exemptions from the civilian human rights standards; that is, to produce evidence to reinforce claims to all-male combat roles and ensure that the CF would be exempted from Section 15 of the Charter.[27]

As the task force delivered its findings, the Canadian Human Rights Commission launched hearings into complaints from three Canadian women and one man regarding limitations on the employment of women in the CF. In February 1987, as the hearings continued, the Minister of National Defence (MND), Perrin Beatty, ordered the Department of National Defence to develop trial options to determine which single-gender units and military occupations could be opened to mixed-gender employment. The Combat Related Employment of Women (CREW) trials were developed to evaluate the impact of women on the operational effectiveness of trial combat units, in a manner similar to the earlier SWINTER trials.[28] Two years after the CREW project was established, progress among the naval occupations was evident. Women were easily attracted to the Maritime Surface and Sub-Surface (MARS) officer occupation and naval operations branch non-commissioned occupations for the CREW trials. In fact, in February 1989 the recruitment of women into the navy trial was put on hold as the number of women participating exceeded trial minimum requirements for each occupation.[29]

In 1989, the CREW trials were superseded by the decision of the Canadian Human Rights Tribunal. The CHRT directed the CF to fully integrate women into all environments and roles, except submarine service, over the following ten-year period. The tribunal further directed that current CREW trials would not be regarded as "trials" and directed the CF to implement internal and external monitoring as it moved towards full gender integration by 1999.[30] Although recommendations had been made in the past to open all military occupations to women, this was the first time that the CF were given legally binding direction and made accountable to an external body in their efforts to implement that direction. The CF explored the possibility of an appeal to the CHRT ruling, based largely on the absence of evidence that gender integration would not harm operational effectiveness. But less than two weeks after the tribunal decision in February, CF senior leadership determined there was little chance for a successful appeal. On 1 March 1989, the Chief of the Defence Staff (CDS), General Paul Manson, shared the tribunal decision with members of the CF through a CF-wide message:

> First, I can tell you that, although I have expressed concern over the legality and substance of the Tribunal direction to terminate the trials, it has been concluded that an appeal act not be undertaken. As a

consequence [emphasis added], we must now accept that there no longer exists a bona fide occupational requirement for discrimination against women through employment limitations.... The main point that I wish to make at this time is that the CHRC decision can be looked upon as the latest (and presumably the last) of a series of developments within the CF over the past 20 years leading to the full equality between the serving men and women of the forces.[31]

The disappointment of the CF was palpable: it would take more than the tribunal decision to reverse the momentum of resistance that had been accumulating, with leadership support, in the previous twenty years.

Negotiating *Gender* in the Canadian Military

For the better part of the previous two decades, CF leadership had placed considerable priority and effort on research and trial programs to evaluate the impact of the participation of women on previously all-male military units and roles based on assumptions about dichotomous sex-based differences between women and men.[32] In response to the ruling of the CHRT in February, strategy abruptly shifted; by July 1989, CF policy was rewritten to reflect a "gender-neutral" force in which women and men shared equally, both opportunity and liability.[33] All women in the military, regardless of the terms of service under which they had enrolled or the length of time during which they had served within the sex-based limitations of those terms of service, immediately became eligible and liable for service in all military units. In spite of the significant concerns that had persisted for the better part of two decades about the potential negative impact of women on operational effectiveness, those concerns were quickly abandoned and new CF employment policies would apply to all serving women and men. Even in cases in which women were involuntary participants and clearly not motivated or well prepared to serve in previously all-male operational units, there was no evident concern that their inclusion would harm operational effectiveness.[34]

In the immediate aftermath of the CHRT no one but the Director of Women Personnel was paying any attention to women's issues.[35] The elimination of the position of the DWP in 1990 was but one in a series of changes to reinforce the new gender-neutral position of the military, changes that significantly reduced the visibility of women within broader demands on the organization for social change and reduced defence expenditures, including significant personnel reductions. In 1989, the CREW team had assumed the internal monitoring function as directed by the CHRT; however, the CREW project was disbanded in 1991, and by 1992, the Director Conditions of Service, along with responsibility for the oversight of a range of personnel issues, had assumed formal responsibility for "overseeing and monitoring issues of integration."[36] Oversight of gender integration from within the CF had been almost completely eliminated.

In February 1990, the MND, Bill McKnight, and the Associate MND, Mary Collins, established the Minister's Advisory Board (MAB) on the Integration of Women in the Canadian Forces[37] to "advise and make recommendations to the Ministers on the progress of the integration of women in the CF pursuant to the Human Rights Tribunal decision."[38] In fulfilling its mandate, the board attempted to remain at arm's length from internal military stakeholders, including policy- and decision-makers. Even though several members of the MAB had served in the CF, few senior military policy and research staff believed that the board had sufficient awareness of the CF or adequate knowledge of the scientific methods and research processes required to produce valid observations and recommendations.[39] In a 1995 mid-term review of the MAB, the Chief of Personnel Resource Management, Brigadier-General Beno, noted that the board played "a credibility role, a validating role that will, *if nothing else*, guard against someone stepping in to tell us how to do our business" (emphasis added).[40] This was not exactly an affirmation of the value of the board's work. The MAB was coming to the end of its five-year term, and advisory committees across government were under review in response to shrinking government budgets. As a result, the MAB was stood down by the MND in 1995.[41]

The ten years following the CHRT were challenging for the CF as the organization struggled to come to terms with the implications of the ruling. During the first five years, barriers to the full participation of women in the CF were addressed through such initiatives as the implementation of harassment policy and personal equipment adaptations.[42] Also, as noted in an earlier analysis of gender integration in the Canadian Forces, the early 1990s witnessed a shift from a focus on the *integration of women* to *gender integration*. Regardless of some recognition of the complexity of gender integration, in 1994, the CF declared that on the basis of "equal opportunity and equal liability policy, governing the employment of women in the CF," *in principle* gender integration was complete.[43] However, the CF "struggled to come to terms with the expectations of the CHRC, including what the CHRC would accept as compliance with the 1989 Tribunal order."[44]

For most of the decade following the 1989 tribunal order, senior leadership remained virtually silent on gender integration. Similarly, military psychologist Rosemary Park describes CF silence in response to the legal inclusion of homosexuals in 1992 as one of "benign neutrality," which signalled qualified acceptance.[45] However, as the 1999 CHRT decision approached, there was an outbreak of senior leadership direction to address the compliance gaps. The CF was also preparing for its new obligations to the Employment Equity Act in 1996.[46] Leadership on gender integration expanded from staff monitoring and research to include several senior leadership initiatives to convince the commission that the CF was committed and capable of delivering fairness and equitable opportunity to all women and men in the military. By 1996, the Department of National Defence had established a Defence Diversity Council to provide senior leadership oversight of all issues related to diversity including employment equity and gender integration. In 1998, the MND, Art Eggleton, also stood up the "Minister's Advisory Board on Gender Integration and Employment Equity in the Canadian Forces," thus re-establishing an external monitoring role.[47]

The Canadian Forces held a press conference on 19 February 1999, exactly ten years after the Canadian Human Rights Tribunal

Order. The army, navy, and air force claimed that major progress had been made in the past ten years and more progress would follow. Indeed, in spite of personnel reductions and overall decrease in the number of women serving in the Regular Force, representation increased from 9.9 per cent in 1989 to 10.8 per cent in 1999 (see table 3.1). Also in February 1999, the Chief Commissioner of the CHRC, Michele Falardeau-Ramsay, told the Chief of the Defence Staff, General Maurice Baril, that while the tribunal objectives had not been met, the commission was satisfied that senior leadership had demonstrated commitment to addressing the remaining challenges of gender integration.[48] As a result, conditions that had been enforced by the tribunal, including external monitoring of CF processes related to gender integration, were lifted. In 2000, the external advisory board concluded that the CF had developed admirable plans but was failing to implement them.[49] The tenure of the board was short; it was stood down in 2000 after delivering just two reports to the MND.

For all intents and purposes, gender integration was now no longer an issue as the Canadian military considered gender integration to be a fait accompli. In 1999, the CF defined gender integration as "the process of facilitating the full participation of women in the CF,"[50] yet in the following years continued to assume a gender-neutral posture. For those inside the military who experienced the transition from outright resistance to the relative acceptance of women in all military roles, gender integration had certainly come a long way. And there were positive indications of change. A harassment survey administered in 1998 to military members indicated that anonymously reported rates of sexual harassment among women had decreased from 26.2 per cent in 1992 to 14 per cent in 1998,[51] and further declined to 9 per cent by 2012.[52] However, in April 2014 sexual misconduct in the CAF was brought to public attention when Canadian newsmagazine *L'Actualité*, along with sister magazine *Maclean's*,[53] claimed that the prevalence of sexual harassment and sexual misconduct in the CAF was much higher than that previously identified in CAF research and data sources. The Chief of the Defence Staff (CDS) responded swiftly, commissioning an external review of sexual harassment and sexual misconduct.[54] The report of the External Review Authority, prepared by former Supreme Court justice Marie Deschamps, was released in April 2015. It described "a prevailing sexualized environment characterized by the frequent use of sexualized language, sexual jokes, innuendos," and "discriminatory comments with respect to the abilities of female members of the military," and further noted that the use of language that belittles women is commonplace and frequently condoned.[55] In response, by August 2015 the CDS established Operation HONOUR to eliminate harmful and inappropriate sexual behaviour[56] along with broader efforts to effect culture change in the Canadian military.[57] A Statistics Canada survey administered to CAF members in 2016 reinforced the insidious and persistent challenge; women were four times as likely as their male counterparts to report experience of sexual assault in the previous twelve months (4.8 and 1.2 per cent, respectively),[58] and LGBT members of the CAF were more likely to report experience of sexual assault than non-LGBT members (5.6 and 1.6 per cent, respectively).[59] This discussion, along with these recent challenges related to sexual harassment and sexual misconduct, raises important questions about the extent to which sex- and gender-based differences have been integrated, or alternatively, assimilated within military culture.

Gender Inclusion?

Gender-neutral approaches are often effective and necessary to demonstrate that all members are equally important to the team and share the load equitably. This approach is also useful in ensuring that personnel are not frustrated by special attention to the female members of the team and in assisting women with blending in or integrating into the team without undue attention. In fact, military women are frequently more adamant than their male peers that they not receive attention because they are different. This is one way in which gender-neutral cultural values undermine the potential added value of gender diversity, including any unique value that difference might bring to a military operation. Military women have learned that, for the most part, their success is based on fitting into a male-dominated culture, not being different.

Gender-neutral assumptions and approaches also satisfy military culture in ensuring that military policy applies equally to women and men, and most importantly women and men share equal opportunity and equal liability in the military. Just as women are afforded the opportunity to serve in all military roles, they are also equally liable for service that puts them in harm's way. Furthermore, all military members are subject to universality of service, that is, regardless of military occupation all must be physically and psychologically fit for deployment to fulfil the defence and security priorities of the government of Canada. These essential principles guide military service and military culture. Military doctrine, values, and culture are nurtured to prepare for war. Military doctrine reminds all military members that operations other than war do not represent the raison d'être of a military organization. And war is a male-dominated and masculine endeavour. To suggest that women bring particular value to military missions in anything other than non-combat, traditional gender-support roles threatens the primacy of the masculine combat role of the military. A gender-neutral culture, however, can accommodate the inclusion of women without undermining that role.[60]

Even so, Canada was one of the first states to permit women to serve in combat occupations, and throughout Canada's combat commitment to Afghanistan, representation increased. By 2011, women comprised 13.7 per cent of Regular Force members. As such, Canada has garnered significant attention in recent years as other countries begin to remove barriers to the participation of women in ground combat roles. Canadian military women served in combat leadership roles in Afghanistan,[61] including now Major-General Jennie Carignan who in 2016 became the first woman with a combat arms background to achieve General officer status in the Canadian military. Canada has first-hand experience with women on combat teams and did use women, when necessary, for functional sex-based tasks, such as searches, involving women in Afghanistan. Having women performing such tasks made the CAF more effective in the field, not less. Such consideration for

Afghan social values also may have helped improve the Afghan public's attitude towards the Canadian military. On the basis of these successes, the Canadian military has largely considered itself to be fully gender-integrated. Indeed, given some of the gender-related challenges faced in Afghanistan, it would be difficult to argue that Canadian military women do not provide unique value to military operational teams. Yet, as noted earlier, soldier responses to the nation's first female combat casualty in Afghanistan persistently denied difference.

Conclusion

In spite of evident progress in the representation of women into a full range of occupations and roles, contemporary Canadian military history is based upon a foundation of significant resistance to expanded roles for women. This resistance, which was most evident until 1989, was based upon the assumption that gender- and sex-based differences were synonymous and reflected a dichotomous, biologically determined construct. Consequently, decision-making reflected commitment to operational effectiveness that depended upon homogeneous all-male combat teams supported by women in restricted roles. CF leadership protected the masculine warrior identity of the combat arms at a time of increasing concern that the military was losing its unique vocational warrior focus. Immediately following the ruling of the CHRT and opening of access to combat roles for women, the CF shifted to a gender-neutral or gender-blind strategy that minimized differences between women and men, thus limiting the extent to which gender differences were celebrated, optimized, and included in previously all-male military cultural domains. These strategies defined sex and gender in ways that served organizational priorities while satisfying public demands for gender equality. Finally, persistent claims to gender-neutral identity within the Canadian military have implications for the effective integration of gender-diverse experiences and perspectives not only between women and men, but among different groups of men and women.

Today the Canadian military is working to address numerous sex- and gender-related challenges, including the promotion of diversity and inclusion as a core institutional value,[62] increasing the representation of women to 25 per cent by 2026,[63] mitigating sexual harassment and assault,[64] and integrating gender perspectives into operations to effectively respond to United Nations Security Council Resolution 1325 (2000) and subsequent UN women, peace, and security resolutions.[65] This chapter suggests that the evolution of gender integration and broader diversity in the military has been instrumental in preparing the Canadian Armed Forces for the complexity of challenges that it faces today; however, it also highlights the need to reconcile traditional cultural assumptions as the military develops new strategies and moves forward to achieve greater gender diversity, inclusion, and equality.

chapter four

Coming Out in Uniform: A Personal Reflection

JACQUELINE LOPOUR AND NICK DESHPANDE

To varying degrees, "coming out" remains a difficult prospect for many lesbian, gay, bisexual, transgender, and queer youth and adults. The LGBTQ+ community has been at the forefront of building alliances in liberal democracies to both gain and affirm their rights. Identity politics has helped push liberal democracies into recognizing the discrimination many people face by virtue of their social grouping or identity markers. The LGBTQ+ community's battle to affirm their rights in the Canadian military mirrors the broader rise of identity politics in social and political life. Yet the Canadian military provides a unique and challenging backdrop in which members of the LGBTQ+ community lead their lives. This case shows that while acceptance has been normalized, at least at a *policy* level since approximately 1992, there remains a wide variance between military members' coming out journeys and their sense of inclusion. As noted in the introductory chapter, while diversity is a fact, inclusion is a choice. The latter has not always been a smooth experience for many LGBTQ+ community members in the Canadian Armed Forces. This chapter contextualizes experiences of coming out in the broader cultural, political, and social environment of LGBTQ+ inclusion in the CAF. Tracing broad themes of diversity and inclusion efforts of the LGBTQ+ community within the CAF provides a unique insight into the challenge and opportunities that identity politics have brought to the organization.

Canada is widely considered a leading nation for the successful integration of LGBTQ+ personnel into the armed forces.[1] In

2014, the CAF ranked sixth of 103 countries on a global index that considered the degree to which inclusionary policies and practices for LGBTQ+ personnel are adopted.[2] Other nations continuously reference the CAF model of integration and diversity, especially in organizational transformation and civil-military interactions. Even though it is a middle power, Canada's viewpoint has enormous bearing on other countries in such matters. Consider, for example, the exposure of foreign military officers to CAF professional development programs, which introduces allies to, in many cases, relatively progressive principles. The CAF serve as a laudable example to international, domestic, and academic audiences.[3] Canada acts as a "norm entrepreneur"[4] in international normative diffusion, promoting normative change by living by progressive principles.

Experiences of LGBTQ+ Personnel

In spite of this progressive stance globally, a 2015 report entitled *External Review into Sexual Misconduct and Sexual Harassment in the Canadian Armed Forces*, led by former Supreme Court justice Marie Deschamps, illustrated the practical shortcomings of current policies by highlighting the plight of LGBTQ+ personnel. The report is based on interviews that focused on sexual harassment and inappropriate workplace conduct, revealing that "there is an underlying sexualized culture in the CAF that is hostile to women and LGTBQ members, and conducive to more serious incidents of sexual harassment and assault. Cultural change is therefore key. It is not enough to simply revise policies or to repeat the mantra of 'zero tolerance.' Leaders must acknowledge that sexual misconduct is a real and serious problem for the organization, one that requires their own direct and sustained attention."[5]

The report places great emphasis on the role that military leaders can have in changing organizational cultures and moving the needle on inclusion. Deschamps goes on to add that there is a "pervasive low-level harassment, a hostile environment for women and LGBTQ+ members, and, in some cases, more serious and traumatic incidents of sexual assault."[6] The report concludes, in part, that "dismissive responses such as 'this is just the way of the military' are no longer appropriate."[7] The Deschamps report prompted a deluge of lawsuits against the CAF on the grounds of permitting a culture of sexual harassment. A civilian entity called the Sexual Misconduct Response Centre, operating apart from the military chain of command, was set up to accept anonymized counselling and provide information to service members on how to escalate their concerns. As the authors of this chapter and others in this volume note, there remains much more work to be done to make the CAF an *inclusive* workplace.

Research into LGBTQ+ members' experiences in the CAF is an expanding field, but there remains considerable room for further documenting individual narratives and how to improve diversity and inclusion in the Canadian military. Many LGBTQ+ community members may still not feel that the military is an inclusive place that allows them to be open about their identity. Research examines the prejudices, harassment, and persecution that gay and lesbian soldiers faced during the ban that prohibited LGBTQ+ personnel from serving openly.[8] Poulin and Goulique, for example, reported extensive academic prejudice, roadblocks, and problems obtaining the funding needed to support their research about lesbians' experiences in the CAF.[9] Other research appears to target specific policy debates, rather than provide a comprehensive assessment of the issue. After the CAF lifted its ban on LGBTQ+ personnel, other Western militaries began to consider their own changes, sparking an increased appetite for working papers and academic studies about the impact of LGBTQ+ soldiers on military cohesion and readiness.[10] While some of these studies draw conclusions from extensive surveys, few focus closely on individual narratives that reflect the experiences of LGBTQ+ service members. This is what prompted us to include Nick Deshpande's story in this chapter.

While the study of data and larger trends is important, it cannot and should not be understood without also considering the individual and personal experiences of LGBTQ+ military personnel. As the barometers of the practical application of personnel policies, personal narratives translate numbers and statistics into real, lived experiences and provide a new way of studying these issues. This approach considers how researchers' personal experiences can yield important new insights and perspectives.[11]After all, policies about diversity and integration are, by their very nature, policies that affect people's professional and personal lives. Personal narratives can help illuminate key policy discussions and offer critical insights to enable policymakers to create effective policies and practices. In this chapter, LGBTQ+ experiences in the Canadian military is juxtaposed with the literature in an effort to evaluate the state of acceptance and CAF inclusion of one form of diversity.

A History of LGBTQ+ Mistreatment

Until 1992, openly gay and lesbian individuals were not allowed to enlist or serve in the armed forces; those already enrolled could be penalized or dismissed if discovered. In 1967, the Canadian military implemented administrative order CFAO 19-20, or "Sexual Deviation – Investigation, Medical Investigation and Disposal." The order stipulated that any CAF personnel suspected of being gay or lesbian must be investigated and removed from the military, preferably with little or no publicity.[12] As a result of these policies, gay and lesbian soldiers faced harassment, prejudice, and outright persecution. Such treatment was not limited to CAF personnel, as LGBTQ+ personnel in the RCMP and other federal department faced similar persecution.

When the ban was in place, the military's Special Investigations Unit conducted intrusive investigations into suspected LGBTQ+ personnel. In the 1950s and 1960s, the Canadian government commissioned research on a "fruit machine," a supposedly scientific test that could be used to identify gay personnel.[13] The program – an abject failure – was defunded in the late 1960s, but even after that, anti-LGBTQ+ investigations continued. Right up to the time when the ban was lifted, soldiers suspected of being LGBTQ+ were harassed, spied on, and interrogated.[14] They were often pressured to expose other LGBTQ+ personnel. Some members reported prolonged physical surveillance, wiretapping of their personal phones, and day-long interrogation sessions where they were forced to recount the most intimate details of their lives.[15] Many of these soldiers lost their security clearances or were transferred from positions in which they excelled. In some cases, they were released from the military altogether.[16] Investigations were so invasive that they could, by some accounts, meet the Canadian Criminal Code definition of torture.[17] Such harsh tactics were increasingly at odds with Canadian society mores, which in the 1980s were becoming more open, inclusive, and progressive. For example, the Charter of Rights and Freedoms enshrined the prohibition of discrimination on the grounds of sexual orientation. This constitutional protection of LGBTQ+ people in Canada was the start of legal victories for equality, but an arduous road still lay ahead.

The negative psychological impact of the harsh anti-LGBTQ+ investigation tactics cannot be understated. Studies have revealed a high correlation between the harassment these soldiers experienced and severe mental health complications, such as depression, social withdrawal, and even suicide.[18] Some service members turned to drugs and alcohol to cope. Others wilted under the stress of trying to live a double life in which they hid their sexuality from workplace colleagues and lived in fear of being outed.[19] Even after the ban was lifted, many LGBTQ+ personnel were afraid to come out, because they feared it could harm their careers or result in an uncomfortable work environment. Only now are the military and the Canadian government beginning to come to terms with this dark chapter.[20]

A trailblazer in pushing the cause of LGBTQ+ personnel was the story of Michelle Douglas, a young service-woman with an exemplary record who was discharged from the Canadian military on the grounds that she was "not advantageously employable due to homosexuality."[21] In 1989, Douglas subsequently sued the Department of National Defence (DND), arguing that her rights under the Charter of Rights and Freedom had been violated. Facing almost assured defeat in court, DND settled the case with Douglas and decided to overturn the ban. While both the DND and the courts were in favour of removing the ban on LGBTQ+ personnel, it is worthy to note that the government of the day faced stiff resistance by members of Parliament.[22]

Despite political pressure, the Chief of Defence Staff, General John de Chastelain, issued a memo noting that "policies restricting the service of homosexuals in the CF are contrary to the Canadian Charter of Rights and Freedoms."[23] Therefore the ban on LGBTQ+ effectively ended on 27 October 1992. General de Chastelain added that this was a policy that some CAF members would find difficult but that "attitudes and legislation have changed. After careful examination and deliberation I am satisfied that the policy no longer serves the best interests of the CF and its members."[24] This became a milestone in the history of not just the Canadian Armed Forces, but for the Western world. Canada became one of the first Western countries to allow LGBTQ+ personnel to serve openly.

Until that time, the official view was that LGBTQ+ personnel posed a threat to unit cohesion, military order, and national security.[25] Again, as the editors' introductory chapter details, the naysayers to diversity often refer to cohesion in their rejection of diversity. The naysayers were even more discriminatory to the LGBTQ+ community. Both anti-communist and anti-Soviet propaganda campaigns were linked to campaigns against homosexuality.[26] Securitizing homosexuality as a national security threat added another layer to the already great prejudice and discrimination that LGBTQ+ had to contend with. Moreover, a number of high-profile trials in England had claimed that its homosexual personnel were spies working on behalf of the Soviet Union, sending a chill and creating a witch hunt for LGBTQ+ personnel.[27] According to official memoranda, homosexual personnel were considered a counterintelligence threat because they were assumed to be susceptible to blackmail or coercion by hostile intelligence services.[28]

These official explanations, however, belied unacknowledged but manifested social and cultural fears that LGBTQ+ soldiers might somehow threaten the military's traditional, conservative, masculine, heterosexual image, a point similarly echoed by Davis in her chapter in this volume on the inclusion of women. The CAF was characterized by an unofficial ideology of hegemonic masculinity that reinforced "deeply rooted heterosexism in Canadian state institutions."[29] This ideology reflected official policies of exclusion and vice versa, leading to the targeting and expulsion of LGBTQ+ personnel until 1992.

After the ban was lifted, a shared sense of duty and professionalism largely overrode personal prejudice of individual soldiers, according to the hallmark study on this subject. Some military officials noted, "It's not that big a deal for us [including gays and lesbians in the military].... On a day-to-day basis, there probably hasn't been much of a change. People who were typically high performers before are typically high performers now."[30] Another common sentiment shared was that gay members of the military had always served and it was really a non-issue. Belkin and McNicol also noted that the timing of this overturn on the gay ban came at the same time as the end of the Cold War, which had similarly forced a rethinking of CAF's mission and raison d'être. As one CAF official told the authors, "Changes in policy have been greatly overshadowed by budget cuts, downsizing, changes in operational roles, operational tempo. This issue of the acceptance of homosexuals into the forces pales into insignificance ... it's a non-issue."[31]

Even if some individuals maintained personal homophobic views, these were found to be moderated by officers who expressed little tolerance for harassment or prejudice. Senior leaders emphasized changes in *behaviour*, regardless of what an individual might personally *believe*,[32] because moderating belief is not necessarily – or practically – within the military's purview. Despite the official policy, however, individual service members' experiences vary widely, ranging from extremely positive to distressing cases of pervasive prejudice and discrimination as a result of persistent underlying hostility towards homosexuality and transgender people.

One disturbing response to lifting the ban on gay personnel came from a Black Watch reserve force officer who said, "There are a lot of guys in uniform who hate homosexuals, and don't want them around in the service. A lot of men are disgusted with the court ruling, but they have to live with it. They don't want to speak up. They're just keeping their heads down."[33] Again these views may have been held by some CAF personnel, but Belkin and McNicol also noted that the expectation was that gay personnel should be treated equally. Diversity was being accepted in the rank and file of the military, but the march towards inclusion continues. An individual narrative follows.

Coming Out

When co-author of this chapter Nick Deshpande joined the military in 2003 at age eighteen, he suppressed his sexuality. He had made the conscious decision not to be gay, as he thought it would preclude many life experiences he wished to have, such as marriage and family. Living openly gay would invite social ostracization, for which Deshpande imagined it was not worth coming out. He learned much later this mindset was common among lesbian and gay youth. When Deshpande enrolled at the Royal Military College, he was unaware of Canadian LGBTQ+ history in general, and of how the military had treated LGBTQ+ personnel in particular. He remained closeted for much of his military career, a little in awe of colleagues and classmates who were openly homosexual. For Deshpande, it was beyond mere suppression to the point of ingrained habit; he had heterosexual relationships and was very conscious of the need to avoid suspicion that he was gay.

This was the case throughout military college and the first three years of Deshpande's career as an officer. Only when he left Canadian Forces base Petawawa, a relatively rural location, and moved to the larger city of Kingston, did he develop a level of comfort and realization that the course he had adopted was not sustainable. He began to acquaint himself with the gay community, while keeping a firewall between his newfound personal freedom and his professional life. Deshpande made the decision to tell colleagues that he was gay, over time, starting in 2013. He encountered no prejudice, though he was very selective about sharing his orientation. That changed with time, as he increasingly identified as gay, though he sometimes felt uneasy about what the reaction might be from other CAF members. Without exception, however, Deshpande received ardent support from peers and leaders.

This positive experience is described in order to show that acceptance and inclusion is possible, and to avoid simply framing the CAF as negative towards LGBTQ+ personnel. Certainly, however, homophobia persists in the CAF, perhaps at latent levels that result in the type of toxic workplaces addressed in the External Review. As Deshpande met many LGBTQ+ colleagues, it was apparent that his uneventful and positive experience of serving as an openly gay member was not necessarily the norm. Colleagues reported vastly different experiences. One in particular faced overt homophobia in his workplace by a superior and vexatious treatment that might fall below a traditional threshold of harassment, but was designed to make working conditions adverse. It was a significant stressor: the prospect of going to work was enough to induce Deshpande's co-worker's anxiety.

Coming out, the act of declaring one's sexuality openly, is a very personal process that is heavily influenced by social milieu. Familial support, friends, the workplace, and other factors all have a bearing on an individual's decision to "come out." Living as openly gay, lesbian, transgendered, or queer is not necessarily a zero-sum affair: some may choose to be out in specific social contexts. Policy change is likely one factor that has an impact on serving members' decision to come out (and of prospective members to join the military in the first place). As a young man, Deshpande was able to come out while still serving, a feat rendered impossible for soldiers like him serving before 1992.

In Canada and the United States, previous exclusionary policies made it impossible to serve while being openly gay, and the emotional and psychological impact of this legacy on LGBTQ+ service members cannot be ignored. The repeal of "Don't Ask, Don't Tell" in the United States in 2011 was itself a remarkable moment, if only for the timing, especially late when compared to other liberal democracies. At the time, the implications were unclear to Deshpande, but it represented progress and made ostracization a more remote possibility. The appointment of an openly gay U.S. Secretary of the Army, Eric Fanning, in 2016 represents another symbolic moment indicative of more widespread acceptance. Highly visible figureheads, regardless of rank, can have a significant bearing on the success of both LGBTQ+ military members and civilians who support inclusive institutions – even across national boundaries.

The CAF's military and civilian leaders have more recently been trying to make amends for past practices. In November 2017, Chief of the Defence Staff Jonathan H. Vance General noted,

> Sadly, and not that long ago, our Canadian Armed Forces was on a different path. We spied on, interrogated, and criminally pursued our own people. We pitted friends against each other to protect their own careers. We stripped away their dignity before we ruined their livelihood. In many ways, those LGBTQ2 members were more worthy of the privilege of service than many of us. They committed to serving Canada by wearing our uniform, despite knowing they could be persecuted for just being themselves. That took courage, but as an institution, we didn't recognize it and we didn't defend them. On behalf of the Canadian Armed Forces, I am deeply sorry to all of you who were ever investigated, charged or released from the military because of your sexual orientation. You showed us honour and dedication, and we showed you the door. No apology or compensation can ever change the shameful way we instilled fear into your lives and took away your career.[34]

Prime Minister Justin Trudeau also issued a formal apology to members of the LGBTQ+ community:

> From the 1950s to the early 1990s, the government of Canada exercised its authority in a cruel and unjust manner, undertaking a campaign of oppression against members, and suspected members, of the LGBTQ2 communities. The goal was to identify these workers throughout the public service, including the foreign service, the military, and the RCMP, and persecute them. You see, the thinking of the day was that all non-heterosexual Canadians would automatically be at an increased risk of blackmail by our adversaries due to what was called "character weakness." This thinking was prejudiced and flawed. And sadly, what resulted was nothing short of a witch-hunt.[35]

Preceding PM Trudeau's formal apology to the LGBTQ+ community in late 2017, the government agreed to provide victims of the "gay purge" nearly $100 million in compensation. This was in response to a class action lawsuit filed against the Canadian military. Nearly a thousand people sought compensation in the lawsuit and the settlement. Along with the formal apology, these can be viewed as victories for those individuals who paid a high price for serving while hiding their sexual orientation or choosing to come out.

The Perils of Inclusion by Exception

Over the past decade, there has been a stronger chorus for supporting diversity, but, unlike the private sector, inclusion as a practice remains elusive. Diversity and inclusion are not synonymous. To use a metaphor, if diversity is asking people from all walks of life to the party, then inclusion is actually asking them to dance. As one private-sector company explains, "Diversity is the mix; inclusion is getting the mix to work well together."[36] Over the past few decades, Canada has undergone a cultural transformation, becoming a more tolerant, diverse, and open society that embraces diversity and inclusion and views members of the LGBTQ+ community as a national strength.

However, leaders' narratives and awareness training reflect, perhaps inadvertently, antiquated thinking. At around the time that "Don't Ask, Don't Tell" was repealed, a narrative of "inclusion by exception" or minimization was promoted by many leaders in the United States, including President Obama. The announcement of the repeal was a remarkable moment, and one that likely had an impact on lesbian and gay soldiers serving in militaries all around the world. Unfortunately, *tolerance* was elevated above *inclusion*. For example, President Obama said, "As one special operations warfighter said during the Pentagon's review ...: 'We have a gay guy in the unit. He's big, he's mean, he kills lots of bad guys.' 'No one cared that he was gay.' And I think that sums up perfectly the situation."[37] To LGBTQ+ service members, hearing that being gay did not matter as long as you performed well is a narrative very different from acceptance of the whole self. Davis, in this volume, makes a similar point about the need to acknowledge the gender of personnel instead of being "gender blind." Inclusion means recognizing the importance of people's gender and sexuality as an inescapable aspect of their personal and professional lives. If we are to ask individuals to put "service before self," we should also have the decency to accept those selves in their entirety.

By failing to matter, identifying as LGBTQ+ is perhaps not worth acknowledging. Yet it should be. "Don't Ask, Don't Tell" policy was essentially discriminatory as it placed a different and greater burden on LGBT+ service members. There is a delicate balance: being gay should have no bearing on others' treatment, and all members of the military wish to be assessed on the merits of their accomplishments. Yet the approach risks relegating characteristics as unworthy of celebration or import. Similar tensions on gender, again as discussed at length in Davis chapter in this volume, were evident at every turn when making women "be like the boys" was the wrong approach. Ignoring sexuality or gender or a taking a neutral or "blind" approach and focusing solely on performance fails to harness the full potential that diverse perspectives generate. Members of the military wish to be assessed on the merits of their accomplishments, but not at the cost of having aspects of their identity disregarded.

Furthermore, the merits of adopting policies that cast a wider net than acceptance and tolerance have a basis in operational effectiveness, especially as mission profiles extend well beyond combat to include capacity-building and human security. Operational effectiveness is the degree to which a team can achieve a given mission, and it is based on the individual performance of service members and the team's collective output. As a means of relating to communities in which soldiers are engaged, the military should be aware of members' characteristics that would engender empathy, conscientiousness, and understanding. In the same vein, individuals may not perform to their maximum potential in circumstances that might undermine trust and cohesion as the result of prejudice. Hence rather than thinking of homogeneity as a means of building cohesion, the modern military needs to see inclusion as a means of building cohesion.

Finally, how the CAF addresses LGBTQ+ inclusion has significant implications for recruitment as well. As clearly laid out in

Leuprecht's chapter in this volume, CAF recruitment has declined in recent years, and to reach out to young urban voters, where not just acceptance but celebration of LGBTQ+ rights has become a growing norm, how the Canadian military is viewed as an accepting and inclusive workplace can determine recruitment levels. In response, the Canadian government in June 2017 announced increased defence spending and a hiring surge underpinned by a comprehensive diversity policy.[38] Such a policy may permit the military to meet recruiting goals. A more progressive military may be more attractive to youth who have come of age in a society in which diversity and inclusion are cultural norms; these youths will likely expect their workplaces to reflect these values, especially as so many others in both the public and private sectors now do.

Conclusion

Coming out is a milestone in the life of a LGBTQ+ person. The military provides a unique backdrop for this process. Until 1992, it was not possible to be openly gay in the Canadian Armed Forces and continue to serve. Today, there is widespread recognition of the adverse impact of such policies. As an institution, the Canadian military has made great strides and today sets an example for similar institutions around the world. However, much work remains to be done.

As the 2015 review of Marie Deschamps reveals, if Canada is to be recognized as a leader on progressive personnel policies, work to prevent prejudice and intolerance from manifesting must continue. While prejudice and intolerance are not widespread in the CAF, they certainly exist and must be addressed. Within the Canadian Armed Forces, minority perceptions persist that acceptance of LGBTQ+ members will affect cohesion. Such perceptions are bolstered by louder voices across the border. In the United States, forces still work against the tide of diversity and inclusion. During the U.S. presidential race of 2016, one candidate declared, "We shouldn't view the military as a cauldron for social experiments."[39] The issue of whether transgendered people should be allowed to serve has also been reignited in the U.S. political discourse. These messages normalize discriminatory practices and have a wider audience beyond the United States.

The emphasis on professional conduct will remain important, because standards create the norms that shape group behaviour and beliefs. At the same time, true inclusion demands something greater than merely painting everyone with the same brush, a challenging prospect for any military. The following recommendations are intended to provoke thinking about how to create a culture of inclusion and an environment where all members feel and are accepted. First, the CAF should promote the implementation and resource allocation for Employee Resource Groups or similar groups, at an installation level. This model is commonly found in the private sector, and it allows for the formation of chapters around common issues and causes in which anyone can be a member. Such groups give rise to mentorship opportunities, another important source of support and stability for LGBTQ+ members.

Second, the CAF should empower the forthcoming Champion of Diversity and Inclusion to address and promote LGBTQ+ inclusion. Such a move will help avoid the pitfall of policies that lean towards assimilation. The CAF should also ensure that the health-care system and Care Delivery Units are equipped, trained, and have processes to support LGBTQ+ members' physical and mental well-being. Narratives of *inclusion*, in line with private-sector practices, which are distinct from approaches that merely highlight diversity and tolerance, and that celebrate and harness unique characteristics to unlocking talent and maximum potential, should be promoted by the CAF. According to Deloitte, inclusion "encompasses the unique beliefs, backgrounds, talents, capabilities, and ways of living of our people."[40] CAF leadership should deliberately look for ways to emphasize these narratives.

Third, the Royal Military Chaplaincy Corps must also be engaged as a resource for LGBTQ+ service members. As a critical stakeholder in the well-being of CAF members, and given their "ministry of presence," chaplains should adhere to a standard of care and maintain an open-door policy that can make them important resources to service members, who may be struggling not only with the professional, but also the social, moral, and religious implications of coming out.

Fourth, institutional leadership is an important element for the strengthening a culture of diversity and inclusion. Officers and the general leadership should be equipped with the tools to temper and stop homophobia in the workplace and ensure that accountability and performance measurement are related to how leaders foster inclusive workplace dynamics.

Last, the CAF must look beyond these short- to medium-term measures, by supporting and facilitating additional research – both internal and external – that explores LGBTQ+ individuals' experiences in the CAF. Future research may consider the personal narratives of transgender service members, in particular, as a way to highlight how individual experiences across the LGBTQ+ community vary widely, and as such, require different recommendations. This chapter provides one perspective. Gathering the views of multiple LGBTQ+ personnel will lead to a more compelling account of the current state of affairs in the CAF, and it could better inform future policy decisions. Aggregating anonymized data may yield additional results as well.

chapter five

The North's Canadian Rangers

P. Whitney Lackenbauer

In the twenty-first century, the Canadian Rangers – an unortho-dox military organization comprising predominantly Indigenous people – have emerged from the shadows to become a highly visible example of diversity and inclusion in the CAF. With approximately five thousand members, Rangers live in more than two hundred Canadian communities and speak "26 different languages and dialects, many Indigenous."[1] As part-time, non-commissioned members of a subcomponent of the CAF Reserves, the Rangers' official mission is "to provide a military presence in sparsely settled northern, coastal and isolated areas of Canada that can-not conveniently or economically be provided for by other com-ponents of the Canadian Forces."[2] Creating an organization that successfully mobilizes Canadians living in remote regions and situates them appropriately within the defence team has entailed moving beyond conventional military structures and practices.

Canada's extensive coastlines and vast northern expanses have presented security and sovereignty problems since the Second World War. As Canada's recently released defence policy high-lights, "Spanning three Territories and stretching as far as the North Pole, Canada's North is a sprawling region, encompassing 75 per cent of the country's national coastlines and 40 per cent of its total land mass." This tremendous expanse, "coupled with its ice-filled seas, harsh climate, and more than 36,000 islands," poses particular monitoring and surveillance challenges. Furthermore, Canada's three northern territories have the lowest population density in North America – a significant constraint on conventional operations that also amplifies the benefits of drawing on access to local resources. *Strong, Secure, Engaged* notes that "the region is spotted with vibrant communities, many inhabited by Canada's Indigenous populations. These communities form an integral part of Canada's identity, and our history is intimately connected with the imagery and the character of the North."[3]

The Rangers are neither a military nor an Aboriginal *program* (as they are sometimes misidentified), but rather a sub-component of the Reserves that embodies the benefits of leveraging the unique skill sets of Canadians from diverse ethnic and social backgrounds to support home defence and public safety. While Indigenous Canadians represented 2.2 per cent of the total Canadian Armed Forces in 2013 (an official figure that does not seem to include the Canadian Rangers, because they are neither Regular Force nor Primary Reserves), they make up more than two-thirds of the Canadian Rangers in northern Canada.[4] Given the defence policy's commitment to "better forecast occupational requirements and engage in more targeted recruiting, including capitalizing on the unique talents and skill-sets of Canada's diverse population,"[5] the successful inclusion of northern Indigenous peoples in the defence team through the Rangers represents an important case study. How can we explain the historical emergence of the Rangers as a diverse and inclusive organization? How do the Ranger role, mission, and tasks accommodate Indigenous and local knowledge and expertise, and how do understandings of diversity shape military practices in remote northern communities?

This chapter provides an analytical overview of the Canadian Rangers' history, their terms of service and roles – both formal and informal, the socio-political contexts in which they operate, their command structure – where community-based patrols vote in their own leadership, and their practical contributions to the defence team in the Canadian North.[6] There are five Canadian Ranger Patrol Groups (CRPGs) across Canada, each encompassing a distinct geographical area. This chapter examines 1 CRPG, the largest military unit in Canada with more than 1850 Rangers in sixty patrols across Yukon, the Northwest Territories, Nunavut, and northern British Columbia.[7] The majority of Canadian Rangers in 1 CRPG are First

Nations or Inuit. They have spent much of their lives on the land, embody the cultural diversity of the North, and represent the wide range of languages spoken by northern Canadians. As the eyes, ears, and voice of the CAF in the North, southern military units rely on and learn from the experience and knowledge of the Rangers to survive and operate effectively in Arctic and Subarctic environments. The Canadian Rangers not only benefit their communities in a direct social and economic sense, they also empower northern Canadians who mentor and educate other members of the CAF on how to manage, respect, and ultimately care for their homeland.[8]

As a bridge between diverse cultures and between the civilian and military realms, the Rangers represent a successful integration of national security and sovereignty agendas with community-based activities and local stewardship. The identity of the Indigenous peoples is tied to the land, and the CAF's decision to gain their assistance in defending that land and that identity has been a fruitful collaboration. This practical partnership, rooted in traditional knowledge and skills, promotes cooperation, communal and individual empowerment, and cross-cultural understanding. Accordingly, this chapter argues that the Rangers represent a compelling case study of the practical benefits of harnessing diversity to enhance CAF capabilities.

Rangers' History

Since 1947, the Rangers' official mission has been "to provide a military presence in sparsely settled northern, coastal and isolated areas of Canada that cannot conveniently or economically be provided for by other components of the Canadian Forces."[9] The actual tasks that they perform in support of this mission have become more complex. Their initial focus was national *security* – protecting their communities from enemy attack in the early Cold War. By the 1970s, their responsibilities became directly linked to the armed forces' role in support of Canada's *sovereignty* in the Arctic. Since the 1990s, the Rangers have also played a more visible nation-building and *stewardship* role in remote regions across Canada.

They represent an important success story for the Canadian Forces as a flexible, inexpensive, and culturally inclusive means of having "boots on the ground" exercising Canadian sovereignty and conducting or supporting domestic operations.[10]

In early 1942, terrified British Columbians facing the Japanese threat in the Pacific pushed the federal government to improve its defences along the West Coast. The army responded by forming the Pacific Coast Militia Rangers, a Reserve corps modelled after the British Home Guard. This unconventional military force allowed British Columbian men who were too old or too young for overseas service, or engaged in essential industries such as fishing and mining, to contribute to home defence. They were expected to use their own equipment and local knowledge so that they could act as the military's eyes and ears, report any suspicious vessels or activities, and do what they could to help professional forces repel an enemy invasion.

After the war, Canada's geographical position between the United States and the Soviet Union drew new strategic interest to remote northern areas. Canada did not have the military resources to station large numbers of regular soldiers in northern and remote regions of the country, but it still needed eyes and ears in those areas. Consequently, officials resurrected the Ranger concept in 1947, this time to span all of Canada's sparsely populated coastal and northern areas. By design, the Rangers would remain in their home communities in both war and peace. Their local knowledge would allow them to serve as guides and scouts, report suspicious activities, and if the unthinkable came to pass, delay an enemy advance using guerrilla tactics until professional forces arrived. Rangers provided intelligence reports on strange ships and aircraft, participated in training exercises with Canada's Mobile Striking Force and other army units, and conducted search and rescue. The diverse mix of Inuit, First Nations, Métis, and whites united in one task: "guarding a country that doesn't even know of their existence."[11] Even then, observers highlighted the ethnic diversity of the force as its primary attribute. This diversity, however, still did not extend to gender. Women, who at that time were not considered as appropriate military combatants, were not eligible to serve as Rangers – a gender barrier that remained until the early 1990s.

Annual resupply and training visits by Regular Force Ranger Liaison Officers during the late 1950s and early 1960s exemplified cross-cultural contact between army representatives and Indigenous Canadians living in the North. By the 1960s, however, the Rangers factored little in Ottawa's defence plans. Northern residents with armbands and rifles could hardly fend off hostile Soviet bombers carrying nuclear weapons. Because the Rangers cost next to nothing, the organization survived – thanks only to local initiative. The "Shadow Army of the North"[12] received little to no direction from military officials, and for many their annual ammunition supplies stopped arriving by the late 1960s. Apart from Newfoundland and Labrador and a sprinkling of northern communities, the Ranger organization was largely inactive by 1970.

The federal government renewed its interest in Arctic sovereignty in the wake of the American icebreaker *Manhattan*'s voyages in 1969–70, which Canadians believed threatened their control over the Northwest Passage. Although this new "crisis" had nothing to do with the Soviet military threat, Pierre Trudeau turned to the Canadian Armed Forces to assert symbolic control. His government promised increased surveillance and more Arctic training for southern troops. It created a new Northern Region Headquarters in Yellowknife responsible for the largest military region in the world, but had almost no operational units under its direct command, except the Rangers, who had been neglected for a decade and needed revitalization. Politicians and military officials in the North recommended upgrades to the Rangers, "so as to [better] use the talents and knowledge of northerners for surveillance purposes and to assist the military."[13] Limited progress was made in getting several northern units back on their feet. The Rangers still seemed appropriate: their members were predominantly Indigenous Canadians, lived in the North and thus demonstrated Canadian occupation, could provide surveillance in their homeland at little cost, and protected sovereignty without being overly "militaristic."

Revitalizing the Rangers in the Far North also fit with a broader federal government agenda to increase northern Indigenous participation in Canadian society. Beginning in the 1970s, the military launched initiatives to increase northerners' representation in the armed forces. By official standards, these efforts to recruit Indigenous northerners for the regular military failed. Few had the required education, and even fewer completed basic training. On the other hand, Staff Officer Ken Eyre noted, taking the best-educated young people out of their communities to serve in the Forces ran against "the developing set of Inuit priorities of that period." Canadian Ranger service, however, avoided this predicament. A northern Indigenous person remained in and served his community while at the same time serving as a Ranger.

Changes to the structure of the Ranger organization supported this new community-based focus. Northern Region replaced the conventional army company-platoon structure with localized patrols named after their communities. Patrols, rather than complicated company organizations spanning a broad area, better reflected the Arctic's demographic and geographic realities following the nucleation of Indigenous peoples into permanent settlements. Furthermore, the emergence of new forms of community-based leadership provided a stronger basis for Ranger activities. An effective – and more representative – Ranger organization in the "new North" would depend on devolving responsibility to Indigenous Canadians who could and would form a strong leadership cadre. Accordingly, the decision to empower community members to vote in their own patrol leaders rather than appoint them according to military criteria, however unorthodox from an army standpoint, proved "highly popular in small Arctic communities."[14] This process ensured that Ranger leadership reflected their northern communities. This system remains in place today, with decision-making within patrols reflecting local cultural and political norms.

Staff from the new northern headquarters in Yellowknife provided basic training to Inuit and Dene Rangers in the 1970s, and these activities also proved highly popular in communities. Regular Force Ranger Instructors, typically combat arms non-commissioned officers, visited patrols across the Northwest Territories and began offering the first training, which focused on practical skills such as marksmanship, map and compass, and basic communications rather than seeking to offer training comparable to that of Regular or Primary Reserve Force soldiers. Although the promised political commitment to expand the military's northern footprint proved more rhetorical than real, as the result of an austere fiscal environment and the absence of acute military threats, the Rangers found favour in Ottawa because they visibly asserted sovereignty at little to no cost.

The Rangers' interactions with the military also contributed to greater cross-cultural awareness and the sharing of skills. Yearly or biannual Nanook Ranger exercises trained individual members to Basic Ranger Standards, and annual ammunition resupply visits provided more sustained contact between the military establishment and the Rangers than had existed for decades. Regular Force units resumed training with Rangers in the North, learned about Indigenous cultures and survival techniques, and stressed that the Rangers taught them invaluable skills, even if they did have "a non-military way of doing things." Rangers possessed an intimate knowledge of the land, borne of experience and traditional knowledge extending back generations. Accordingly, the Rangers and southern soldiers developed a sense of cohesion as members of the Canadian defence team. The Rangers did not replicate the expertise of Regular and Reserve Force units, but they supplemented it with their local and Indigenous knowledge, experience navigating the land, and cultural intelligence that allowed them to share information with southern soldiers.

Sovereignty, rather than the practical relationships on the ground, served as the pretext for subsequent growth in the Ranger organization. When the U.S. Coast Guard icebreaker *Polar Sea* pushed through the Northwest Passage in 1985, Canadians once again worried about sovereignty and demanded a bolder military presence in the Arctic. Brian Mulroney's Conservative government promised a host of big-ticket investments to improve Canada's control over the Arctic, from acquiring nuclear submarines to building a Polar Class icebreaker. At the same time, and on a much lower key, the Canadian Rangers drew attention as an important grassroots way to keep Canada's "true North strong and free." Until that time, defence assessments had focused on the Rangers' military utility. In a changing political climate, however, other aspects of the organization made it even more attractive. Although several Indigenous leaders called for the demilitarization of the Arctic on social and environmental grounds, they always applauded the Rangers as a positive example of northerners contributing directly to sovereignty and security. Media coverage began to emphasize the social and political benefits of the Rangers in Indigenous, particularly Inuit, communities. Now the Rangers enjoyed tremendous appeal as an inexpensive, culturally inclusive, and visible means of demonstrating Canada's sovereignty.

Most of the government's promised investments in Arctic defence evaporated with the end of the Cold War. Conservative and Liberal governments, however, did follow through and increase the number and geographical scope of the Canadian Rangers in the 1990s – despite downsizing in the CAF more generally. Ranger patrols were re-established in the Yukon and in communities along the Mackenzie River, with most new growth directed to Indigenous communities. This reflected the importance of building and reinforcing Indigenous-military partnerships, particularly at a time when confrontations at Goose Bay, Oka, Gustafsen Lake, and Ipperwash strained relations with Indigenous peoples in southern Canada.[15] Furthermore, journalists applauded the Rangers' role in teaching the military and in encouraging elders to share their traditional knowledge with younger people *within* Indigenous communities. This was clear in the creation of the Junior Canadian Rangers (JCR) in 1998, which has grown to become the largest federally sponsored youth program in northern Canada.

By the twenty-first century, Canadian Ranger patrols were found in nearly every community in the territorial north. Popular descriptions of the Rangers have persistently emphasized their Indigenous composition and typically equated Rangers with Inuit defending their homeland.[16] In the media and in political discourse, northern voices often emphasize that the most appropriate "boots on the ground" are mukluks on the tundra, planted during regular hunting activities or Ranger-led sovereignty patrols. The Rangers' established record of operations, extending back more than seven decades, affirms the interconnectedness between Indigenous and local knowledge, identities, and practices, on the one hand, and the nation's interest in exercising its sovereignty on a continuous basis, on the other. Over the past decade, when national political interest in the Arctic surged in response to broadened awareness about climate change impacts in the Arctic, visions of increasingly accessible natural resources and navigable polar passages, insecurities about sovereignty, and our responsibilities as stewards of a homeland with intrinsic value to northerners and to Canadians more generally,[17] the Rangers became an increasingly regular fixture in the Canadian media. Growing and strengthening the Rangers featured prominently in the Harper government's plans to bolster Arctic sovereignty and enhance the safety and security of northerners,[18] with the Canadian Rangers reaching an average paid strength of 5,000 by 2013.[19] This number has been sustained since that time. Well-publicized Ranger involvement in signature "sovereignty" initiatives, such as the annual Operation Nanook summer exercises and Nunalivut winter operations in the High Arctic, consolidated the Rangers' place as icons of Canada's efforts to assert sovereignty and promote security. "If Canada's Arctic sovereignty has a brand, it's the red Rangers hoodie," journalist Tim Querengesser observed.[20] Under the Ranger hoodies, Canadians find a representative cross-section of northern Canadian society – a visible and celebrated example of diversity in action.

Diversity as a Force Multiplier

Canada's three northern territories are a diverse human geography, with Indigenous peoples comprising a substantial portion of the population. Combined, Canada's three territories were home to just over 113,600 people in 2016, representing 0.3 per cent of the total Canadian population. Outside of the territorial capitals, most residents live in small, dispersed communities, many without road access, with concomitant challenges of economies of scale and the delivery of government services. Whereas Indigenous people – First Nations, Inuit, and Métis – made up 4.3 per cent of the total Canadian population in the 2011 census, they comprised 23.1% of the population in Yukon, 51.9 per cent in Northwest Territories, and 86.3 per cent in Nunavut.

The lack of Ranger self-identification data in 1 CRPG does not allow for firm statistics, but conversations with Ranger instructors and headquarters personnel, as well as my own fieldwork over the past fifteen years, affirm that more than two-thirds of all Canadian

Rangers across the territorial North are of Indigenous descent. The rates of Indigenous participation are highest in Nunavut and NWT, with Yukon having higher numbers of non-Indigenous members, as broader demography would predict. At the local level, individual patrols represent their communities' ethnocultural and linguistic diversity. These are important considerations, given the government of Canada's strong focus on the centrality of northern Indigenous leadership and the defence policy statement that "Indigenous communities are at the heart of Canada's North" and the military will "work to expand and deepen our extensive relationships with these communities, particularly through the Canadian Rangers and Junior Canadian Rangers."[21]

To facilitate the inclusion of a diverse range of northern Canadians, the Rangers have unique enlistment criteria. The only formal entry criteria for men and women who wish to join the Rangers stipulates that they be over eighteen years of age; Canadian citizens or landed immigrants who reside in a remote, coastal or isolated area; in sufficiently good health to carry out their duties; knowledgeable about the local terrain and competent to operate on the land; and free of any legal prohibitions. There are no fitness or aptitude tests that Rangers must take prior to joining, nor do they face any hard medical criteria. Given social indicators that reveal significant health and education gaps between northern and southern Canadians, these important accommodations allow the Ranger organization to include a more representative sample of northern society than might otherwise be the case. As Brigadier Kelly Woiden, the Chief of Staff, Army reserve, told the House of Commons Standing Committee on National Defence on 18 February 2015, "More than anything else, [Rangers] have a very clear and strong understanding of local community and their environment. Many of them are individuals who have prominence. They can be an elder within the native community with their local Inuit or other ... First Nations peoples across the country. However, they could also just be rank-and-file folk because of their background and knowledge, for instance, the local snowmobile mechanic who has done well and he's the best guy."[22]

Ranger enrolment criteria also respect the local and Indigenous knowledge and practical experience operating in their homelands that recruits bring to the organization. Upon enrolment, Canadian Rangers are considered to be "trained, self-sufficient, equipped, and clothed to operate as self-sufficient mobile forces in support of CAF sovereignty and domestic operations in Canada in their local area of responsibility (AOR)." This AOR is generally described as a 150-kilometre radius around their home communities.[23] New Rangers are generally provided with a ten-day orientation course, provided by Regular or Primary Reserve Force Ranger Instructors, which focuses primarily on marksmanship and learning basic facts about the history and structure of the CAF. There is no "basic training" akin to the Regular Force or Primary Reserves, and Rangers are not required to undertake annual training. Accordingly, Rangers do not conform to the principle of universality of service, because knowledge of the military and conventional "soldiering skills" are not prerequisites for their participation. Their role is not to serve as combat forces, but rather to serve as enablers for other elements of the defence team in a warfighting scenario. This precludes the need to incorporate them into more typical modes of military culture and training – an important consideration, given the sensitivities around a long history of state-led assimilationist agendas seeking to eradicate Indigenous cultures and recast Indigenous people into Euro-Canadian moulds.

The organization is also unique in that there is no compulsory retirement age for Rangers. Instead, Rangers are considered non-effective only when they can no longer patrol their AOR in the process of their individual normal routine; they do not reflect good credit upon their community, their patrol, and the CAF; they are not accepted as equal and participating members within their respective patrol; or they no longer provide tangible advice and guidance to the patrol that is grounded in experientially based, traditional knowledge. If the patrol membership decides by consensus that an individual is non-effective, the commanding officer of the patrol group can release the member.[24] This process not only reinforces the community-based philosophy of the Ranger organization, it also reflects a deep-seated respect for the role of elders in Indigenous communities. As long as individuals contribute to their Ranger patrol, in the eyes of the other patrol members, they can remain in the organization and make positive contributions. For example, people unable to travel on the land can serve as communication contacts back in the community. Elders also serve as important cultural mentors and subject matter experts, lending traditional and local knowledge to the planning of operations, management of relationships within a patrol, training of other Rangers, and mentoring of youth. Accordingly, the absence of compulsory retirement age not only brings greater generational diversity[25] within the Rangers than in the Regular and Primary Reserve Forces, it also facilitates the trans-generational transfer of knowledge within northern Indigenous communities.

The decision not to impose an age cap or strict medical conditions on Ranger service can lead to confusion. Overzealous media stories in recent years that suggest a crisis in the organization because of the number of Rangers who have died while still serving (forty members in 1 CRPG from 2012 to 2015) seem completely unaware of these policies.[26] While the tragic death of Ranger Donald Angoyoak of Gjoa Haven during Exercise Polar Passage was operationally related and prompted Prime Minister Stephen Harper to remind Canadians that this demonstrated how the Rangers and other CAF members faced "real dangers as they safeguard Canadian sovereignty in the Arctic,"[27] the other thirty-nine Rangers had died as the result of non-duty related causes. Most passed away from natural causes, including old age. For example, Ranger Alex Van Bibber passed away in November 2014 at the age of ninety-eight, having served with the Rangers since the late 1940s – and having still run his trap line only weeks before he died of heart failure.[28] Although these deaths have a significant impact on the Rangers and their communities, the military cannot influence the number of Rangers who die of natural causes. Unacceptably high suicide rates in the North also have an impact on the Rangers, both directly and indirectly. There is no evidence that stresses related to Ranger service have any correlation with suicides, and some observers suggest that more military-supported activities, providing northerners with a sense of purpose and self-worth, might actually reduce suicide rates.

The Rangers organization has also become a more inclusive place for women since the first women broke the gender barrier in 1991. As of December 2016, there were 408 female Rangers in 1 CRPG, representing 22.7 per cent of the unit strength – a much higher percentage than in the Regular Force or Primary Reserves. Eight of the sixty Ranger sergeants (patrol commanders) in 1 CRPG are women (13.3 per cent), as are 52 of the 237 Master Corporals (21.9 per cent) and 46 of the 181 Corporals (25.4 per cent).[29] These statistics affirm that women feel that they can and should lead in the Rangers, as well as be accepted by their peers (who elect them into these positions). They also reflect the prominent role of women in overseeing the Junior Canadian Ranger patrols in their communities, which is typically done by a Master Corporal. For example, Master Corporal Therese "Dollie" Simon, a Ranger since November 1994, leads the JCR program Fort Resolution, NWT. In her "day job" she is a coordinator for the Deninu K'ue First Nation Community Wellness Program, where she works with local people with addictions. "Basically, I was looking to do something different but little did I know that it was something I was missing – going out onto the land, hunting and reconnecting that way," she explained about her decision to join the Rangers. "I enjoy it and I now have lifetime friends that I have made all over the Yukon and Northwest Territories. And, we are always learning something new." She describes the Rangers as a uniformly "positive experience – a break from the busyness of the day, though we do work hard. The bonus is that we get paid."[30]

Although southern Canadian media commentators often criticize the lack of pay, equipment, and clothing provided to Rangers compared to their Regular and Reserve Force counterparts, my extensive conversations with Rangers from across the North over the last two decades suggests that these remarks are generally ill-informed or misplaced. Although Rangers are not paid for their year-round service as "eyes and ears" on the land, Rangers are paid for force generation activities such as annual training patrols, local meetings, and leadership workshops, with an average of twelve paid days per year. Furthermore, they are paid when they participate in force employment activities such as Operations Nanook, Nunalivut, and Nunakput, as well as when they provide support to southern units on northern training exercises (NOREXs) or are officially tasked to conduct search and rescue. Although the influx of several thousand dollars into a community at the end of a Ranger patrol or military exercise might appear paltry, this Ranger pay can constitute a substantive part of an Indigenous economy that balances short-term paid labour with traditional harvesting activities, thus supporting a social economy that does not conform to Western models.

The diverse landscapes in which Rangers live and operate also prescribe different equipment and clothing needs. The philosophy of treating the Rangers as self-sufficient, lightly equipped members of the defence team recognizes this reality as well as the military's limited capability to provide logistical support and sustenance to community-based patrols distributed across the territorial North. The Rangers are known for their much-publicized "red hoodie" and are also provided with T-shirts, a ball cap, Canadian Disruptive Pattern (CADPAT) pants, military boots, and red jackets intended for parade. On operations, however, Rangers are expected to use their own environmentally appropriate clothing, which they deem best-suited to local conditions, rather than being assigned standard military gear. While media commentators often dismiss the Rangers as "rag-tag forces" as a result, they fail to observe that this lack of uniformity embodies a respect for diversity, allowing Rangers to make their own decisions about what they should wear to operate comfortably and effectively in their home environments. This same logic extends to transportation and camping equipment. During training and official taskings, Rangers are paid for the use of their own equipment and vehicles such as snowmobiles, all-terrain vehicles, and boats according to an established Equipment Usage Rate (EUR). This arrangement provides Rangers with some tax-free reimbursements that they can invest in their own equipment and tools, appropriate to their local environment, which they can then use in their everyday lives without having to ask the government for permission to do so. By allowing individuals to invest in their own, privately owned equipment, this approach represents a material contribution to local capacity-building.

Inclusion in Practice

The Rangers have proven their value in recent decades by striking an appropriate balance between their military and community contributions.[31] The combat role originally assigned to Rangers in

1947 has been removed from their official task list, because they are neither trained nor equipped for this role, leading some commentators to declare that they are not a "real military force" and using this as a prime example that the CAF is unprepared to defend Canada's Arctic from foreign adversaries.[32] This logic is problematic on several levels, revealing a profound misunderstanding of the Rangers and how they fit within the defence team.

The Rangers' national task list (see table 5.1) encompasses three broad aspects: conducting and supporting surveillance and presence patrols; conducting and assisting with domestic military operations; and maintaining a Canadian Armed Forces presence in local communities. This includes reporting unusual activities or sightings; collecting local data for the CAF; land-based and maritime patrolling – in winter by snowmobile and in summer by boat; training and guiding Regular and Primary Reserve Force units operating in remote regions; assisting in search-and-rescue efforts and in local emergencies; and assisting with natural disasters such as forest fires and floods.[33] The Army considers the Rangers "a mature capability" and "the foundation of the CF's [sic] operational capability across the North for a range of domestic missions."[34] In emphasizing their myriad contributions, the Army notes that the "Rangers will remain a critical and enduring presence on the ground, valuable in many roles, including amongst others, the CAF's eyes and ears for routine surveillance purposes, its guides, local cultural advisors, interpreters, and the core of our liaison capacity in many locations, while remaining immediately available to support local government or other agencies."[35]

The key Arctic defence documents produced by the Canadian military over the last decade all emphasize integrated defence team and whole-of-government approaches to meet challenges across the mission spectrum.[36] Within these concepts, the Rangers are situated as facilitators or enablers for other military components providing combined response capabilities. Lessons learned or post-exercise reports regularly highlight the benefits of this partnership and the need to leverage the Rangers' knowledge and capabilities to facilitate operations and further develop Regular and Primary Reserve Force units' operating skills in remote areas. Rather than dismissing the Rangers for not simply replicating existing army capabilities of southern-based units, these exercises affirm the value of having access to experts with extensive experience operating in austere conditions who are willing to share their local and traditional knowledge about lands and waters and provide practical support for activities in what southerners consider to be "extreme environments."

As members of their local communities, the Rangers also represent an important source of shared awareness and liaison with community partners[37] and, by virtue of their capabilities and location, regularly support other government agencies in responding to the broad spectrum of security and safety issues facing isolated communities. For example, their leadership and training makes them the de facto lead during states of emergency in their communities – from avalanches, flooding, extreme snowstorms, and power plant shutdowns to forest fires and water crises. Accordingly, they are the CAF's first responders in most safety and security situations.[38] Rangers are also called up to assist with search and rescue in their communities, both as volunteers who know how to work effectively as a group and, when called upon, as an official military tasking. In many cases, their leadership and training makes them the de facto lead during states of emergency in their communities. Their familiarity with local cultures, fluency in Indigenous languages, and vested interest in the welfare of their fellow community members make them valuable, trusted assets.

The Rangers provide an important outlet for Indigenous peoples and other northerners who wish to serve in the defence of their country without having to leave their communities. Ranger activities also allow members of Aboriginal communities to practise and share traditional skills, such as living off the land, not only with people from outside their cultures but also across generations within. These skills are central to Indigenous identities, and there is a persistent worry that these will be lost unless individuals have opportunities to exercise them and share them with younger generations. By celebrating traditional and local knowledge and skills, and encouraging and enabling community members to go out on the land and share their knowledge and expertise, the Rangers can play an important role in supporting the retention or expansion of core cultural competencies. In turn, the Ranger concept is inherently rooted in the idea that the unique knowledge of northern peoples can make an important contribution to effective military operations. It is this partnership, rooted in mutual learning and sharing, that has made the Rangers a long-term success on the local and national levels. It also reflects the achievement of inclusion, building on an appreciation of northern diversity.

Conclusion

The Canadian Rangers are a strong example of how a sub-component of the Reserve Force can harness the benefits of diversity, ensuring that northerners are integrally involved in the defence team when it operates in the North and developing local capabilities that both reflect and support the interests of local communities.[39] Although commentators often associate military practices, and those of the state more generally, with physical dislocation, environmental degradation, political disruption, and culture shock for Indigenous peoples,[40] the interconnectedness between the military, remote communities, and Canadian society is respected as a constructive force in the case of the Canadian Rangers. It serves as a striking example of what can be achieved when policies and practices are rooted in a spirit of accommodation, trust, and mutual respect.

Promised investments to enhance Ranger capabilities and training can be well directed as long as they respect the Rangers' long-standing roles and mission and are rooted in a robust awareness of how and why the organization has evolved into its current state. Tensions between commentators who want to convert the Rangers from their current role into a more conventional Primary Reserve mould, as well as those who would seek to expand the Rangers into a work-training program to create more employment for northern Indigenous communities, threaten to break an organization that is not broken. Seldom do outside proposals appreciate how and why the organization has assumed its unique form or how the Rangers' role, mission, and tasks translate across national, regional, and local scales, addressing both military and local civilian needs. Instead, various stakeholders have pushed to repackage the Rangers into a form that fits their agendas, without recognizing the broader implications for the organization. Canadians must be careful not to set the Rangers up to fail by asking too much of them, unravelling their ties and relevance to the military, or, conversely, trying to over-militarize them to face the highly unlikely prospect of a military adversary challenging our Arctic sovereignty or territorial integrity in the foreseeable future.[41]

Canada's defence policy *Strong, Secure, Engaged* commits the Defence team "to enhance the Canadian Armed Forces' ability to operate in the Arctic and adapt to a changed security environment" by "enhance[ing] and expand[ing] the training and effectiveness of the Canadian Rangers to improve their functional capabilities within the Canadian Armed Forces."[42] This marks a subtle but important shift from the minister's mandate letter released in November 2015, which had directed the military to "increase the size of the Canadian Rangers."[43] Rather than seeking to increase the number of Canadian Rangers at this point, military resources should be allocated to increasing the number of Ranger Instructors and clerks that support the Ranger organization. The recent expansion to 5000 Rangers across Canada has already over-stretched human resources in various patrol group headquarters, which provide critical administrative, training, and staff support to the Rangers. In consolidating previous growth by strengthening the CRPGs and resourcing them properly, the government can improve the effectiveness and sustainability of the Rangers while improving the health and wellness of the military members who support them. Addressing gaps in Ranger access to health care, including mental health services, available to other CAF members, clarifying the appropriate class of service that Rangers should be on for the tasks they perform, and processing compensation claims for damaged equipment in a timely fashion should help to remove barriers that affect the overall well-being of Rangers and their families.[44]

Maintaining the balance between operational and socio-political benefits continues to lie at the heart of sustaining the Rangers as both a diverse military formation and as a community-based organization. As the Rangers continue to evolve, however, there are opportunities to increase diversity and ensure more equitable opportunity within the organization. While I have depicted 1 CRPG as a model of successfully mobilizing Indigenous peoples to participate in a military organization, this does not preclude the need for concerted efforts to recruit Rangers from Indigenous communities that are currently unrepresented or underrepresented in specific patrols. While the lack of statistics on the ethnic background of Rangers in 1 CRPG remains a hindrance to deep analysis, a formal diversity assessment would help to identify potential barriers that may be preventing some people from participating more fully or equally within the organization. A study on the roles and status of women in the Rangers would also be helpful. Furthermore, while the contributions of Inuit serving as Rangers in the Far North, where Canadian sovereignty is allegedly imperilled, are well reflected in national media coverage, First Nations and Métis in the Northwest Territories and Yukon, as well as non-Indigenous northerners serving in 1 CRPG, receive less attention. Celebrating the diversity of the Rangers means expanding our understanding to include a more nuanced portrait that reflects the wide range of northerners serving in the unit.

The evolution of the Rangers suggests a political environment and a military institutional atmosphere in which Indigenous peoples' contributions to the defence team are seen as both proper and legitimate, reinforcing the "value of inclusion in a culture of uniformity."[45] Accordingly, the Department of National Defence should make greater effort to publicly acknowledge the Rangers' myriad forms of service to their country, heighten political and public understanding of the ethnic and gender diversity of Rangers, and articulate how diversity and inclusion can serve as a "force multiplier" for security and public-safety missions. As the 2015 Canadian Joint Operations Plan for the North notes, "Military forces operating in the North face a number of unique challenges not typically faced operating elsewhere in Canada or around the world. While not insurmountable, these challenges require unique solutions and approaches."[46] The Rangers, an example of successfully mobilizing diversity in remote regions through an unconventional form of military service, are a prime example of a unique and inclusive approach that demonstrates the merits of diversity in the defence and security sectors on functional grounds.[47]

Table 5.1. Canadian Ranger Tasks

The tasks in the following table may be undertaken by a CR member on duty when authorized by their CRPG HQ:

Tasks	Examples
Conduct and provide support to sovereignty operations	• Conduct and provide support to surveillance and sovereignty patrols, including training in Canada • Conduct North Warning System site patrols • Report suspicious and unusual activities • Collect local information of military significance
Conduct and provide assistance to CAF domestic operations	• Conduct surveillance of Canadian territory • Provide local knowledge and CR expertise (i.e., advice and guides) • Participate in search and rescue operations • Provide support in response to disasters and support in humanitarian operations • Provide assistance to federal, provincial, territorial or municipal government authorities
Maintain a CAF presence in the local community	• Instruct, mentor, and supervise Junior Canadian Rangers* • Participate in and support events in the local community (e.g., Yukon Quest, Canada Day, Remembrance Day, etc.)

The following tasks may not be assigned to a CR member, except when placed on active service under section 31 of the *National Defence Act*:

1. undertaking tactical military training;
2. performing immediate local defence tasks, such as containing or observing small enemy detachments pending the arrival of other forces;
3. providing vital point security (e.g., dams, mines, oil pipelines, etc.);
4. assisting federal, provincial, territorial or local police in the discovery, reporting and apprehension of enemy agents, saboteurs, criminals or terrorists; and
5. serving in aid of the civil power.

* When assisting with the conduct of the activities of the Junior Canadian Rangers' Program, CR members are contributing to national goals of the government of Canada by significantly improving the quality of life of Junior Canadian Rangers across the country, especially in the most isolated areas of Canada.

Source: Defence Administration Order and Directive (DAOD) 2020-2, Canadian Rangers, 21 May 2015, http://www.forces.gc.ca/en/about-policies-standards-defence-admin-orders-directives-2000/2020-2.page.

chapter six

Diversifying the Canadian Armed Forces' Chaplaincy

BIANCA ROMAGNOLI

After being posted to Canadian Forces Base Trenton, Padre Baldwin developed a good understanding of the base and its personnel. Working within a unit of hundreds of soldiers, Padre Baldwin prided himself on being able to recognize all the troops by face and knowing most soldiers by name. He could recount personal details about each one. After walking the unit lines and speaking with some of these soldiers, it was obvious that his presence in the unit was felt and appreciated by most. However, what makes Padre Baldwin so interesting is that as the first Ukrainian Orthodox priest since the Second World War, his success in being recruited was not guaranteed and exists as an anomaly. With almost eight years of service as a Regular Force Chaplain, Padre Baldwin believes that even in his own short career, tremendous changes have occurred in the Chaplaincy. While Baldwin affirms that the Royal Canadian Chaplain Services' current mandate is to match the religious composition of Chaplains to that of the Canadian public, the statistics reveal another story.[1]

With almost forty denominations identified within the CAF, only select denominations of Protestantism, Catholicism, Judaism, and Islam are represented in the Chaplaincy; the last two have shockingly low numbers of Chaplains.[2] As the religious "face" of the military, padres – an affectionate name for Chaplains that has its origins in British military tradition – represent religious diversity for both soldiers and the public.[3] Despite increased societal secularism, the Chaplaincy is an established and valued element of the CAF. But like modern organizations grappling with diversity and inclusion, the CAF Chaplaincy and padres also face many challenges in meeting the needs of CAF personnel. There remains a lack of non-Christian Chaplains. While this could persuade Canadians to question the legitimacy of the Chaplaincy within the military, this is not the case. The Chaplaincy is being asked and tasked to diversify its recruitment to be more inclusive, but challenges and opportunities abound. This chapter discusses some of the obstacles in meeting the diverse religious and spiritual needs of an armed force that is itself diversifying.

Historical Development of the Chaplaincy

When Canada declared its support for Britain in the First World War, the CAF did not have an official Chaplain corps. Regardless, 33 volunteer members of clergy were deployed alongside soldiers in the role of Chaplains. Over the course of the war, as the branch was established and developed, that number rose to 524, with 447 serving overseas.[4] These 524 Chaplains hailed from mostly Protestant traditions, particularly English-speaking Methodist, Anglican, and Presbyterian ministers, with a few rabbis.[5] These men were sent overseas with no military training or support and were often left in dangerous combat conditions for extended periods of time for lack of replacements from Canada. Many Chaplains were attached on a ratio of one Chaplain for every thousand troops and were stationed in camps, hospitals, casualty stations, and battalions.[6] Because there was no established organization to administer these clergymen at the beginning of the war, many were sent overseas haphazardly. They were simply attached to units as they left Canada and travelled around Europe, moving between units as they were needed. However, when the war ended, the Office of the Director of Chaplain Services and the Canadian Chaplain Service were closed. While many of these clergymen gained honourable distinctions, the branch was disbanded, and the clergymen returned to their own congregations in Canada. Similar to the hundreds of thousands of

Canadians who joined the military for the duration of the war, only to resume their non-military lives at its conclusion, military Chaplains returned to their lives before the war.

With the outbreak of the Second World War in 1939, Chaplains were quickly returned to active duty, with 1,400 Chaplains, once again predominantly drawn from Protestant traditions, enlisted to accompany Canadian soldiers to the frontlines. The CAF was able to quickly re-establish the Chaplain Services, and Canadian Chaplains returned to support fighting troops. Naval Chaplains were introduced to ships and began to minister onboard Canadian vessels.[7] Once again, Chaplains were understood as integral to trench warfare as they allowed for the administration of burial, sacraments, and last rites to troops who died overseas, facilitated through the military for the first time.[8] Chaplains also provided comfort and support to family members back in Canada.

After the war, when it became clear to the military that Chaplains provided a critical service, the Chaplain Services were established as a permanent fixture. The branch was renamed the Royal Canadian Army Chaplain Corps in 1948,[9] and two distinctive branches, one Roman Catholic and the other Protestant, were established with a division of 137 Protestant and 162 Roman Catholic padres.[10] While most clergy continued to have no military training, their role as religious leaders in trench warfare won the trust and admiration of the troops, and their legacy as "one of the boys" continues today.

Since the end of Second World War, the Royal Canadian Chaplain Service has gone through tremendous changes. The Canadian Forces Chaplain School and Centre was established in 1993[11] to provide Chaplains with basic military and survival skills, helping to integrate Chaplains into the units with which they worked. In more recent years, the school has focused its efforts on providing education on religious diversity as it struggles to keep up with the changing demographics of military personnel. However, as religious, racial, and gender minorities continue to join the CAF, the Chaplaincy finds itself struggling to remain representative of the diversity found in the Canadian population.

Religiosity in the Canadian Military

Outside of historical research, very little is known about religion in the military and the Chaplaincy, largely because there has been almost no research into religion in the CAF by either internal or external sources. Joanne Rennick and Michael Peterson present two comprehensive studies on the topic. Through semi-structured and unstructured interviews conducted over the course of a year with Canadian Armed Forces personnel, this chapter provides more detail and describes the challenges in diversifying the CAF Chaplaincy. As a member of the CAF with seven years of service with two reserve units in Southern Ontario, the author was uniquely situated in her research as an insider and did not face some of the restrictions faced by other military researchers.[12] However, despite personal access to CAF personnel, bureaucratic hurdles such as ethics approval were successfully navigated.

Over the course of a year, ten interviews with CAF personnel, including unit, brigade, and division-level Chaplains, and retired, reserve, and Regular Force soldiers were conducted. The author engaged in participant observation with her own unit and at work and social events with military personnel. Demographic signifiers, such as race, gender, age, and language play an important role, and signifiers such as marital status, urban versus rural, and education levels are informative when describing difference in the CAF.[13] All except one of the participants were white male anglophones.

Research was conducted through phone and email conversations, along with analysis of academic and personal work written by some interlocutors. Interviewees included soldiers whose identification varied from religious personnel to atheists and agnostics and everything in between. The beliefs of two soldiers who belonged to the same Wiccan coven, Anthony and Thomas, were central to their identities. While they are content with the religious services provided by current Chaplains, they hope that during their careers they may encounter a Chaplain of their own faith. Others, like retired sergeant Jeffrey, believe that religion has absolutely no place in the CAF and has become completely obsolete. While this remains the opinion of only a few soldiers, it highlights Rennick's assertion that without proper statistics, the only way to gain insight into the religiosity of soldiers is through personal interviews.[14]

Until recently the majority of Canadian immigrants came from Europe, bringing with them Christian belief systems. As immigration patterns shifted to Asian and Middle Eastern regions, the proportion of the population adhering to other religions expanded accordingly. Religion in Canada today is marked by this diversity, and the CAF, along with other institutions, have been faced with the challenge of addressing these changes. Scholars of religion in Canada argue that the importance of religion to Canadians has not decreased, but has simply changed its form.[15] However, the most complicated part about writing policy on religion and religious diversity remains that, despite its familiarity, *religion* remains undefined.[16] This ambiguity is played out on two stages in the CAF: in the everyday lives of soldiers, and within the political realm of policymaking. Fuelled by this ambiguity about religion and its position in society, the CAF has simultaneously demonstrated an inability to remove religion as a category from policy, while increasingly calling for the removal of religious practices from public space.

The Charter of Rights and Freedoms provides Canadians with fundamental rights. However, when Canadians join the military they surrender some of these freedoms for conformity and operational success. Religious liberty is one freedom that soldiers can retain, a freedom that allows them to deviate from military convention when they adhere to a religious requirement. Examples can be seen with the introduction of hijabs, turbans, and yarmulkes; the authorization of beards and braided hair for practising Muslims and Indigenous peoples; and the introduction of kosher and halal meals for Jewish and Muslim soldiers. All of these exemptions are made possible only because the CAF has recognized these practices as necessary for the religious adherence of service members. These, along with other exemptions, are outlined in the 2001 *Canadian Forces Dress Instructions*, stating that as long as there is no danger to personnel or mission success, religious service members can follow religious practices. However, at the same time as more religious practices are being introduced into the CAF under this religious freedom exception, there has been a rejection of formal institutionalized forms of religion.[17] Instead soldiers are moving towards more personal and private understandings of spirituality. Rennick demonstrates how, while there is a general decline in religiosity within Canada, belief, particularly in the form of spirituality, has become increasingly important and relevant.

As the Chaplaincy evolved from its historically Christian tradition, it transformed its emphasis on serving individuals through the ministry of presence, which downplays religious canon, to instead accommodate personal beliefs. This shift created a tension between the traditional Christian practices and the fact that soldiers, echoing the pluralism of broader society, are increasingly identifying themselves as "spiritual" rather than "religious." A soldier interviewed by Rennick believes that "[the Chaplaincy] need[s] to have more of a sense of religion as something that's personal for people" and that religion does not have a place in public space.[18] This shift has also brought with it soldiers' desire to move away from religious dogma in ceremonies where "the rejection of traditional religious authority as well as the very private nature of personal spirituality makes some of the 'old military traditions' distasteful experiences for many personnel."[19] While the Chaplaincy has attempted to address this within the Chaplain's handbook citing that participation within religious service is completely voluntary, the reality is that religious language and practices are masked within other formal events that are not voluntary. As one service member explained it, "You have to go on parade and a lot of times there are prayers and, even if the Chaplain's not with us, the captain or first officer or someone will say the prayers, and they're prayers to Jesus.... You're required to be at the parade, and therefore, you're required to listen to the prayers."[20] This tension between public and private religion is exacerbated by the Chaplaincy's inability to introduce religious diversity within its own rank.

This tension has caused service members to demand that manifestations of religion be limited to expressions based on spirituality with universal appeal, or be consigned to the private sphere if they cannot be representative of all soldiers. A major barrier to the inclusion of other traditions is that the unit padres perform the ceremonies on the basis of their own traditions, and consequently the ceremonies are usually performed from within a Christian denomination.[21] The transition towards a multifaith identity, however, is full of obstacles. While this shift is motivated by organizational survival and the desire to remain relevant, it has also created tension among Chaplains who are trying to cater to this pluralist approach and minister to soldiers with disparate beliefs while also adhering to their own tradition.[22]

Chaplain Recruitment and Diversity

Chaplain recruitment is rigorous. Padre Andrew Tremblay, for example, an ex-infantry soldier turned officer turned padre, seemed like a recruitment expert after ten years of experience working both within and outside the Chaplaincy. He notes that Chaplains are held to the same military fitness, psychological, and health standards as all other soldiers.[23] During an interview, he described this as being recruited green and purple:[24] "So green is army, purple is Chaplain, and so the Chaplain always has that dual chain that they're operating around ... but what it does for recruiting is you gotta do all the officer things, but there is a whole other ecclesiastical thing." While all officers in the CAF must have at least an undergraduate degree,[25] Chaplains must also be ordained or mandated by a nationally registered faith group; have a master's of divinity degree and maintain support from a local ecclesiastical authority and the Interfaith Committee on Canadian Military Chaplaincy (ICCMC); and have two years' experiences in a civilian ministry.[26] While some exceptions are being made to loosen the MDiv requirement through Prior Learning Evaluations, which individually evaluate a candidate's qualification, the process to become a Chaplain remains long and exhausting. For Padre Malek Talbott, a divisional Chaplain working in policy at a headquarters in Western Canada, these challenges come from a bureaucratic perspective:

> It's about a level of experience and expectation that we have for the people that we serve. Also it's recognition that the government of Canada said [the MDiv] is a professional qualification that they don't want to move from. So don't get me wrong, there are wonderful Baptist ministers or evangelical ministers that have been serving in the church for twenty years, that are fantastic pastors and probably have a shit load of experience, more than someone who has two years' experience, but we're caught now because we don't have the degree ... we're trying to find ways, where their experience can match up to that. But it's a huge time effort and resource to discern every individual that applies to us. Takes a lot of time and a lot of effort. Which we do, but we don't have the resources to do it like that [*snaps fingers*].

Padre Talbott also emphasizes that the distinction is not between educated and uneducated. Even individuals applying with a PhD in theology are not desirable because they lack the practical and experiential training the MDiv provides. Furthermore, the military lacks the ability and resources to properly train individuals in any given tradition. Having candidates come to the military with their religious training already completed absolves the military of responsibility for the religious practices of Chaplains, placing the onus of religious management on the religious institutions. This creates two streams of accountability – one through the military chain of command and another through the religious group to which the Chaplain belongs. The greatest challenge inherent in this arrangement is that many traditions, such as Sikhism, Sunni Islam, Hinduism, and Indigenous spirituality, do not have a simple hierarchical structure. It is only through the imposition of the MDiv requirement that the military believes they can ensure the status quo across the CAF. As new belief groups join the CAF and apply to the Chaplaincy, maintaining the status quo allows the military to control how belief is understood and administered, but does little to help with diversity.

Within the CAF, belief is defined as being sincerely held, and it is the Chaplain's responsibility to advise the chain of command whether the belief will hinder operational success.[27] Having external accountability as the backbone of the Chaplaincy allows it to better determine which beliefs are considered sincere. As Padre Andrew Trembley explained it,

> There needs to be accountability, 'cause otherwise this is where the sincerely held beliefs comes in. You could come in and say "I am going to be a *hu-ga bu-ga* Chaplain." You just make something up. "It's my sincerely held belief. Here's my religion, here's my credentials." And if there is no structure or accountability that you answer to, then there is absolutely no way to vet that and you step over the line, and start doing things that are not kosher, then what? There's no way, 'cause you can just say, "That's within my religious practice." No matter how weird it got, "It's within my religious practices."

The idea that malicious people would join the Chaplaincy in order to destroy its integrity and cause havoc seems to be closer to fearmongering than reality; however, this does little to loosen the strict guidelines. Padre Brian Sanderson, a brigade Chaplain, explained that accountability is necessary because the military is unable to adequately monitor and discipline Chaplains who go outside their religious mandate: "It's really important that there are lines of accountability. Because if I make a misstep, religiously, [the army may or may not] but I will definitely be disciplined by the church, and that gives the institution that sense of security that there are lines of accountability that will always be observed." However, because many traditions are not organized with this clear structural hierarchy, it becomes very difficult for prospective Chaplains coming from minority traditions without this formal approval process to prove that they have clear lines of accountability and support.

With approximately 400 Chaplains serving 68,000 soldiers and 27,000 reservists, the Chaplain branch constantly struggles to maintain its recruitment numbers. In addition to the relative inaccessibility of the branch to many traditions, rigorous recruitment means that most Chaplains are recruited relatively late in their careers. With the retirement of Chaplains at sixty years old, many Chaplains find that they must retire before they are able to achieve meaningful career goals. Fulfilling the educational and ecclesiastical requirements can sometimes take entire careers, hence joining the CAF can sometimes be a midlife career change. Brigade Padre Brian Sanderson expressed his own frustrations at this predicament: "There's always going to be a need because ... the youngest people that can apply are early to mid-thirties. Maybe, if you've got a family, early forties. So, for a lot of people it comes as a mid-career thing. So the aging out or the average age of Chaplains is a constant concern for the leadership in terms of ... well, there's so many billets; so many places that Chaplains are needed, but do we have enough? So there's always a constant need for new people."

The Chaplaincy seems to be at an impasse. On the one hand, they find themselves in desperate need of Chaplains, but on the other they greatly limit their own recruitment and enrolment. Regardless of these strict regulations, a select group of individuals has managed to slip through and is working to reshape the Chaplaincy, while also demonstrating their invaluable contributions to the armed forces.

In 2010, the demographic of the Chaplaincy remained predominantly, if not exclusively, Christian. Out of the 220 Regular Force Chaplains enlisted that year, 218 were either Roman Catholic or Protestant.[28] This religion distribution within the Chaplaincy contrasts with the demographic trends in Canada, where Christians (69 per cent), atheists (23 per cent), Muslims (3 per cent), Hindus (1.5 per cent) and Sikhs (1.5 per cent) constituted the main religious groups in 2011.[29]

Only during this past decade has there been any increased diversity of religion of Chaplains, and while progress is extremely slow, the effort cannot be completely discounted. Padre Brian Sanderson believes that during the war in Afghanistan the Chaplaincy started to become diverse, particularly with certain Christian denominations. "It used to be dominated by Anglicans and Roman Catholics, and in Afghanistan it started to open up. There's a lot [more] of evangelical denominations than there used to be." Similar to traditions such as Islam, Buddhism, and Hinduism, many evangelical denominations do not have formal or recognized educational streams, and therefore have struggled to fulfil the educational requirement of the Chaplaincy. Instead of getting a formal MDiv like Roman Catholics or Anglicans, many evangelicals attend Bible college, which makes them ineligible for the Chaplain branch. While the MDiv requirement has become increasingly lenient and has allowed for certain types of expansions, the need for formal ecclesiastical support remains a seemingly impenetrable barrier. This is made particularly evident in Rennick's investigation of Indigenous spirituality. Faiths such as Indigenous spirituality are unable to fulfil the requirements mandated by the military, because they do not have an accepted centralized authority, and while there are Indigenous Chaplains, they belong exclusively to Christian denominations.

In recent years, symbolic changes to the Chaplaincy have made it more inclusive. Through initiatives such as the Prior Learning Evaluations, the Chaplaincy has allowed for some leniency. These changes are evidenced not only by those who can join, but also in how the Chaplaincy represents itself to the public. Inclusion of non-Christian badges, changes to the Branch motto and official hymn, allowance for religious diversity in ceremonies, and creation of interfaith centres have all been part of the expansion.[30] Regardless of these accommodations, many candidates spend months, if not years, trying to fulfil the requirements for the CAF. Bethany Helms, a converted Muslim, spent nearly a year repeatedly tweaking and manipulating her curriculum vitae to make her a desirable fit. As she explains, "Even if from these questions ... what is the year of your ordination? That doesn't apply to me. Where did you get your master's of theology? Well, I had to show that I had Islamic studies. Islamic studies is different than a department of theology because it is not meant necessarily for the practising Muslim. Then I also had counselling psychology, so again I had to mix and match and show how this was." Bethany would become the first Muslim pastoral associate, but her struggle follows in the footsteps of others who have attempted to make the Chaplaincy more diverse.[31]

While Padre Carl Baldwin hopes that others will also "blaze a trail," he understands that for many this future may remain a pipe dream. With so many requirements to become a successful candidate, and many candidates coming from traditions whose structure is still too far from the Christian-oriented one on which the Chaplaincy is based, the future of successfully diversifying seems distant.

Even within the few traditions that have made a space for themselves in the Chaplaincy, there remains a struggle to achieve proper representation. In an interview with CBC News, the first CAF imam, Padre Suleyman Demiray, states that while he was happy to have joined the Chaplain Branch as a Regular Force padre, it was a "big responsibility to represent a faith and ... be [a] good model."[32] At one point, Padre Demiray was the only Muslim padre, who represented approximately 200 Muslim soldiers within the Canadian Armed Forces.[33] Similarly, Padres Chaim Mendelsohn and Lazer Danzinger, who joined as the first rabbis in the CAF, the former as a reservist and the latter in the Regular Forces, see their role as twofold: first, providing religious worship to those who adhere to their faith and facilitating service for all other members; and second, allowing for a greater understanding of their faith to non-believers.[34]

It is not only Muslim and Jewish candidates, however, who find it difficult to join the Chaplaincy. As noted, even certain Christian denominations struggle to join or gain proper representation. A candidate currently being recruited, Padre Brian Sanderson, has spent over a year attempting to demonstrate the validity of his qualifications as a Romanian Catholic priest. As Sanderson's degree comes from a Romanian school, his transcripts had to be obtained, translated, and compared to a recognized Canadian institution. However, as Padre Malek Talbott pointed out, the Chaplaincy must examine each case separately, and the military lacks the resources to do so quickly and efficiently. While those interviewed were committed to following through with this arduous process, the inaccessibility of the Chaplaincy and the impositions on candidates can be deterrents.

Progressive overtures by the Chaplaincy to other faith denominations must be further pursued. This will entail relaxation of certain requirements for other religious groups that are currently based upon the particularities of the Christian faiths. The provision of religious services must not be considered an "organizational burden" but rather a benefit for CAF personnel. Everyday religious practices such as prayers, rituals, and fasts play an important role in war, along with the spiritual yearning of soldiers on the battlefield for a narrative meaning.[35] Individual religious and spiritual needs must be catered to, as long as they do not conflict with organizational goals.[36] This is particularly important as spirituality and religion have been found to be strong coping mechanism for post-traumatic stress disorder.[37] Military Chaplains have adapted to this change in the religious experience of soldiers, which has become more individualized and less "organized," but they have not fully adapted to the diversification of religious beliefs within the military, which echoes national demographic trends. Removing the obstacles to the recruitment of non-Christian Chaplains remains imperative for a truly diverse military Chaplaincy. The Interfaith Committee on Canadian Military Chaplaincy must work to remove administrative requirements, such as those faced by Padre Brian Sanderson, in order to meet its commitment to a religiously diverse Canadian Armed Forces.

Allowing for more diversity would likely require a complete reformation of the Chaplaincy, and current Chaplains can understandably feel insecure about dramatic changes. To achieve this transformation, the CAF would need an alternative method of establishing external accountability. Losing direct ecclesiastical support would remove their unique access to two streams of accountability – through their church and through the military command structure – and could damage their legitimacy in freely moving along the chain of command. But given the need to provide services to all its members, the Chaplaincy must engage with the Interfaith Committee on Canadian Military Chaplaincy, members of the CAF, and the main religious groupings within Canada. Rather than being an organizational burden imposed by legal imperative, religious diversity within the Chaplaincy could complement the public image of the CAF and improve the quality of management decisions, while providing superior solutions to organizational problems. This approach is consistent with perspectives on the positive impact of diversity on human resources when differences in gender, sexual orientation, and religion are viewed as positive attributes rather than potential organizational challenges.[38] Leadership is crucial to positive change in the CAF organizational culture, and the CAF must be ready to confront broader changes in religious practice among its members by removing barriers to full inclusion.

Conclusion

The Chaplaincy is as one of the most complicated parts of this Canadian Armed Forces, continuously advocating for expansion and diversity, but seemingly unable to remove the barriers that could make this expansion a possibility. Regulations implemented after the Second World War worked for what were then predominantly Christian personnel. However, as religious diversity spread throughout Canada and in the CAF, the Chaplaincy found itself struggling to loosen rules about who could join this branch. For the soldier interviewed by Rennick, who wishes to be the first Indigenous spirituality Chaplain, they distort and limit understandings of diversity in Canada: "They keep saying you need some kind of degree, but my response is 'That's in *your* world, not in *my* world.'"[39] Even if this soldier could become a Chaplain, many Chaplains believe this would only heighten a new problem. Many traditions could never be properly represented by the few Chaplains the military could employ.[40] Expanding the Chaplaincy would not be as simple as merely stating that "more religions can join." Instead, a restructuring of how the military understands religion, spirituality, and itself may be the result of expanding the Chaplaincy.

For the Canadian Armed Forces, it is worth considering the consequences of the status quo, which may harm efforts in the CAF to recruit from untapped demographic communities. As many chapters in this volume demonstrate, the demographic reality of where Canada is moving makes diversity an imperative for CAF sustainability. Religious diversity in the Chaplaincy is similarly necessary to achieve diversity in regular CAF ranks. Without conclusive data, one can only speculate about the effects of religious expansion in the Chaplaincy upon the organization; however, there have been repeated calls from several faiths to expand the Chaplaincy to better and more efficiently serve Canadian soldiers. This approach will invariably strengthen its legitimacy as an organization that reflects the country and personnel it serves.

chapter seven

Francophone Inclusion and Bilingualism in the Canadian Armed Forces

STÉPHANIE CHOUINARD

The issue of managing linguistic diversity within a country's armed forces is not new. For hundreds of years, multilingual and multi-ethnic states throughout the world have had to deal with the dilemma of commanding an army that may not speak the same language; Canada is not an exception.[1] The CAF has legally embraced bilingualism, thanks in part to the rise of identity politics of francophone communities who have pushed for greater recognition. By 1969, Canada had granted official and legal recognition to the languages of the country's two national groups: French and English. As a federal institution, the CAF, and the Department of National Defence (DND), must comply with the Official Languages Act (OLA) – a legal obligation with which it has struggled in the past.[2] Notwithstanding this legal recognition, the growing multicultural reality of Canada has raised new questions about the place of bilingualism in the CAF.

The CAF has historically been a predominantly anglophone institution, in language spoken and in culture. Despite the relatively smaller presence of francophones, the role of bilingualism has been important for the Canadian military, but not without challenges. Recruitment from francophone communities comprised a significant portion of the citizenry, and bilingualism helped to promote allegiance and unity. Nevertheless, the CAF has faced significant reprimands from the Commissioner of Official Languages for its failure to comply with the OLA, as CAF personnel have complained of their inability to work in their official language of choice and as CAF communications with the Canadian public have not always been equally offered in French and English. Canada's language regime has influenced the development of language policies in the CAF, including its most recent Official Languages Action Plan (OLAP).

As noted throughout this volume, the composition of Canadian society is indeed changing and becoming more diverse. This may invariably mean a decline in the number of people who speak both of the country's official languages. Yet, as this chapter shows, Canadians have an enduring attachment to bilingualism, despite the growing share of newcomers who are more likely to be – or to become – anglophones. Beyond the legal responsibilities for the CAF through the federal language regime, bilingualism and diversity within the Canadian military corps are not mutually exclusive. In fact, they are imperative for the Canadian military to continue to "reflect the values and composition of the larger society that nurtures it."[3] More precisely, as Canada becomes a flagship of "deep diversity," bilingualism policies of the CAF remain relevant in light of its legal obligations and of new Canadians' understanding and expectations of their new country. Reconciling the goals of recruiting a more ethnically diverse and more bilingual body of Canadians in the CAF has its challenges; this chapter discusses some of the ways the CAF may achieve diversity and inclusion, in order to strengthen its public legitimacy.

The Politics of Bilingualism in the CAF

The use of language (or languages) in government institutions, whether the armed forces or otherwise, is rarely a neutral policy decision. Often, adopting a language is a political choice, with implications for government institutions. As noted by Cardinal and Sonntag, "Language policies are political. They have political and social consequences. Language policies can reinforce or diffuse conflict between language groups. They can be instruments of inclusion or exclusion.... They can be implicated in civil strife and war."[4] Canada was built in English and French, but the two languages have not always been equal. For the first 100 years after Confederation,

Canadian language rights were marked by a political compromise between two "founding nations," extended to include four founding provinces, and later joined by six others.[5] This political compromise was born from a tradition of mutual accommodation between the political elites of its two dominant ethnic groups.[6] Section 133 of the Constitution Act, 1867, stipulated that both French and English languages were official in the Parliament and the courts of Canada and Quebec. At its entry into Confederation, Manitoba adopted the same protections.[7] In the rest of the Canadian state and in provincial governments outside of Quebec, English was the official language. This linguistic compromise encountered many crises, such as the school crises where many provincial governments forbade the teaching of French.[8] Among other events, this lead to the first conscription crisis in 1917, followed by another in 1942, where French Canadians then refused to enrol and serve in the CAF as a sign of protest for what was perceived as unfair treatment of their language and culture by the state.

As an institution that embodies Canadian state traditions and signals certain values and national myths of Canadian society, the CAF has promoted and upheld this tradition of an imperfect compromise between French- and English-speaking political elites. The historical relationship between French Canadians and the CAF has been tense. French Canadians have been under-represented in higher echelons of the military ranks, and the issue threatened Canadian unity, particularly during the First and Second World Wars. To illustrate, "at the time of the First World War, French Canadians made up almost one-third of the Canadian population, [yet] they constituted only 12.6 percent of the effectives in the Canadian Armed Forces. In the Second World War that percentage rose, but only to 19 percent." The percentage of French Canadians was even smaller in the Air Force and the Navy.[9]

Efforts were made to address the underrepresentation of French Canadians during the Second World War, when there were fifty-seven French-speaking or bilingual units in the army and infantry.[10] Nevertheless, at the end of the Second World War, the Royal 22e Régiment became the only permanent francophone unit in the CAF.[11] Moreover, there were no provisions to allow francophone schooling of children or provision of services to military spouses on Canadian bases. Many francophone serving members and their families felt like second-class citizens within the armed forces – and in their own country.[12] As a result, many French Canadians felt excluded, and both the CAF and the Canadian state lost some legitimacy in their eyes. Eventually, many francophones became assimilated or turned to using English in the CAF, but this then created a recruitment challenge where French Canadians felt further excluded from the forces and were less interested in enrolling.[13] As Labrosse notes, the situation was so dire that "the vicious circle of low French-Canadian enlistment constituted a danger to national unity and national security."[14] Simply put, Canada and the CAF were losing public legitimacy in the eyes of one of the two national communities in the country.

Attention slowly turned to francophones' exclusion from the CAF ranks, as francophone communities increasingly fought for their recognition. For a few decades after the Second World War and up to 1971 with the adoption of the Multiculturalism Act, Canada searched for a new identity, and "nation building" became a main preoccupation of successive Canadian governments. As Martel and Pâquet noted, "A new consensus slowly emerge[d] ... to redefine national collective references.... A new symbolic order [appeared] within which the linguistic issue will take a different significance, starting in the 1960s."[15] The 1960s and Quebec's Quiet Revolution shook the Canadian linguistic status quo. Demands for broader recognition of the French language, as well as for linguistic equality more generally, were being increasingly heard. French Canadians wanted their language to be acknowledged and better represented nationally. Tensions arose as the previous consensus between the country's two linguistic communities was quickly fading away to tumultuous identity politics and a looming national crisis, which the Royal Commission on Bilingualism and Biculturalism noted "were it to persist and be accentuated, could lead to the destruction of Canada."[16]

The Laurendeau-Dunton Commission, as it was also known, was appointed in 1963 and published its final report six years later. Its mandate had three main points of enquiry: the breadth of bilingualism in the federal civil service, the role of private and public institutions in the promotion of better cultural relations, and the possibilities offered to Canadians to become bilingual.[17] The results of the Canada-wide enquiry underlined exclusion faced by French speakers everywhere in the country, with a special focus on Quebec, and the overall underrepresentation of the French language. Commissioned research demonstrated that French Canadians were widely under-represented in the civil service and were facing economic discrimination. The final report recommended several measures, including that:

- Canada, as well as New Brunswick and Ontario, become officially bilingual (book 1);
- French-speaking and English-speaking parents have an opportunity to have their children educated in their mother tongue everywhere in the country (book 2);
- The civil service seek out a linguistic balance between French and English employees (book 3); and
- Ottawa, the federal capital, become officially bilingual (book 4).

While the Pearson government did not act on the Bilingualism and Biculturalism Commission's recommendations, the Trudeau government, elected in 1968, swiftly adopted an Official Languages Act (OLA) in 1969, as did the Robichaud government in New Brunswick. The substance of the "compromise" on which Canada's language rights rested had thus been altered, from where French had little space outside of Quebec and in very few federal institutions, to one where French would be on equal footing with English throughout all Canadian and New Brunswick governmental institutions. This law conveyed an important political message to Canadians – and most specifically to Quebec nationalists – that francophones were at home from coast to coast and that French was a viable language for use everywhere in Canada.

In parallel to discussions on the place of the French language within Canadian society, the "problem" of French-Canadian representation in the CAF also started to be taken more seriously following the end of the Second World War. The 1950–1 Committee for the Study of Bilingual Problems requested that the senior officer of each corps assess the reasons why French-Canadians were poorly represented in the CAF and present options to resolve this issue. While some officers proposed to create francophone-only units, especially in Quebec, others feared that opting for that solution would "create two unilingual armies" rather than one bilingual force.[18] Indeed, various studies have brought to light the "adverse effects of the language barrier on the information structure within international [military] organizations."[19] In part as a result of this committee's findings, the Royal Military College Saint-Jean was created in 1952 to provide French-language instruction to francophone recruits. This sent a strong message throughout the CAF on the importance of bilingualism, despite an enduring perception that English would remain the working language of the military.[20]

In 1966, a French-Canadian became Chief of Defence Staff for the first time. General Jean Allard used his leadership to address the systematic under-representation of francophones in the CAF. Allard was very sensitive to the issues faced by French-Canadians in the military and wished to resolve them, wanting to "ensure that Francophone military personnel would enjoy the same opportunities as Anglophones."[21] A number of the programs he initiated included recruitment and training of francophones in French and the creation of a Bilingualism Secretariat office in 1967.[22]

Allard's changes were introduced when the 1969 OLA also came into force. Despite its relative independence from the rest of DND, the CAF also came under the purview of the OLA. This mandated the CAF to become a bilingual institution and comply with OLA obligations – including the need to communicate with Canadians in the official language of their choice, and more generally, to ensure equal respect and status of the French and English languages.[23] The 1971 White Paper on Defence[24] also clarified the government's position on the CAF as an institution that "had a significant role to play in promoting national unity" and its need to "reflect the bilingual and bicultural nature of the country."[25] The Department of Defence responded to the White Paper in its 1972 "Implementation Programme and Plan to Increase Bilingualism and Biculturalism in the Armed Forces"[26] The latter had ten objectives, of which the following were the most important: "firstly, to ensure that both the

English and French languages became equal in status, rights and privileges 'as to their use in the Canadian Forces'; secondly that 'the linguistic and cultural values of both English-speaking and French-speaking Canadians' would be reflected in the organization; and, lastly that by 1987, the two official language groups ... became proportionally represented 'throughout the rank structure at all levels of responsibility and in all trades and classifications of the Canadian Forces.'"[27]

Important changes were being made to make the CAF more inclusive of francophones and to recognize the deep challenges that francophone alienation would have on the country's armed forces. Hence, in 1976 the Language Centre was created at Royal Military College to assist in officer-cadets' language training and to facilitate their graduation from RMC as minimally bilingual. In 1980, the CAF's language program was updated and renamed the Official Languages Plan (Military), in order to differentiate the military and civilian arms of DND's bilingualism requirements. With the revision of the OLA in 1988, which now included the right of all civil servants to work in the official language of their choice, as well as the possibility to enforce the OLA through court remedies, the CAF needed to adapt once again. Its new Master Implementation Plan, published in 1989, introduced a broad "universal approach" underlined by two principles: "that service members should be able to pursue meaningful careers in their first official languages and, that leaders should lead in the official languages used by those they lead."[28] As Gaudet explains, this new implementation plan was in fact recognizing bilingualism as an asset for officers and suggested that it would be required to advance beyond certain rank levels. The measure created some resentment amongst many unilingual anglophone officers, who argued that they were now at a disadvantage for career progression, compared to their francophone peers, as many felt that "they had been denied access to [second] language training."[29] In 1995, Royal Military College Saint-Jean ceased providing university-level education, which had a considerable impact on the linguistic duality of the CAF, as it had given anglophone Officer-Cadets an opportunity to learn French in a distinctively francophone environment.[30]

Despite pushback from some CAF members, and following the federal government's 2003 Action Plan for Official Languages, DND responded with its own Strategic Plan 2003–2006, which reinforced the universal approach put in place since 1989. This document created a language requirement of advanced reading, intermediate writing, and advanced oral interaction (C-B-C) for all the senior leadership within the CAF, mandating advanced bilingual proficiency for reading and oral interaction, as well as intermediate-level bilingualism for written communication. That approach was replaced in 2007. The National Defence Official Languages Program Transformation Model advocated a functional approach to official languages in the CAF, whereby "the unique roles and responsibilities of the Canadian military and the fact that for operational reasons, its uniformed members are required to move from posts to posts" are taken into account.[31] Hence, "to obtain compliance with the OLA, DND now sees the bilingual capacity of a unit measured 'as a whole' rather than on 'an individual positional basis.' As long as there is bilingual capacity somewhere within the unit, when and where bilingual functions are required, DND considers that the OLA requirements ... can be satisfied."[32] In practice, this meant, among other things, that only senior positions at the rank of Brigadier-General and above need to meet the C-B-C language requirement.

These changes drew harsh criticism from the Commissioner of Official Languages (COL), outlining that despite the uniqueness of the tasks performed by DND and the CAF, "the Official Languages Act does not confer special or preferred status on the Department of National Defence and the Canadian Forces. The Act applies equally to all federal institutions" and "the Canadian Forces must reflect Canadian values, including linguistic duality. The Forces must promote this duality and comply fully with the Official Languages Act."[33] A few years later, the COL published a 2011 report on the progress made by the CAF and found more work was needed to comply with the OLA.[34] While the COL acknowledged some improvements, especially in light of DND's five-year Official Languages Action Plan 2017–2022, parts of the audit revealed continuing challenges. Areas that needed improvement included bilingual in-person services, email responses in both languages, and access to English services on Quebec bases.[35] The new OLAP reiterates many of the previous concerns but also talks about fostering cultural change at the CAF in promoting the official languages.[36] Time will tell if OLAP succeeded in its goals. The announcement that Royal Military College Saint-Jean will resume its functions as a degree-granting institution should also prove beneficial in attaining these goals.

Promoting and advocating for francophone rights in the CAF has brought significant legal and policy changes to help recruitment and retention of this population in the ranks. These efforts seem to have paid off. Consider that the 2011 census shows that 23.2 per cent of Canadians had French as the first official language spoken, and 30.1 per cent said they were able to conduct a conversation in French.[37] Statistics regarding the first official language of CAF staff revealed that 27 per cent of the military personnel and 21 per cent of the Reserve personnel identified their first language as French.[38] Moreover, 42.2 per cent of Regular members and 33.9 per cent of Reserve members reported to be bilingual.[39] While French-speakers in the CAF are no longer under-represented, bilingualism in the armed forces is relatively higher than the general public, as it is in the Canadian civil service at large.

Reconciling Bilingualism in Multicultural Canada

While the number of French-speakers has increased in Canada since the 1960s, the *proportion* of French-speakers in Canada has slowly but steadily decreased (see table 7.1). This is in large part because of the evolution of the country's ethnic make-up over the previous decades – with international immigration being the main driver of population growth. Indeed, the vast majority of newcomers have been anglophone rather than francophone.[40] As pointed out by Leuprecht and others in this volume, while the CAF is seeking to increase its recruitment of ethnic minorities and urbanites, and to move outside its traditional recruitment base, this would seem to pose a challenge to CAF's bilingual policy. Indeed, new

Table 7.1. Canadians' French-Speaking Ability and Growth of Population, 1981–2011

Year	Canadian population (millions)	French-speaking population (millions)			
		Native language	First language spoken	Primary language at home	Conversational ability
1981	24.08	6.18	6.34	5.92	7.67
1991	26.99	6.56	6.81	6.29	8.51
2001	29.64	6.78	7.14	6.53	9.18
2006	31.24	6.89	7.37	6.69	9.59
2011	33.12	7.17	7.69	6.96	9.96
Population growth, 1981–2011 (%)	37.5	16.1	21.3	17.6	29.9

Source: Canadian bilingualism outside of Quebec, 2006 Census + CAF 2002 Characteristics of Military Personnel.

potential CAF recruits are more likely to speak or adopt English as their language of choice. As the ethnic and linguistic face of Canada changes, how will the CAF embody the Canadian ideal of "multiculturalism within a bilingual framework"?[41]

Canada has incontestably become a country of newcomers, with thousands of new immigrants and refugees arriving each year. It is estimated that in fifteen years, a quarter of Canadians will be first-generation immigrants.[42] In major cities like Toronto and Vancouver, the majority of the population was born outside of Canada. These newcomers have gradually altered both the ethnic and linguistic composition of our country. Indeed, as of 2011, 58 per cent of Canadians identified English as their mother tongue, while 22 per cent identified French, and 21 per cent identified a non-official language. "Canada is at the cusp of an historical shift, with Allophones [people whose first language is neither English nor French] likely to surpass the number of Francophones in the next census."[43] The decreasing proportion of francophones in Canada can be attributed to high immigration rates, along with a sharp decline in the birth rate of French Canadians since the 1960s.

The vast majority of newcomers in Canada who do not already have French or English as either a mother tongue or a learned language will choose to learn English over French. Moreover, immigration has led to an overall decline in bilingualism in the country, as most newcomers do not know both official languages.[44]

Official bilingualism in Canada has been implemented for close to fifty years. Since 1969, all federal services are available in both official languages, everywhere in the country, as well as in the province of New Brunswick. As mentioned above, different federal institutions, such as the CAF, have struggled to meet the expectations laid out by the OLA. At the level of individual bilingualism, progress has also been slow. "Whereas 12.2% of Canadians considered themselves bilingual in 1961, that is capable of conducting a conversation in both French and English, the number has increased to 17.5% in 2011," with francophones being significantly more likely to be bilingual than anglophones.[45] This slow increase in the individual capacity to speak both official languages has not, however, hindered general support for bilingualism.

While these new demographic trends appear to suggest that support for bilingualism would decline, in fact the views of new Canadians on this topic may tell a different story. Semi-directed interviews conducted with nearly 200 first-generation immigrants from cities across Canada between 2007 and 2012 revealed that they place a high value on the ideal of "bilingualism within a multicultural framework" expressed in Canadian legislation since the 1970s. "Canada's policy of bilingualism – not only the right to services but also the encouragement and incentives for all Canadians to learn a second official language – is a uniquely important means of cultivating a tolerant and open attitude toward other cultures and languages from around the world."[46] In that sense, bilingualism was a source of "civic pride" for new Canadians and part of "the Canadian dream."

The surveyed population had another reason to emphasize the value of bilingualism in Canada: knowledge of both official languages was also perceived as a professional asset. Bilingualism was considered to be a useful tool for professional advancement, in Canada and abroad, as English and French were perceived to

be international languages, especially among the younger generations. "In today's increasingly globalized society, there is a sense
among young immigrants that speaking several languages is a
standard expectation ... multilingualism is modern."[47] Canadian
newcomers value bilingualism and have a deep understanding of
bilingualism as being part of Canadian identity and a "natural corollary and facilitator of multiculturalism."[48] Hence, despite the rise
of allophones in Canada, there is a deep attachment to bilingualism as a source of national pride.

It would appear that support among first- and second-generation
immigrants for official bilingualism in Canada equals or even
surpasses support among Canadian anglophones.[49] Results of a
recent survey show that 69 per cent of allophones, a category that
comprises new immigrants primarily, either "strongly agree or
somewhat agree that it is important to preserve French and English
as Canada's two official languages," as opposed to 67 per cent of
anglophones.[50] When looking at the rest of Canada, outside of
Quebec, the support for bilingualism stands at 66 per cent.[51]

Overall, these different sets of data show that, despite the lagging
rates of bilingualism among Canadians, mostly due to Canada's
yearly intake of immigrants and refugees, bilingualism is still highly
valued among Canadian citizens and newcomers for a variety of reasons. Beyond its legal obligations, as an institution intent on reflecting
both the *composition* and *values* of Canadian society, the CAF therefore has good reason to maintain bilingualism as a core principle.

Conclusion

This chapter laid the base for a broader discussion on the management of bilingualism and diversity goals in the CAF. This question comes at a crucial time in Canada's history, as the country
is inching away from the traditional French-English dichotomy,
which defined much of its history, towards "deep diversity."
Francophone Canadians have put pressure on Canadian institutions to gain more rights and services, resulting in OLA obligations
across the civil service, including the CAF. Bilingualism may be

demographically threatened, but despite changes in the country's ethnocultural make-up, Canadians hold bilingualism as a valuable part of Canadian identity. It is therefore still important to the CAF's public legitimacy.

Not only is bilingualism culturally valuable, but the knowledge of two official languages is also perceived to be advantageous to one's career in Canada. The policies of the CAF, and of the federal public service as a whole, seem to vindicate this belief. These observations bolster the argument for the reconcilability of the CAF's dual goals of bilingual and multicultural representation in its ranks. CAF bilingualism is not only culturally valuable and legally binding in Canada's federal institutions, but also holds an operational value. First, several studies in the field of psychology have highlighted the positive impact of bilingualism on working memory and on the management of complex tasks, requiring executive function demands such as problem-solving, mental flexibility, and task switching.[52] These studies reinforce the necessity of developing policies within the CAF favourable to the acquisition of language skills, not only at the operational command level but also in the rank and file. Second, as the editors' introductory chapter notes, CAF are increasingly being deployed to lead and participate in international coalitions and multinational operations. CAF bilingualism gives our forces a global comparative advantage in these deployments. The optimal way for the CAF to prove the importance of bilingualism within its ranks would be to revise its conception of "bilingual capacity" by promoting and offering the possibility of learning one of the country's two official languages to all of its personnel.

chapter eight

Race and Belonging

TAMMY GEORGE

Typically, Western militaries in general, and the Canadian Armed Forces (CAF) in particular, have not been narrated as institutions that are organized or understood along racial lines. While there has been ample research and scholarly work conducted on race and the military from a variety of perspectives such as employment equity, racial patterns in enlistment, officer promotion rates, and administration of military justice, particularly in the American context, very little scholarship has brought together bodies of work that centre on the *lived* experience of racialized soldiers and how they negotiate national belonging within the Canadian multicultural context.[1] Literatures on war and soldiering have largely dealt with markers of identity such as race, gender, and sexuality, rather than focus on the practices of racialization and gendering as they are produced institutionally and lived out daily. How wars and armed conflict produce, naturalize, and maintain race, gender, and ethnic hierarchies are also instrumental to understanding the racial underpinnings of citizenship and notions of diversity in the contemporary moment. The lived experience of racialized soldiers within a multicultural framework is a key component to understanding how the state has attempted to neutralize systemic racism.

Using qualitative interviews with racialized soldiers, this chapter reveals how the notion of diversity is negotiated among racialized soldiers in the CAF. In doing so, the analysis demonstrates how the Canadian military is constructed as what I term a "white space" for racialized soldiers, and illustrates how they grapple with everyday encounters in an institution that is not made in their image. What the soldiers' narratives reveal is how this space in which they live, train, and work is experienced as "white," both in terms of demographics and through the specificities of the military culture they negotiate. For them, the military encounter is racial. Racialized soldiers are made through everyday encounters with whiteness, where such encounters constitute "the ambivalent site where whiteness is constituted, or where race happens."[2] While there are practices and policies that call for a strict standardized culture in the Canadian military, racialized soldiers embody the "other" and come to know themselves as other through colonial legacies of whiteness and their encounters with white Canadian soldiers.

Questions posed here about diversity discourse are: What are the techniques and mechanisms by which institutional whiteness is produced? How do soldiers of colour secure a subject position in such a space? And what are the material effects of the encounters with whiteness, and hence the relationship to diversity? To answer these questions, the experiences of racialized members of the Canadian military are related to highlight what Victoria Basham describes as the "co-constitutive links between the everyday and the geopolitical."[3] The chapter demonstrates how formal and informal practices, as well as institutional logistics, have contributed to the preservation of a culture of whiteness in the Canadian Armed Forces, while further exploring how racialized bodies negotiate this space in a multitude of ways. In doing so, the production of whiteness and how it "quilts together various racial practices" in the Canadian military are grounded in colonial history that is ultimately connected to how we wage war in the present.[4]

Recruitment of Racialized Canadians

Several feminists of colour have offered strong critiques of the language of diversity.[5] For Mohanty, diversity is a discourse of "benign variation," which "bypasses power as well as history to suggest harmonious empty pluralism."[6] Building on these claims, Alexander suggests that diversity as a practice functions by "manufactur[ing] cohesion" and creating the impression of "more diversity" than "actually exists."[7] Puwar maintains that diversity has come to "overwhelmingly mean the inclusion of people who look different."[8] Inclusion is understood to mean that institutions do not have a problem with racism and that they are in fact post-racial. Thus, as Ahmed has argued that diversity and its attending mechanisms have instead become "about *changing perceptions of whiteness* rather than *changing whiteness in organization.*"[9] As suggested below, racialized soldiers are deemed good for business and the CAF's image or brand; however, as their narratives reveal, diversity initiatives do not address racism, and racialized soldiers who join the military often feel that the organization frequently fails to deliver on promises and that ultimately it is engaging in a surface celebration of difference.

The Canadian military's relationship to diversity in its recruitment efforts reflected the historical and political struggles in Canada for justice, the legitimacy of different Canadian identities, and the expansion of citizenship rights in the 1960s and 1970s. Much of the political legislation of the period "aimed to bring the federal government and public institutions in line with the values of multiculturalism, bilingualism and gender equity – values that were a core part of the Canadian 'rights' revolution."[10] Attention to francophones in the military emerged as the first priority. French Canadians served in the military in large numbers and did not need to be recruited. However, they were often restricted to the lower ranks and subjected to persistent and institutionalized racism.[11] As noted in Chouinard's chapter in this volume, growing separatist sentiment in Quebec prompted the federal government to implement a number of measures aimed at francophones. Importantly, these measures concerned language issues only, and did not include attention to racism. In 1963 the Pearson government struck the Commission on Bilingualism and Biculturalism, and with the release of its final report enforced bilingualism as a central component of the CAF. As a result, as Cowen shows,[12] francophones did not become an employment equity group targeted for recruitment. Instead, language conditions improved. Presently, bilingual francophones comprise a sizeable proportion of the CAF – approximately 4 per cent are unilingual francophone, whereas bilingual soldiers are approximately 43 per cent of all members of the CAF.

In the 1980s, the Charter of Rights and Freedoms and the implementation of Employment Equity laws further pushed the military to diversify. With respect to racialized groups, specialized programs to recruit Indigenous peoples into the Canadian Forces were longstanding and have a complex history,[13] as Lackenbauer's chapter in this volume elucidates. The Oka crisis of 1990, an Indigenous revolt, marked a low point in modern Canadian military history and its relationship with Indigenous peoples. Canada deployed almost 14,000 military personnel at the height of the crisis to put down the revolt.[14] The late 1990s witnessed several Indigenous uprisings in across Canada. Throughout this turbulent period, the Canadian military continued to recruit Indigenous peoples into the CAF, but did so cautiously and with minimal reference to the "Oka Crisis" and other Indigenous uprisings.[15] While the Oka crisis remains a contentious issue for Indigenous communities, the Canadian Forces nonetheless invests heavily in its recruitment campaigns targeting Indigenous communities.[16]

Targeted recruitment among non-Indigenous racialized groups did not occur until the 1980s. Cowen demonstrates that the Canadian Forces Personnel Applied Research Unit (CFPARU) was trying to grapple with ethnicity and how that would affect targeted recruitment. As Cowen explains, "Ethnicity was furthermore conceptualized as something of an obstacle to recruitment. It was constantly conflated with immigration status in CFPARU reports, as though they were interchangeable concepts, well into the 1990s."[17] A lack of engagement with racism in the ranks persisted, even though there was a growing interest in recruiting racialized citizens. In fact, "the CFPARU initially attributed the low participation rates of people of colour in the military to the failings of their own cultures rather than the systemic racism or hegemonic whiteness of the military."[18] Cowen also explains that racialized groups were perceived as difficult to recruit because of, in the words of the military, a "built in resistance to any move that will take the youth away from the cultural group to which they belong."[19]

The 1990s marked a difficult time for the Canadian Forces as they joined the U.S.-led coalition in the first Gulf War but were faced at home with budget cuts and subject to the Force Reduction Plan. These cutbacks and the enquiry into prisoner abuse by Canadian peacekeepers in Somalia further impeded the recruitment of racialized soldiers.[20] The enquiry exposed racist hazing and white supremacist subcultures within the military, and a cover-up of abuses across the ranks. As a result, committees were struck and diversity task forces were created to improve the Canadian military's internal diversity and to devise sensitivity protocols. While the CAF was more immediately concerned with improving the public image of the military and increasing recruitment from targeted segments of Canadian society than they were with improving military culture, several outcomes of this event produced an increased awareness of the depths of structural racism in the CAF. These changes had a direct impact on Indigenous people, members of visible minority groups, women, and people with disabilities. The CAF were required to diversify.[21] However, as Cowen explains, "Ironically, though these initiatives were a failure in achieving any significant diversification of the military workforce, or even in raising recruitment rates, through this work the military became one of the most important sources for diversity discourse in Canada"[22]

Understanding Race and Spaces of Whiteness in Canada

Race can be defined "as a social construction, a human contrivance used to frame and rationalize hierarchical divisions between population groups in the modern world."[23] Racialization sets the stage for pointing out specific groups for unequal treatment on the basis of real or imagined features.[24] More importantly it is the process of turning physical differences into social markers, and then enforcing them in a regime of oppression, that gives race its significance.

Racialization also has been described as an individual's tendency to "see oneself, one's past, present, and future, through the colour of one's own skin."[25] It also refers "to the historical emergence of the idea of 'race' and to its subsequent reproduction and application."[26] I refer to the social construction of race and gender and the historical, economic, political, and cultural processes through which modernist categories of race are (re)produced.

It is important to distinguish between how racism is structurally embedded and how it is embodied in social structures of society. Critical race scholars who have critiqued the state in its role in racist and/or exclusionary acts[27] are central to examining how racism operates historically and currently. Drawing on these scholars, I trace the connections between the state and racial exclusions, and examine how they manifest conceptually, theoretically, materially, and spatially through military spaces. Price addresses the intersection between embedded structures of whiteness through critical race theory and how whiteness is embodied using critical geographies of race.[28] She asks us to be mindful of the differences between the two schools of thought and how they intersect. Before we can attempt to negate racialized discourses, we must understand how deeply structured and embedded white supremacy is in our colonial histories, economic institutions, and political structures and how this continues to have a bearing on the present.

Several scholars have documented the existence of racism in Canadian society that is grounded in different historical events involving racialized groups in Canada. They have examined and theorized how these encounters with racism continue to operate.[29] Himani Bannerji argues that the labour market acts as a barrier for racialized individuals because Canada itself is constructed as a "white" nation, thereby discriminating against racialized bodies in its social, political, and economic spheres.[30] In this context she argues that "'Canada' then cannot be taken as a given. It is obviously a construction, a set of representations, embodying certain types of political and cultural communities and their operations. These communities were themselves constructed in agreement with certain ideas regarding skin colour, history, language (English/French), and other cultural signifiers – all of which may be subsumed under the ideological category 'white.'"[31] The problematic stereotypes that are created about racialized groups in Canada contribute to the social construction of a vision of whiteness that permits white Canadians to maintain a specific place of privilege.

How do we understand and theorize this notion of whiteness, and how does it operate in contemporary Canadian social life? Offering a historical and spatial analysis of how Canadian society and its laws were founded on the basis of a "white settler society," Sherene Razack describes how mythologies of Canada's origins paint a picture of white European settlers as the "bearers of civilization" and that people of colour arrived in this country after most of its development transpired.[32] It is through these national mythologies whereby European settlers become the bearers of civilization, that the racial distinction between who has and has not participated and contributed in nation building is made.[33] This process is deeply connected to the Canadian landscape and largely informs the racialized hierarchies that situate white settlers as fundamentally national subjects. Although they can differ at times, each of these narratives props up white European settlers as being entitled to occupy and use this land, and then uses the governing power structures to make this entitlement into law.

It is the production and reproduction over time of these myths, grounded in the disavowal of the role of Indigenous and people of colour in the building of the Canadian nation, that permits white settlers in Canada to assert themselves as overseers of the nation. It is these individuals, who maintain positions of power, who can organize their space to sustain unequal social relations and in turn use these relations to shape racialized spaces. Through social and political means, they determine who can and cannot legitimately belong to the nation. Exposing the association between racialization and (geographical, social, political) space is critical to analyse space as a site of power relations. White Canadians obtain senses of selves through the construction of rigid boundaries that establish specific spaces – in roles or positions of power and authority – as places reserved for national subjects. It is this cycle of knowledge production that further outlines the boundaries of a space that is inhabited by the racial "other."[34]

Kobayashi and Peake refer to the concept of "geographies of whiteness": they bridge critical race theory and geography by suggesting that place contextualizes the construction of race and the nation, generating geographically specific ideologies of racism and nationalism.[35] Certain places assume more powerful roles than others by restricting or controlling spatial access. The CAF has been selected as the investigative terrain because they are often an "overlooked form of national work and belonging" in academic and popular discourse.[36] This terrain is under-researched as a matrix of racialized national belonging and citizenship in the West. The Canadian military is an important site of analysis because it has been considered as a crucial nerve centre for the formation of Canadian identity and the historical construction of the Canadian nation, notions that are deeply racial. According to Kobayashi and Peake, spatial interpretation also needs to take into account "empty spaces" that result from silence, exclusion, and denial, and that serve as a basis for reproducing normative whiteness. The bridging of geography and critical race theory offers a nuanced exploration of racialized individuals' experiences navigating and negotiating the Canadian Forces.

Theoretical and Methodological Considerations

This chapter is informed by critical race and feminist post-structuralist theory.[37] From this standpoint, individuals' subjectivities are made possible through the already gendered and racialized discourses to which they have access. I thus attempted not only to map the range of discourses to which racialized soldiers have access in constructing their meanings, but also to investigate how they position themselves in relation to these discourses. For example, there is a specific set of discourses for what it means to be a "good" and "loyal" soldier, which are articulated by individuals to define themselves as such. The construction of what has been termed as the "military ethos" demarcates the boundaries within which soldiers can negotiate what it means to be a "good," "effective," and "dutiful" soldier within the military context. As a result, it is these discourses that individuals engaged with when coming to understand themselves as soldier-citizen subjects, reflecting the notion that reality is made and not found; racialized soldiers then construct "reality" through language and cultural practices.

With respect to "identity," I understood it as being dynamic, multiple, and shifting.[38] Identity is negotiated in relation to meanings and practices that individuals draw on as they participate in the culture and come to understand who they are.[39] As for "discourse," like Foucault,[40] I understood this concept as not being about objects but as constituting them. Discourse refers not only to the meaning of language, but also to the real effects of language use. Discourses are "regimes of truth,"[41] and as such, they specify what can be said or done at particular times and places, they sustain specific relations of power, and they construct particular practices. It is through discourse that meanings, subjects, and subjectivities are formed. Although discourse is not equivalent to language, choices in language point to those discourses being drawn upon by speakers and to the ways in which they position themselves and others. Like Weedon, I understood that experience is given meaning in language and through a range of discursive formations that are often contradictory and that constitute conflicting versions of social reality.[42]

One-on-one semi-structured interviews were conducted with thirty soldiers who identified as racialized in the Canadian military situated in the regions of Toronto, Ottawa, and Halifax. The conversations with the participants lasted between one and three hours. The soldiers interviewed included men and women serving in all three branches (Army, Navy, and Air Force) of the CAF, and varying in age, rank, and their commission status. Throughout this study, I sought to understand how these soldiers' racial positioning shapes their experience of the military, their relationship to military life, citizenship, and organized violence more broadly. This process entailed posing questions to explore the values placed on military service as a profession, what it means to be a soldier in the post-9/11 moment, their experiences with training (specifically with The Standard for Harassment and Racism Prevention Program and cross-cultural training pre-deployment), and their encounters with racism. I asked about their experiences of being a racialized subject in a predominantly white space, and how they themselves constitute "diversity." Moreover, I asked questions about their nuanced encounters with racism with fellow soldiers, superiors, civilians, and during their deployment overseas, to trace the complex expressions of whiteness operating in the Canadian military and in the post-9/11 moment. To insure anonymity, self-chosen pseudonyms were used in the transcriptions and in the current chapter.

Understanding Diversity Discourse in the Canadian Forces

While the recruitment advertisements deployed during Canada's mission in Afghanistan attempted to display the CAF as a diverse institution, my research indicated a more complex experience within the CAF, that has remained insufficiently recognized or understood. For some of the soldiers interviewed in this study, the military was diverse, while others felt that the efforts were merely tokenistic. Here, Blaze reflects on how the CAF has tackled diversity, and its impact on the institution:

> Now that I'm retired, I see things around recruitment a little differ-
> ently. On the one hand, I understand why the military works its way
> into ethnic communities and events. They really are trying to fulfil its
> numbers, which is maybe not the best way of going about it. But on
> the other hand, when that's your focus, it's not about them and what
> they bring. So yeah, you could say the military has an ethnic soldier
> now and it might look good, but what's the point if the military isn't
> changed by this?

Blaze raises an important point about diversity, and diversity initiatives. While he understands the need for the CAF to raise its profile and recruit racialized soldiers, he also understands that if numbers are the sole focus, then little attention is paid to life conditions in the military for racialized soldiers.

Many of the soldiers I spoke with expressed the view that the military is very good at symbolism, celebrating diversity in terms of certain days or months, but that it is not attending to real change. For example, Black History Month is observed, as is International Women's Day, and the Day for the Elimination of Racism, to name a few. These days are often replete with posters, speeches, displays, photo opportunities, and events. However, some of the soldiers I spoke with understood these practices as being largely tokenistic rather than representing the existence of real change. Maya comments, for instance,

> They'll have the posters up. I personally just ignore them because I don't care, but they have posters up. I'm pretty sure I saw one for Asian Awareness Month. I laughed my ass off. I was like, "Wow, we got one of those? Why am I not on the poster?" There's a Black History one, of course, there's the Women's one and the International Day we just had. So yes, they are big on it, for sure. I just ignore most of them because I don't have time for that. The military is open to that, but you also got to wonder why only on those specific days or months.

Ruban offers an interesting contrast to the current recruitment campaigns we have witnessed. While these recruitment posters seek to portray racialized soldiers as a central feature to the Forces, Ruban's narrative offers a very different reality through his experiences of racism both inside and outside of the Canadian Armed Forces. Ruban describes his reason for joining the military as due to having few options available him outside of the military, despite his education and experience.

> I came out with degrees, with keys to the city, but we couldn't get employment, there was a few of us ... and the common denominator is racism. So I didn't join the military as my first choice, I joined the military because I had a young family and I wanted to eat, but the military didn't factor, didn't get contrived in my mind to make a better life. That said, once in there, I applied myself and I did exceedingly well. The

only thing I couldn't anticipate was the level of racism encountered by me and my colleagues. It was just overwhelming.

Ruban is a retired African Nova Scotian who began in the army and then served in the Royal Canadian Air Force. He attained the rank of Sergeant after seven years of service and served in Israel and Germany. In 1991, he was diagnosed with post-traumatic stress disorder and had to be released because the CAF found that he was "unfit" to perform military duties. Ruban emphasized early on for me that he would like to say that he acquired his condition in battle, but instead he openly attributes his PTSD to the blatant and systemic racism he faced during his time in the Forces.

Ruban's experience in the Canadian military was complex in that he was a very successful soldier, excelling in most areas during his service, but his experiences were constantly marked by the racism he faced at all levels. Eventually, Ruban was granted stress leave and sought the assistance he required to become whole again. In 1995, he was released from the CAF, but today Ruban continues to do advocacy work for those who may suffer racial injustice in the Canadian military. Despite having left the CAF in the mid-nineties, Ruban's experiences speak to a historical culture of whiteness in the military that has led to subsequent diversity initiatives in the CAF. Most recently, Ruban Coward and three other former service members were involved in a class action law suit against the Canadian Armed Forces, citing that it was racial discrimination that forced them to end their careers in military service.[43]

Negotiating the Canadian Armed Forces as a "White Space"

According to *The Canadian Armed Forces Employment Equity Report (2014–2015)*, of all currently serving members, 91.5 per cent are white Canadian, 6.0 per cent of serving members identify as a visible minority, and 2.5 per cent identify as Indigenous. While there is an argument to be made about the bodily constitution of the armed forces, there were other ways in which "whiteness" was experienced in the Canadian Forces among racialized soldiers. Several conversations with soldiers involved their telling me that the Canadian Forces is a fairly welcoming place. Others struggled to find their place. While sharing with me their experiences in the Canadian military, many soldiers articulated that they were warned of racism and that it was "so white"[44] or a "not a very diverse place"[45] but "might get better over time."[46]

Chester, an Engineer in the Reserve Force, understood the Canadian military to be a "white space."

> I was thinking about joining for a long time. I really enjoyed the idea of being part of something bigger, but a lot of my friends and family warned me that the military is really "white" [*laughs*].

When I asked Chester to describe what he meant by "white" in this context, he responded,

> Well, you know, not very multicultural or diverse, and that you wouldn't see many people that look like you and me around. Also, being a soldier means that you have to be a certain way, there's a strict way of being with little room for anything else.

Chester conceives of institutional whiteness in terms of the bodies present and the company he is surrounded by in the CAF. According to Chester, a "white space" is constructed by the absence of diverse bodies. He also addresses the idea that to be a soldier one must perform a soldier's identity, one that allows very little room for different ways of being. Racialized soldiers deviating from the cultural norms and practices within the CAF are quickly reminded that they are not part of the norm and are encouraged to conform to ensure operational effectiveness.

Throughout this research study, one of the more commonly expressed views of the military as "really white" was the lack of racialized bodies in the senior ranks. Several soldiers remarked on the difficulty of moving up in the ranks, or noted that they had a hard time imagining their careers expanding because they did not see themselves reflected in the senior membership. According to Alfred,

> I got jaded, because I don't see myself in the leadership. There were also a couple of other experiences. I mean, whether it was the terms of service, or having to fight tooth and nail for every single promotion that I've gotten, or whether it was various office crap. I realized their system is not going to change. Learn to live and work within the system. And hopefully try to thrive, just do your best and whatever happens, happens. I just stopped caring.

When I asked him if he thought that the lack of people of colour had an effect on people of lower ranks and what they want to achieve in the military, he responded,

> I think it does. No one will admit it.... When I want a role model, I look for the qualities that people have. But with other people it does matter. And even within the unit it does matter. I'm sitting here telling you that there are no black people that I can look up to and say I want to be just like him. All the successful black people I know are my friends. And they're outside of the military. And they make major moves. It's like I can't do that here. And you try. And you just can't get it done. After a while you decide, yeah, it's time to leave.

Alfred reveals a number of important points about his tenure in the Canadian Forces. He began his journey in the military as a reservist "beaming with optimism" and desiring "to make a difference." As I continued to speak with him, his experience appeared to be marked with struggle. Six years into his service, by now a full-time member of the force, he recollects, "Something just switched off in me and I stopped caring." He describes apathy and disappointment that built over the years about the lack of people of colour in the upper ranks, which seems to have affected his overall morale as a member of the Canadian Forces.

My interview with Alfred demonstrated that he is affected by not seeing his body reflected in the leadership; he believes that this affects his career mobility, and as a result he feels limited in the contribution he can make to the organization. While he emphasizes that he looks at qualities and values in a role model, rather than race, in this instance he may also be accommodating the neo-liberal discourse about qualifications that are constructed largely outside of race and entrenched in this idea of colour blindness. He notes that all his friends of colour succeed in other institutions outside of the military, but suggests that while an individual can try to climb the ranks in the CF, it is very difficult for racialized individuals.

Alongside the visible representation Alfred speaks about, experiencing the Canadian Armed Forces as a "white space" often encompassed the contexts or places where racialized soldiers worked, lived, and trained. Racialized soldiers' concerns, both anticipated and lived, are felt through the often-rural spaces of military labour and life. Maya explains how belonging was tenuous for her through a historical reminder of whiteness that continues to imbue the present:

> Let me tell you one of my first days when I was in Pet [Petawawa], I was driving on the main road, because there's always just one, and I passed by this tow truck. I'm like saying in my head, "Oh my God, this is where I live. I actually live here now." I've been to Petawawa before and I passed by this tow truck company and I see a Confederate flag and it says, "Proud to be a hick." And then I think I cried. I think I had a tear come from my eye. I think it was one of the first few days I was in Pet, and I was like, "This is where I live. Oh my God." But to them the Confederate flag is not like how I understand it in my head. I'm like, I know the Confederate flag wasn't initially supposed to be a racial thing, but over the years, guess what? And now it's on a business in Petawawa and I was like, "Oh God, this is where I live. Got it."

Maya's experience of racism in Petawawa, and her resulting deep distress, goes to the heart of the paradox experienced by soldiers of colour. In that moment, while sitting in her car and coming face-to-face with the Confederate battle flag, she is starkly reminded that national belonging is tenuous, even as a soldier. Belonging neither to military space nor to the public space of the town where the base is located, for Maya this racist encounter is an emotional moment when the eviction from citizenship is palpable and when not even the Canadian military uniform can shield her.

The presence of the confederate flag for Maya and so many other racialized bodies is symbolic of the presence of white supremacy, demarcating who belongs and who does not. The Confederate battle flag, also known as the "Southern Cross" or the Cross of St Andrew, has much significance in the United States, where it has been described both as a proud emblem of Southern heritage, and as being a shameful reminder of slavery and segregation. In recent history, the Confederate battle flag has also been appropriated by the Ku Klux Klan and other racist hate groups. According to the Southern Poverty Law Centre, more than 500 extremist groups have appropriated the Confederate flag as one of their organizations' symbols.[47]

In Canada, however, there is a tendency to fly a significant number of Confederate flags, primarily in rural areas of Alberta and parts of Ontario. A recent American company has started selling bumper stickers and decals merging the Canadian flag with the Confederate battle flag. What this signals in the Canadian context is a heavy rural sentiment that figures closely with both Canadian national identity and the racist history of the United States that this flag symbolizes for so many.

Exploring the connection between whiteness and rurality is especially meaningful with the election of U.S. President Donald Trump, where it has been argued that his victory was due in significant measure to support from rural white voters.[48] Similarly, Shannon conflates this notion of military tradition with Canadian-ness and whiteness, and expresses the difficulties she has navigating the inflexibility of military tradition in the face of including racialized bodies for service:

> Go to Kingston and you'll see what's important. And in the CAF it is curling, it's hockey, and it's darts. You know, that's been my experience, and those are sports of interest to your typical white person in the military. So, they set up social events around those things, right? So, while

you can sit here by yourself and have no friends or you can get in there and throw a rock down the ice and have a beer and just try to like it because that's what the dominant crowd is doing. That's kind of what I mean by just fitting in. Just kind of accepting what already exists and just trying to be part of it.

I asked Shannon if she found this experience to be really difficult at times, and if there were moments where she couldn't do it anymore:

Yeah, there are times that it's difficult, but you can always do it. You don't go into this blind, and it doesn't take long for you to see what the situation is. So, either you get out or you make the decision you're going to stay.

The Limits of Diversity: Naming Racism

Naming race and racism is often met with pervasive claims of colour blindness. That is to say, that one does not see race and/or institutional racism operating and relegates these ideas to issues of the past. As a result, the power dynamics associated with understanding the operation of racism and white supremacy remain unexplored. Under such conditions Goldberg argued, "It is not that race is simply silenced, if silenced at all. It is shifted to less formal domains for the most part, embedded in structures, without being explicitly named, where it is more difficult to identify, more ambivalently related to, more ambiguous."[49] This situation can permit racism to continue or even to flourish, permeating beyond detection of the general public.[50] In this way, racism remains embedded within the military structure and has been increasingly difficult to recognize.[51]

One of the main ways in which the discourse of silence operates around race in the Canadian Forces is to redirect blame onto soldiers of colour, where they are portrayed as being responsible for their hardship and oppression because of their inability to "handle it" or "work it out." This was most visible through the claim of playing the race card. My conversations with Liza and Alfred illustrate this point:

> *Alfred:* A white female private, less trained than I was, literally, applies and she gets the job. And there's a pattern of that throughout. So, you see all of this. You raise your hand. You say, "What the hell's going on?" And they say, "Oh you're trying to pull the race card." They go on to say, "Don't worry, no one is racist, I have a best friend who's black," and so now I'm the one who is responsible.
>
> *Liza:* I've thought many times about mentioning something about race. The problem is every time you try to bring it up someone is saying that I'm too sensitive or that I'm playing the race card or making a bigger deal of the issue than needs to be. I have a problem with someone, and then it turns into me being the problem. I don't get it.

Simply suggesting that race and racism are part of some of the issues that arise in the CAF, is met with strong opposition as evidenced by Alfred and Liza. Instead, they are considered disloyal and unpatriotic for "rocking the boat."[52] Behind the statement "playing the race card"[53] is the moral assertion made within the Canadian Armed Forces and in other neoliberal institutions that race is unmentionable. The assertion of the "race card" is not compatible within Canadian multicultural spaces. The very accusation of "playing the card" has become a way of disqualifying the attempt to discuss past and present racial injury.[54] As Chen has observed,[55] the rhetoric of the race card betrays a peculiar logic where a winning hand has been identified with a handicap. Therefore, to succeed in naming the race card is to lose in the larger game of life. Consequently, policing the use of the race card aims to discredit racialized suffering and turn it into a (supposed) advantage.

This tactic contributes to the culture of silence around race, and works to consolidate whiteness. In my conversation with Shannon we discussed how issues of racism are handled in the military:

> There's a saying in the military and it has existed forever: it's "Handle at the lowest level." Like, they don't want things escalating. If you don't get along with your boss, you're the one who gets the bad PER, which

is your personal evaluation assessment. You get the bad one. You learn right from the get go that in order to succeed it's up to you to get along with your superior. Perhaps rightly so, your superior doesn't have to get along with you.... So, many people who have had conflicts with their bosses and not everyone will say he or she is a racist, but maybe their jokes are.... I'm not going to say, "You're racist," but you just displayed tendencies of insensitivity, if that's what you want to call it now days, right?

I then prompted her on what she was going to do about it and what her options were in this context. She answered,

And if you do, just be prepared for the walls to come down on you. If you're going to bring something forward like that, I mean, you'd almost have to be like, really hurt in order for it to be worth your while to come forward. Like something would have had to happen to you where it was visually documented so you could say, "Look at this. This is what happened and this was him who did this." But if it's all psychological, I mean, good luck. If you don't have it on tape that someone is over the line, and saying all of these things to you....

The burden of proof is on you. That's really what I'm saying. In this system, you have to prove it. Yeah, you really do, because if they want to go with the zero tolerance, that means someone's career is over, and I'm not just going to do that.

Shannon describes how difficult it is to name racism or confirm racist acts when they do occur, because there is enormous pressure on an individual for ending someone's career. The soldiers I engaged with often employed mitigation strategies, which refer to "the processes through which individuals seek simultaneously to downplay or deny incidences of racism and to exonerate those accused of engaging in such acts (whether that be themselves or others). This involves offering alternative explanations with the purpose of refuting intentionality and responsibility on the part of the person(s) under scrutiny."[56]

According to Doane, these strategies of denial are central to the framework of colour-blindness: "Given the general social consensus that racism violates social norms and the strong negative valuation attached to the 'racist' label, charges of racism are a significant rhetorical and political weapon. In the twenty-first century, no one wants to be accused of racism or to be called a racist,"[57] particularly in a context that espouses diversity or multiculturalism. Doane's point is relevant here and relates to what Shannon reveals. She also goes on to highlight how the burden of proof is placed on racialized bodies, which gives way to mitigation strategies.

Conclusion

What is revealed in this research is that while the CAF may present itself as diverse and appealing to the multicultural mosaic, the *lived* reality for racialized soldiers can be quite different. The implications are that we must seriously interrogate the theoretical, practical, and political work of the concept of diversity. Moreover, the findings ask us to think through what we might want to accomplish when advocating for new CAF (or other) initiatives and policies on cultural diversity. Hence, this research also challenges us to rethink the impact and effectiveness of diversity, particularly on those who are "diverse." More importantly, identifying how diversity discourse is manifested and lived in the CAF offers constructive ways to rethink how conceptually and practically this concept is being deployed, and perhaps offers insights into contemporary multicultural Canada more broadly.

While some of the soldiers in this study were critical of the military, viewing diversity initiatives as merely superficial and arguing for the need to address racism more concretely, some also hoped to secure for themselves a sense of national belonging. More importantly, the narratives of these soldiers reveal the deep-rooted nature of whiteness in the CAF in culture and geography. The soldiers negotiate this space in a number of ways but mostly by accepting racism as a term and condition, and only occasionally naming it. It is striking how much they have to come to terms with it in order to live and work in this space.

While the Canadian military has made efforts to promote racial progress through its appeals to diversity, its complex recruitment history of racialized soldiers and subsequent integration of racial minorities reveal that the opposite often is the outcome. The continued inability to name racism officially and unofficially reveals the real limitations of this integration and the work of diversity. Given these limitations, what then is the role of diversity work in the modern era? If whiteness is integral to the Canadian military and its fundamental form and nature is not addressed, "diversity" can never mean anything beyond being a tool of governance and racial management, thereby assisting – or obliging – racial others to learn to function within it.

chapter nine

Canadian Muslim Youth and Military Service

MELISSA FINN AND BESSMA MOMANI

Despite contemporary tensions between racialized communities and both police and military institutions, ethnic minorities can also derive benefits from their participation in military service, including legitimacy, integration, membership, and formal citizenship status.[1] As the introductory chapter in this volume also notes, the corollary holds where Western militaries derive benefits of legitimacy when recruiting members of ethnocultural communities.[2] Diversity in the armed forces is an asset for Western countries, because contemporary militaries are expected to have an array of cultural competencies, and, as noted in the introduction, militaries that serve in foreign countries can utilize diversity to improve their overseas operations and relationship with locals. Ethnocultural diversity also provides Western militaries, like the Canadian Armed Forces, an opportunity to challenge the propaganda of their enemies, to meet the social expectations for inclusion by new Canadians, changes in social norms, and/or to fulfil the objectives of public policy.[3] As the introduction of this volume also noted, a diverse and inclusive CAF allows it to be more effective in international missions and multicultural settings. Beyond these considerations, as Leuprecht's and Chouniard's chapters in this volume also showed, several Western militaries, including Canada's, are facing shrinkage in their traditional recruitment pools as the result of declining populations. By reaching out to ethnocultural communities and newcomer Canadians, Western militaries can fill these gaps while becoming more reflective of the demographic characteristics of the societies they are supposed to defend.[4]

The Canadian Armed Forces (CAF) has included diversity as one of their priorities and has intensified their recruitment efforts towards minorities, with targeted goals. Given the importance of military service in fostering a sense of belonging of minorities, as evidenced in the academic literature on the U.S. military,[5] greater national inclusion can be achieved by having a more diverse Canadian military that includes its Muslim youth. Using qualitative evidence, this chapter shows how Canadian Muslim youth (eighteen to thirty-four years of age) vary in their perceptions of the value or benefit of service in the armed forces, and that although many of them do not view service necessarily as a duty, they do believe that Canada and its society and values should be defended. In a global context marked by rising populism, violent Islamist extremism, and Islamophobia, the sentiments of young Muslims are an important factor in the tone of public debate in Canada. Moreover, as CAF are likely to deploy in some of the troubled regions that have Muslim-majority populations, how the armed forces include Canadian Muslims and how the latter perceive the former is important to the public legitimacy of the institution. Themes of duty, citizenship, trust, militarism, and life choices emerged in conversations with Canadian Muslim youth on joining the Canadian Armed Forces.

Benefits of Diversity in the Armed Forces

As the editors noted in their introductory chapter in this volume, the benefits of diversity in the armed forces extend beyond institutional accountability to the larger society from which militaries are composed and to increasing manoeuvrability in high-stakes conflicts. In their participation in the armed forces, soldiers from ethnocultural minority groups contribute to and shape a military's collective values, normative priorities, decision-making, cultures of loyalty and solidarity, and institutional project management.[6] Having personnel with multiple backgrounds can improve decision-making and increase the effectiveness of humanitarian missions and civil-military cooperation.[7] Further, "if majority members have a positive attitude towards cultural diversity, minority members may feel more strongly accepted, which enhances their well-being in the country and the likelihood that missions and civil-military benefit from their unique contributions."[8]

The benefits of diversity in militaries extend to minorities themselves who pursue involvement for personal and career gains. In the effort to enhance inclusion in Western societies, immigrants have long looked to the diversification of militaries as a way to prove their loyalty to mainstream society through participation in its defence; moreover, in some societies, immigrants have used military service as a way to gain formal citizenship[9] – a principle now applied in the CAF. Through inclusive policies and broadening interest among potential recruits, militaries are diversifying. The recruitment of volunteers for military service has transformed the make-up of many Western militaries across racial, religious, and ethnic lines. American minorities, for example, not only actively sought placements in the military, they agitated when they were denied the opportunities, knowing that the struggle was for legitimacy that would ultimately lead to enfranchisement.[10] The nature of the risks that minority group members take in the line of military duty, moreover, has been shown to have a significant and commensurate impact on the cohesiveness and loyalty of their particular units[11] and the discourses that emerge from these experiences.

As noted by Leuprecht in this volume, the Canadian military struggles to maintain its recruitment numbers among its all-volunteer armed forces, which it manages to maintain at 68,000 personnel and 27,000 reservists with thousands of recruits per year.[12] As a result of these gaps, many services of the CAF are understaffed. Recruitment is complicated by young people's pursuit of postsecondary education, "the cyclical fluctuations in civilian job opportunities, and the occurrence of international and domestic events that can lead to periods of heightened concern."[13] The propensity to serve is related to a number of factors that depend on the time period and the characteristics of the youth population under study. In the past, the intention to enlist was influenced by economic factors, the desire for self-improvement, needing money for education, wanting to give service to country, wanting to escape from circumstances that may involve social and political problems, seeking opportunities to travel, searching for educational opportunities or to gain new perspectives, and wanting to advance one's career (especially among women). The top six goals identified by Eighmey that differentiate military service from civilian employment include: physical challenge, development of self-discipline, development of leadership skills, gaining opportunities for adventure, job security, and gaining money for education.[14] Among the Muslim youth who participated in this study, none who were open to joining the Canadian Armed Forces spoke of these specific issues as factors motivating their interest. We enquired into why that is.

In a longitudinal study on American youth, Segal et al. found that the American all-volunteer force went through several phases that were dependent on the events in the global sphere, the state of the U.S. economy, and the availability of recruiting resources. Access to education benefits for service members, relative youth unemployment, the state of entry-level civilian wages, the size of youth populations, and the perceived purpose of military missions all had an impact upon recruitment in the U.S. Armed Forces. The authors also discovered that only 5 per cent of youth respondents from 1991 to 1997 said that they "definitely will" serve in the armed forces, and that "students who are definite in their feelings about military service as early as the eighth grade are unlikely to change during their high school years. However, those who are less certain, whether they are leaning in favour of or against military service, tend over time to resolve their indecision in a negative direction."[15] They also found that propensity to serve is not constant across social groups, including variations along gender, racial, and educational lines – a point also alluded to in George's chapter in this volume. For some groups, their expectation to serve exceeded their desire to serve, insofar as the military was perceived to offer them opportunities denied in civilian work, thus inclining them to military service despite their reservations. For other groups, their desire exceeded their actual expectation to serve insofar as obstacles or compelling alternatives impede their entrance into military service.[16]

Eighmey argues that some people are motivated by "occupational" factors to join the military and some are motivated by "institutional" factors. Occupational motivation is related to material and professional advancement; it is movement towards material factors and extrinsic concerns such as comparative pay, acquisition of technical training, improved working conditions, and enlistment incentives. For American youth, tight competition in the labour market led many to see military work as a way to enhance their livelihoods and professional experience, so their decision to enlist was based on economic motivators.[17] Institutional motivations, on the other hand, involve the pursuit of intrinsic values and norms that separate military and civilian work. Eighmey clarifies this motivational framework: "Selfless [social] motives such as duty to country, loyalty, and commitment are seen as organized around a concept of readiness to sacrifice oneself on behalf of others."[18] This chapter shows that Canadian Muslim youth who are inclined to serve with the Canadian Armed Forces appear to embrace intrinsic values rather than extrinsic benefits.

Canadian Muslim Youth Views on Military Service

The majority of young Canadian Muslims were either born in Canada or immigrated at a very young age and are therefore an important newcomer community. As a result of their demographic rise and their education levels, they constitute a population of interest for the CAF. According to the 2011 National Household Survey, Muslims accounted for 3.2 per cent of Canada's population, standing at 1,053,945[19] and constituting the fastest growing religious group.[20] This population is, in its majority, foreign-born (68 per cent), urban, and educated. Ninety-five per cent of Muslims lived in Canada's metropolitan areas, with two-thirds of this population residing in Toronto and Montreal's metropolitan areas, and 44 per cent of working-age Muslims (twenty-five to forty-four years old) have a university degree, compared to 26 per cent of the general Canadian population.[21] In its efforts to diversify its composition and to meet its recruitment needs, young Canadian Muslims constitute a valuable resource pool for the CAF, and their belonging to the CAF can contribute to their integration within Canada. The population of young Canadian Muslims is, in its majority, urbanized, and shares many of its views with the broader youth population in Canada. Although religion constitutes a common identifier, the cultural background of Canadian Muslims is very diverse, ranging from Southeast Asian, Arab, to African. Their views and experiences on the military are, therefore, informed by their own particular familial histories, their individual interests, and their political awareness.

The analysis of the perceptions of Muslim youth in Canada and their sense of belonging is based on two distinct studies. The first is based on two surveys conducted by the Environics Institute for Survey Research, in partnership with several other organizations. The first survey, "Focus Canada: Surveys of Muslims in Canada 2016," assessed how the experiences of Muslims in Canada has changed over the years, and how it varied across segments of the Muslim community in Canada. For this study, the views and experiences of young Muslims in Canada[22] ($N = 225$ out of 600 surveyed) was extracted from the Environics study, and analysed. The survey was undertaken between November 2015 and February 2016, in English, French, Arabic, and Urdu.

The final data of the survey sample were weighted so that the findings are proportionate to the population of Muslims in Canada, based on the 2011 National Household Survey.[23] Given the size of the sample, we can expect results to be accurate, in 95 out of 100 cases, to within ±4 per cent. The margin of sampling error is greater for results for regional and other subgroups of the population, including Muslim youth (eighteen to thirty-four years of age).

The Environics Study conducted a second study on the perceptions of Muslims in Canada by non-Muslim Canadians, between 6 and 15 February 2016. The same weighting adjustments were done for this study, leading to a greater margin of sampling error for subgroups of the population. Findings from these two surveys can be contrasted, to highlight the views of young Muslim and non-Muslim Canadians. To complement these survey findings, focus groups with young Muslims (eighteen to twenty-nine years of age), living in Toronto, were conducted to unpack some of the complexities in the ways that Canadian Muslim youth perceive life in Canada and describe their ideas on military service.

When the respondents were asked to rate their appreciation ("Satisfied," "Dissatisfied," "Don't know or refused") with the ways things were going in Canada, the vast majority of Canadian Muslims showed their satisfaction (89 per cent) with the general direction of the country. This appreciation was much higher than the one found among the same age group among the non-Muslim Canadian population (63 per cent). At the other end of the scale, 7 per cent of young Canadian Muslims showed dissatisfaction with the general direction of the country, compared to 29 per cent of young non-Muslim Canadians. Respondents were also asked to rate their pride in Canada. The choices of response were "Very proud," "Somewhat proud," "Not very proud," "Depends," "Not Canadian / Do not consider self as Canadian," and "Don't know / No answer." An additional choice "Not at all proud" was included in the Public Opinion about Muslims in Canada survey, targeting non-Muslim Canadian respondents. The vast majority of Canadian Muslims youth (94 per cent) described themselves as either "very proud" (81 per cent) or "somewhat proud" (13 per cent) of Canada. This percentage was similar to the sentiments expressed by young non-Muslims Canadian (72 per cent described themselves as "very proud" and 18 per cent as "somewhat proud") but was lower, compared to older age groups, whether Muslims or non-Muslims.

Muslim respondents were asked to describe their sense of belonging to Canada, with the choice of answers being "Very strong," "Generally strong," "Generally weak" or "Very weak." The survey also measured the changes in this sense of belonging to Canada, over the last five years. Non-Muslim Canadian respondents were not asked this question. Of young Canadian Muslims, 92 per cent expressed a strong attachment to Canada, with 41 per cent describing their sense of belonging as "very strong" and 51 per cent as "generally strong." Although this percentage is very high, older Muslims are more likely to report a greater sense of belonging to Canada (97 per cent among thirty-five to forty-four; 95 per cent among forty-five to fifty-nine, and 98 per cent among those over sixty). Yet 55 per cent of young Canadian Muslims described their sense of attachment to Canada as stronger over the past five years. The 2016 Survey of Muslims in Canada shows that young Muslims express great pride in their Canadian identity and are satisfied, for the most part, with the conduct of affairs in Canada. Indeed, many young Muslims were either born in Canada or immigrated at a young age; they have thus grown with the promise of diversity and inclusion and expect to benefit from the same freedoms and accommodations as their fellow non-Muslim Canadians.[24] How this strong sense of belonging and pride in Canada is when translated into feelings about military service was the point of our focus groups comprising 100 Muslim youth in Toronto.

Out of 106 focus group participants, 72 participants (70 per cent) responded on private cue cards to the question, "Would you consider joining the Canadian Armed Forces? Why or why not?" Of those participants, thirty out of seventy-two (42 per cent) said that they would join the armed forces, eleven respondents (15 per cent) were either undecided or willing only if military action is not conducted in Muslim or homeland countries, and thirty-one respondents (43 per cent) said that they would not take up military service.[25] In the analysis that follows, we focus on Canadian Muslim youth's perceptions of military service in relation to differing notions of duty, trust of the military/Canadian government, impact of militarism on homelands, citizenship, and their own life choices.

Most denominations of Islam were represented during the focus group session, including Sunnism, and within Sunnism, the Ahmadi sect, and Shi'ism, and within Shi'ism, the Ismaili sect. The focus group facilitators were able to report back on denominational backgrounds of participants because of the nature of the answers provided during the discussions. Youth participants were drawn from a wide range of ethnic ancestries, including South Asian, Arab, African, and Persian backgrounds, reflective of the Canadian Muslim demographics.

Among those Canadian Muslim youth who wrote in the affirmative to the cue card question, several who supported military service frequently tied it back to a sense of duty, but this sense of duty was varied in its expression. For example, for some, military service was presented as a self-evident duty, whereas others felt that people had to be primed by context or raised on the importance of military work before that duty would be inculcated. Participants discussed military service as way to "protect the country" or, in expressing their love for Canada, expressed the view that being in service of "this great country" was a matter of honour, that "joining the forces ... would be a great opportunity to serve my country," or that, as an Ahmadi Muslim, he or she was required to "support [his or her] country and protect it." A common theme here was the idea that if the country required help, many said that they would rise to meet the expectations of this call. Another participant wrote that he or she would never decline service [if asked] because service to country means protecting "loved ones."

Another view expressed was the idea that military service is repayment for the protection the Canadian government provided during immigration: "Yes, for sure. I support my country Canada, and would fight for it and defending it no matter what my religion is. They gave me the chance to have a new life and safe haven." Another respondent made a similar remark: "Yes, I would because Canada has given me a lot of opportunities." One respondent appreciated the freedoms he or she enjoyed in Canada and perceived the history of Canadian military missions as focused on humanitarianism, and because of these two factors, expressed the view that military service would not violate his or her ethical standards: "I definitely do [agree], because this country has given me rights I could only dream of in my home country. I am free to practise my religion, express my thoughts, and vote, so if anything threatens this amazing place, then I wouldn't mind standing up for it. Given the history of the Canadian Forces, the missions they engage in are humanitarian. So, becoming a part of it would not go against my personal ethics." Other focus group participants described protection of nation and sacrifice of self for other people as a matter and requirement of faith as Muslims. One participant said that the Prophet Muhammad had taught that "love of country is part of faith" and another said that, "as a Muslim, I believe that love for your country is part of your faith." Tying devotion to country and nationalist sentiment to self-sacrifice for other people, another person answered the cue card question by writing that "we should always sacrifice ourselves to help others."

The participants also expressed the idea that they had something unique to offer and were therefore obliged to support the Canadian military based on a sense of duty. One participant said that he or she would join in an engineering role, and in an interesting turn of phrase, said that he or she owed it to Canada (to join because of some unnamed debt) in order to "help us [all Canadians]." Also expressed was the idea that Muslims have a role to play working with the armed forces because they are uniquely suited to broker the chasm between state actors: Western military forces / Western foreign policy decision-makers, and non-state actors, such as Muslim actors who use political violence as a form of activism: "I would join the armed forces. I love Canada, the values of Canada, etc. Do I agree with all of the missions they do? Not always, but it would be an honour serving the armed forces. I believe as a Muslim I could be the peacemaker between the Canadian Forces and the extremists who call themselves Muslim. If only I was more fit and didn't have poor eyesight." One way in which military service is framed is in terms of citizenship, with Canadian Muslim youth uttering affirmations similar to those among the African American community that service would help validate their presence in Canada. For example, one participant said, "Yes, it will be a good opportunity [to be in the military in order] to spread knowledge and good reputation [that] Muslim[s] can also join the Army." Others expressed their commitment to their Canadian identity and formal citizenship (and membership) in a commitment to the defence of Canada: "Yes definitely [I would join]. As a Canadian, who strongly identifies as a Canadian, I would be willing to defend *my* country." In some cases, duty to faith was linked to a duty of citizenship that might be fulfilled partly through military work, identified in statements such as "Loyalty to my country is part of my faith," "Canada is my country," and "It's a great country."

On the other end of the duty spectrum, one participant felt that feeling at home in Canada was central to feeling a duty to serve in the military, and since he or she did not yet feel at home in Canada, he or she did not feel a concomitant obligation to serve. In one case, military work was regarded as "a waste of time and useless," thus the participant indicated that he or she would never join the armed forces in Canada or in his or her "own" home country either. Several other youth participants seemed to imply that dual citizenship meant that they had obligations to countries other than Canada that impeded their ability to engage in military service ("No [I would not join], I have dual citizenship").

Trust is a hinge-point that either favours Canadian Muslim youth's reception to military service or not. This trust factor is captured poignantly in the statement of one participant who wrote, "If this country believes in me, then I would definitely believe in it, and contribute in the armed forces." Here, the individual expresses the view that societal faith in ethnic, religious, and racial minority youth inspires a reciprocal sense of faith in country and a concomitant obligation to stand up to protect it. One individual showed great trust in the military, saying that he or she had already "submitted an application for the Canadian Armed Forces" in order to "enhance my technical skills." Another view expressed was that having a presence in the military might ensure that Muslims can give input on the direction and nature of military interventions abroad to mitigate either their overreach or their problematic impact upon local populations: "I would love joining the Canadian Armed Forces if it means gaining more control over the chaos happening in states with Muslim majority. This [participation] can lessen the biasness [sic] and racial crimes that are infested when such a country is attacked."

Commitment to join the armed forces and having trust in military institutions was also expressed as contingent upon the nature of the military missions themselves. Framing military service in a recreational rather than serious manner, one young person wrote that being part of the military "should be fun," but qualified his or her enthusiasm saying, "As long as I / the army forces would be fighting for something worthwhile," and a different participant clarified that he or she would join the military, "only if I was allowed to know (a) what we are fighting for and (b) the right to choose not to fight."

Other Muslim youth have described what they feel would be worthwhile endeavours to justify their involvement in the armed forces, and many of their views relate to their respective levels of trust in the institution. One individual said that his or her participation in the Canadian military would be contingent on protecting the country only, fighting oppressive regimes, and "not harming innocent people." Another participant suggested that he or she might consider military service but "would consult a local [religious] scholar about joining the forces."

Many other Muslim youth were more reflexive in outlining why impaired trust prevents them from joining the Canadian Armed Forces. One youth said that he or she was on the fence about this question of joining the military because, on the one hand, he or she is "passionate about the military and the defence industry," while on the other hand, he or she does "not want to get involved in any killing/destruction, whether Canadian Forces or not." Other reasons for hesitancy came from concerns "about being locked in a tour," not wanting to be part of something controversial and not wanting to "support or trust any affiliation with the U.S. Armed Forces, for obvious reasons," not trusting that the decisions that the Canadian government "will make will be correct" and not wanting "to be involved in killing innocent civilians," and finally not knowing the activities and purpose of the military ("what they're fighting for").

A different youth explained that her or his lack of trust in military institutions is derived from the experience of having watched his Syrian kin suffer under both armed resistance groups and Bashar al-Assad's army. His or her lack of trust in the Canadian military stems from a lack of trust in militaries and militarism in general. He or she writes, "No, I don't trust armed forces in general. I am against weapons. Coming from Syria, I simply hate all the deaths armed forces from both sides (rebels/Bashar) have caused. I don't know what the Canadian Forces go through, but regardless I would not want to be a contributor to any violence."

Canadian Muslim youth's interest in participating in the Canadian military often hinged upon the politics and impact of militarism on homeland(s) and perceived kin populations. One participant clarified that his or her interest in the military was contingent on not being pulled into activities of the U.S. War on Terrorism: "I would not mind joining the Canadian Armed Forces. I consider Canada as my home, just as much as I consider Syria my home. I would be happy to serve my home. However, I am against it in one case only. If the Canadian troops are deployed in the Middle East to fight along with the U.S. troops [in] what they call 'terrorism,' then I am against it. I will not be forced to fight my people." This opinion is strongly correlated with the findings of the Focus Canada Survey of Muslims, where young Muslims singled out Canada's foreign policy as what they liked the least about their new country after the climate/cold weather and taxes.[26]

Despite recognizing Canada as their home, many Muslim youth also expressed disagreement with the activities of the Canadian Armed Forces in "Muslim countries" who were, are, or might be involved in "killing innocent civilians" or "fellow Muslims." One person poignantly described how the trauma of not getting support from the Canadian government when caught in a war in the Middle East had an impact upon his or her interest in being involved in the Canadian military:

It is hard to say if I would join the Canadian Armed Forces. I am a proud Arab Canadian, but to join the armed forces is debatable. I had a traumatizing experience growing up [as a] Canadian while fleeing war in 2006. Under the Conservative Government, the armed forces provided more service to the Christians first, rather than Muslim individuals fleeing war. Although this does not represent Canada, now, it can happen. It is also hard to say as an Arab if I would have to go fight against other Arab countries, then I cannot go against my people.

The Canadian government's approach to Palestinian rights had a direct impact upon Muslim youth's interest in military service. One participant appeared open to the idea of joining the military, especially if Canada had to go to war or be defended, but indicated that the Canadian government's lack of intervention in the plight of Palestinians blunts his or her interest: "The Palestinian struggle and cause are important to me and I feel that the government does not portray any [Palestinian] voices in the matter." Another participant summed up his or her reservations differently:

> I am a pacifist, and so I don't agree with armed forces and war. I am particularly wary of the Canadian and American Armed Forces. I barely know anything about the Canadian Armed Forces, and so I don't feel that confident about expressing my thoughts. I would like to know more about the ideologies they follow, who they fund, where they are deployed, etc. As a Palestinian Arab, I do not feel comfortable [being] part of armed forces that fund the destruction of my homeland. I do not feel comfortable being part of armed forces that bomb Iraq so that they can restore "peace" and perpetuate their own ideology.

Another participant felt that military interventions in the Arab world were counterproductive and that this undermined her or his interest in military service: "I don't think I would join because we have witnessed first-hand how the military of the West interfered in many of the Arab countries and created the refugee crisis. I feel it [military missions] did not solve anything. If anything, it has made things worse and more complex to solve." While Canada does not have a national draft system, the nature of the military is becoming more postmodern, and the societal perceptions towards it are changing.[27]

Like many young Canadians, Muslim youth often perceive military service as enabling or impeding their futures on an existential level. Thus, military service was seen as a critical expression of their own personal politics and self-perceptions. Participants would affirm their respect for military service, while simultaneously affirming their lack of interest in personally serving. For example, one participant said, "I don't have a military bone in my body, but I respect [those] who serve my country." And another wrote, "Nope [to joining], I am not fit for battlefield (LOL). If I have a fit son ... I would send him! I want to finish university, get married, and work for the better of this *ummah* [Muslim community]." Another common thread to statements was the view that military work was life-endangering and thus frightening ("No, I have never been interested in such a scary career") or that they might die being involved in the armed forces ("No [I would not join the CAF], because I am not ready to die"). For others, they had simply not considered such a line of work ("I have honestly never ever thought of this as an option just because it was never a thought to have crossed my mind").

Many participants held the view that serving in the armed forces required bravery or commitment (to specific action) that they do not perceive to have: "[Military service] is too much work," "Sure [I would join], but I doubt that they would want me," or "I'm not capable of this job." Youth also equated military service with militarism and viewed the work of the Canadian Armed Forces as requiring killing, which violated their personal ethics, advanced "materialistic wars/struggles," and/or involved the pursuit of counterproductive actions that do not solve problems. Some said that such work fails to provide an appealing alternative to formal education or the current careers they are pursuing. This latter view was captured thus: "No [I would not join], because I'm [a] pacifist person and I'd be more productive in academia, which is my skillset," or "No [I would not join] simply because that is not the career path I want." Some felt unsuited for a military career because of their perceived inability to follow chains of command: "I would love to but I don't think I qualify. I would always consider what I am fighting for, or the vision of the military."

One youth expressed the view that participation might require him or her to give up something from his or her Muslim identity, and a female respondent indicated that her interest in participating would be contingent on her ability to continue observing her religion: "Yes, I would consider joining the Canadian Armed Forces. It would be a great way serve Canada and Canadians in general. One thing that might hold me back, however, would be whether I would be allowed to wear hijab or not. If I could serve in the Canadian Armed Forces without losing my identity as a Muslim then I would take that opportunity."

One Muslim youth made contingent her or his involvement in military service on the basis of Islamic principles and the assurance that any activity would be designed to protect peace:

One underlying principle of Islam is that no person should assist in acts of cruelty. This command should always be at the forefront of any

Muslim mind. If a Muslim country was attacked because it itself acted in a cruel and unjust way and took its first steps to aggression, then in such circumstances the Quran has instructed Muslim governments that they should stop the hand of the oppressor, this means they should stop the cruelty and endeavour to establish peace. Thus, in such circumstances, to take action as means to end cruelty is permissible. However, when a nation that transgresses reforms itself ... its people should not be taken advantage of, or be subjected, on the basis of false pretences or excuses, instead [they should] be granted normal state freedom and independence once again. The military ambition should thus be to establish peace, rather than to fulfil any vested interests ... [many] non-Muslim countr[ies] are permitted, on the basis of defending peace ... to [go to] war. However, if vested interests are to disrupt peace then one should not join the army, if [someone is] already a part [the army], then he/she must choose to opt out.

Here, this participant problematizes his or her own potential involvement in relation to the purpose of military work and militarism in general. While militaries are ostensibly designed to protect and prevent oppression, this individual recognizes that he or she can lose touch with this purpose and transgress personal values. They often fail to establish peace and instead cement political, economic, and corporate interests.

Conclusion

Although a significant proportion of Canadian Muslim youth are open to the possibility of joining the Canadian Armed Forces, there are enormous roadblocks for this population, mainly because of their critical perspectives on Canada's foreign policy and alliances, especially in relation with Muslim-majority countries. Even though a direct causal link cannot be established, 5 per cent of young Muslims identified Canada's foreign policy as what they liked the least among fifteen choices of possible answers.[28] The statistical significance of this relation is stronger, depending on the gender and the level of education.[29] It is not lost on Muslim youth that militaries can be forces of destruction for their kin. Military recruitment is a formal litmus test for a government's ability to persuade and defend its populations.[30] Impediments to military recruitment among Muslim youth should signal to governments that they have yet to convince this demographic that "nationalisms, domestic histories and mythologies of warfare" are persuasive frameworks for their potential self-sacrifice, and that the work of the armed forces can "mediate anxiety, threat and otherness"; especially given that Muslims are on the receiving end most of the "anxiety, threat, and otherness" mitigating activities of the Western militaries and directly targeted by them.[31] The Canadian Armed Forces have broadened their recruitment efforts towards minority groups, and as Chouinard's chapter in this volume showed, have accommodated other religious practices in its chaplaincy system.[32] Yet, in a demographic context where religious experience becomes increasingly "individualized," the CAF must consider adapting to the possibility of accommodating reasonable objections by its personnel towards its political and military policies. Rather than being a departure, this would make concrete the CAF's commitment to promote policies that support diversity and inclusion.

Beyond their views of the military, young Muslims constitute a demographic of interest for the CAF, which is in need of strengthening the diversity of its personnel, but also in need of recruiting highly skilled individuals. The most recent Defence Policy Review has highlighted the necessity for CAF to expand its capabilities in space and cyber warfare, and to "promote an institution-wide culture that embraces diversity and inclusion."[33] By reaching out to Muslim youth, the CAF would fulfil its diversity commitment towards visible minorities, but also recruit highly skilled individuals to meet the challenge that technological advancements in warfare present. Recent studies have shown that in response to demands of the labour sector, young Canadian Muslims, irrespective of gender, tend to prefer community college and the acquisition of technical skills in IT and engineering.[34]

The complexities of the issues related to young Canadian Muslims and military service are captured in the themes we discovered while talking with Canadian Muslim youth. They link military service to duty, citizenship, trust, militarism, and the expansion or contraction of their life choices, and are therefore motivated more by intrinsic rather than extrinsic (occupational) concerns and values.[35] Although Muslim youth contest the value and purpose of military service, and certainly do not share strong desires to participate, most are very strongly attached to Canada and agree that Canada, Canadian values, and Canadian society are worth defending. They are optimistic that they have a role to play in brokering the divide between Western governments and Muslim militant groups, and that they are suited to mitigating military overreach through their presence and interventions.

chapter ten

Introspection on Diversity in the Canadian Armed Forces

ALAN OKROS

As clearly illustrated in the chapters in this volume, there are a range of ways in which the concept of diversity can be understood and, from there, ways in which organizations can seek to address diversity within. Several authors emphasize that, in the Canadian context, there are strong social, legal, and instrumental rationales for federal agencies to adopt broad understandings and proactive approaches in both policy and practice. As is presented in the editors' introduction and by Leuprecht, there are many reasons why this is even more critical for the Canadian Armed Forces (CAF). Professionally, and as reflected in this book's title, the military doctrine on the profession of arms articulates the social imperatives of ensuring that the military's demographics reflect the population it serves to protect, and that the values in practice are broadly endorsed by society at large.[1] Legally, the CAF, along with the rest of the federal government, is required to comply with relevant legislation, including the 1996 Employment Equity Act (EE) requirements for appropriate proportions throughout the organization of members of designated groups, specifically, women, Indigenous peoples, visible minorities, and persons with disabilities. Practically, however, as enumerated by Leuprecht, the CAF has struggled to fill its ranks with suitable numbers of any type of enrollees, let alone increasing the proportions of EE-designated group members.[2] Against these imperatives, with the 2016 publication of the Canadian Armed Forces Diversity Strategy,[3] the CAF has signalled an important shift in how the institution seeks to address diversity within. This chapter will draw on key ideas presented in the preceding chapters, along with additional perspectives on evolving understandings of diversity to provide comments on the new CAF Diversity Strategy as promulgated by the Chief of the Defence Staff (CDS).

The CAF Diversity Strategy replaces the previous Employment Equity Strategy documents which had been updated on the basis of internal research and policy reviews; feedback from governmental and parliamentary agencies; and negotiations with the Office of the Chief Human Resources Officer.[4] Consistent with the former title, the focus from 1996 to 2015 had been on achieving appropriate proportions of three of the four EE-designated groups.[5] The net result was an emphasis on representation: collating personnel records and conducting a regular census of CAF members to determine the percentage of each of the four groups in the ranks. In the new Diversity Strategy, the CAF recognizes that this approach reflected a "compliance-based model" with the statement that the military would now adopt a "values-based" one.[6] Further, the CDS Foreword to the Strategy states that it incorporates the legal objectives of employment equity but "adopts a broader, more holistic approach ... designed to be an enduring feature of not only the composition of the CAF but how we operate," with direct references to both social and operational imperatives.[7] The social aspects cited are the similar ones of reflecting the society it serves and ensuring the citizenry accepts the CAF as a legitimate institution while, aligned with the chapters by Mangat et al., Leuprecht, Lackenbauer, and Davis, the operational elements emphasize the benefits of a diverse workforce with individuals bringing unique perspectives, work experiences, lifestyles, and cultures. It is in the latter context of establishing "as a matter of practice, policy and institutional culture [the intent to] embrace and actively promote diversity as a core CAF institutional value" that the new strategy is seen as a marked departure from the previous ones.[8]

The History of Diversity in the CAF

Prior to augmenting the ideas presented in the previous chapters with additional views on the types of perspectives that the CAF may wish to recognize and embrace, it is worthwhile to look back prior to the EE Act, as there is a lengthy history of public policy that informs the social imperatives to reflect society and earn public trust and support. To start, two legal proceedings must be noted. As presented by Davis, the first was the 1989 Canadian Human Rights Tribunal ruling on gender integration related specifically to the then-policy of excluding women from combat roles.[9] As highlighted by Lopour and Deshpande, the second was the 1992 out-of-court settlement of the Michelle Douglas case, which led the CAF to abandon discrimination based on sexual orientation and, in doing so, to develop inclusive policies for variously gendered and sexually oriented identities.[10] The reality, however, is that the CAF has been under long-standing requirements to comply with diversity-focused legislation, including the 1988 Multiculturalism Act; 1982 (and 1985) Charter of Rights and Freedoms; 1978 Canadian Human Rights Act; and, as detailed by Davis, the 1970 *Report of the Royal Commission on the Status of Women*, which contained specific recommendations for changes in military policies on the employment of women. On linguistic recognition, the relevant legislation is the 1969 Official Languages Act; however, importantly, and to extend on Chouinard and Leuprecht, the Official Language Act arose from the 1963 *Royal Commission on Bilingualism and Biculturalism* (emphasis on Bicultural). There are elements related to both bilingualism and biculturalism enshrined in the 1867 British North America Act as well. Finally, if fully understood, the Crown's obligations to Canada's Indigenous Peoples extend a further two centuries and more to the Royal Proclamation of 1763.[11]

On the basis of these considerations, the new CAF Diversity Strategy can be seen in some ways as overcoming the myopia of the EE Act's focus on four designated groups with a return to considering the lengthy history of Canadians' expectations that government institutions should be inclusive and reflect the society they serve. To extend on Chouinard's chapter, it is informative to note the period identified in Pariseau and Bernier's work "French Canadians and Bilingualism in the Canadian Armed Forces," as volume 1 covers 1793–1969.[12] There are several reasons why they selected 1793 as the beginning of their study; however, given this starting point, a mere 220 years later the Commissioner of Official Languages continues to "encourage" the CAF to take steps to achieve a minimal standard for bilingualism within. On the basis of a 2011 report, the 2013 follow-up audit by this office concluded that of twenty-four recommendations for initiatives to improve CAF bilingualism, only five had been successfully implemented, with the majority annotated as partially implemented, and two deemed not to have been addressed.[13] Similarly, while the 2015 report by Mme Deschamps[14] is seen as the catalyst for the current CDS directive "Operation Honour," which is intended to address harmful and inappropriate sexual behaviour, it was in 1980 that DND employee Bonnie Robichaud filed her complaint of sexual harassment involving military members – a case that ultimately ended up before the Supreme Court, which not only confirmed that the employer was responsible for addressing cases of sexual harassment but also pointed out that "only an employer can remedy undesirable effects and only an employer can provide the most important remedy – a healthy work environment."[15] Thus, while most would agree that the CAF has made progress in addressing diversity internally, few would suggest that the military has solved the puzzle on how to do so in a substantive and sustainable manner, let alone in a timely fashion. The following two sections highlight possible explanations for the challenges encountered.

From History to Social Construction

As indicated, woven through the chapters in this volume is confirmation that the CAF approach is moving in the right direction, with the need for diversity to be seen primarily as an aspect of incorporating and valuing differences in perspectives rather than in enumerated physical characteristics. As noted by the editors in the introductory chapter to this volume and this author elsewhere, the call is for the CAF to shift from "demographic" diversity to "identity" diversity.[16] This requires understandings of, and appreciation for, different world views, values, and belief systems – facets of individual and group identity that are difficult to comprehend by those who do not share them and do not fit neatly on a spreadsheet. A challenge is that identity, ethnicities, world views, values, and belief systems are all socially constructed – that is, they are created through the use of context-specific human interactions, languages, and symbols that we use to derive meanings from our experiences and to create labels or assumed characteristics to describe ourselves and others.[17] These meanings, labels, and characteristics become accepted as "fact," hence "reality," and often become so deeply embedded in our way of seeing the world that we spend little time, if any, actually thinking about them. Processes of social construction can result in broadly shared ideas and assumptions about what is correct, true, or inevitable, and, particularly when related to human conduct, often to what is seen as good, right, or proper.[18]

Many of the chapters speak to the issues that arise when the constructed social reality or status quo becomes disrupted. As Davis and Leuprecht identify, the introduction of women into the military, especially in combat roles, meant that they – directly or indirectly – confronted the construction of "soldiers" as having always been, hence always must remain, male and masculine. Romagnoli discusses similar disruptions now occurring as the dominant group within the military has had to recognize those whose belief system(s) are not based on Judeo-Christian principles. Lackenbauer's chapter touches on the implications of the CAF dealing with individual and community world views reflecting Indigenous perspectives, while Lopour and Deshpande address issues when individuals' gendered identities or sexual orientation did not fit notions of "normal" or proper. At a deeper level, the chapters by Finn and Momani and by George highlight the point that the CAF has yet to recognize that ethno-cultural blindness prevents the military from understanding the ways in which members of specific communities experience military service or why some who are interested in serving the nation choose not to do so in the current socio-political context. A logical extension of these considerations is to assess other areas where "mainstream" society, organizations, or, particularly, the military may have constructed broadly shared understandings that may not hold true, remain valid, or even distort the ways that the dominant group interprets the views or actions of marginalized groups.

Thus, in recognizing that increased diversity within the military has caused – or will cause when understood – disruptions to the constructed status quo, it is suggested that there are several reasons it would be of value for the military to attend to the processes and products of social construction. The first is that the previous approach to diversity and, in particular, the focus on members of four defined subgroups actually served to allow the majority group to project identities onto "others." One result is that the categories that the CAF constructed were assumed to be useful for the CAF when, in fact, they are almost meaningless for those ascribed the label. Identifying someone as an Indigenous person highlights one specific way in which that person *might* differ from the majority, yet, amongst First Nations, Metis, and the Inuit peoples, this label is virtually meaningless.[19] The broad grouping of "everybody with a skin colour different from ours" is even more problematic, as is the conflation of a range of sexual identities and gendered expressions under LBGT+, along with the dichotomous "man" or "woman" category. Thus, to expand on several of the chapters and, in particular, that by George, a key question arising from the new CAF Diversity Strategy is how diversity will be constructed and how the experiences of those in underrepresented groups will be understood. Of note, diversity is now defined for the CAF as "respect for and appreciation of differences in ethnicity, language, gender, age, national origin, disabilities, sexual orientation, education, and religion."[20]

As an illustration of the challenges presented when social construction is effectively understood, there are several issues with the reporting of the CAF EE census with results broken down by "male" and "female." As currently conducted, the assumptions are that, first, these are the only two gender options possible, and second, that the organization can provide these data without consulting the individual.[21] In separate research undertaken for Defence Research and Development Canada examining the current youth cohort,[22] one noted aspect is the reference in the general media to this group as the "gender-fluid" generation.[23] A 2015 poll of one thousand U.S. millennials by Benson Strategy Group revealed that half of respondents viewed gender as a spectrum rather than a dichotomous male vs female categorization, with the spectrum response endorsed more by respondents who identified as female than male (57 vs 44 per cent).[24] As highlighted in several chapters, how gender is constructed and performed in the military is deemed to be of importance, and this recent research suggests this will become even greater.

Another reason to attend to social construction is that the military engages in this process in a very intentional manner. In order to transform the "civilian" into the soldier, sailor, or aviator, the CAF constructs the "ideal" member through multiple reinforcing activities. As a key mechanism for internal social regulation, the espoused shared identity, values, and beliefs are articulated in *Duty with Honour*. To operationalize this doctrine, the military seeks, in both theory and practice, to apply transformational leadership approaches to inculcate and reinforce the espoused ideal;[25] evoke professional closure to regulate its own affairs, including the creation of the espoused identity, maintenance of a unique culture, including the use of powerful social customs, traditions, and symbols;[26] and, most importantly, independently regulate the entire entry-level processes of attraction, selection, formative training, and rites of passage that are designed to ensure cultural self-perpetuation by seeking to find the "right" applicants and then moulding them into the espoused and practiced "ideal."[27] As reflected in Goffman's description of a "total institution," the military uses social pressures to practise a deliberate form of assimilation.[28] As summarized for the U.S. military, RAND authors Lim, Cho, and Curry state, "Assimilation implies unity and conformity; inclusion implies preserving identity and maintaining individual differences. While assimilation is important for unit cohesion, inclusion is an essential value for a diverse workforce."[29]

Together, the application of EE-designated group classifications and military socialization have had two important consequences. The first has been the artificial creation of differentiations within the military between "us" and "like us but different in some way," with a range of policies from uniforms for women through Aboriginal Entry Programs to religious accommodation intended to help minimize the differences identified by the dominant group.

Although generally unwritten and unspoken, the underlying philosophy, however, is to help acclimatize the "other" to become as close as possible to "us." As argued by Davis in this volume and this author elsewhere,[30] when combined with internal myths such as adoption of "gender-neutral" policies, the results have been to create systematized assimilation rather than effective integration, and, importantly, the enactment of professional practices that close off any space for informed discussions of real and valid differences.[31]

An illustration is the CAF Operation Honour, which seeks to address sexual misconduct with a focus on structural changes to minimize incidents and increase reporting.[32] It is worth noting that the August 2016 comprehensive summary of steps taken under Operation Honour is virtually silent on why individuals who have been subject to sexual misconduct and/or gendered discrimination choose not to report such an incident.[33] Nor does the summary suggest the need to create spaces for those subject to sexual misconduct to communally discuss, debate, or examine the power dynamics that produced these hostilities, potential coping strategies, or changes to organization policies or professional culture. An understanding of the ways in which "victims" of sexual misconduct are being categorically constructed would illustrate the types of research needed to advance the CAF Diversity Strategy objectives.

The second consequence of past practices is that the visible product of military socialization and "accommodations" is that everyone in uniform can be seen to "perform soldier/sailor/aviator," specifically, to learn to produce the appropriate behaviours to demonstrate they fit the prototype ideal military members; however, the military has assumed that these behaviours reflect an internalization of the core values that the military seeks to inculcate.[34] Again, the conclusion from the youth cohort research is that by the time they enter the military, many will have learned to become effective "mirrors" and "chameleons," reflecting back to authorities what the seniors expect to see and blending into the military culture through normative conformity, but some are likely to knowingly not internalize the identity, values, or world view that the military seeks to imprint on them.

From Social Construction to Social Privilege

Social construction not only results in the artificial creation of categories, stereotypes, and reproductions of particular understandings of identities, ethnicities, world views, values, and belief systems but, in doing so, contributes to social structures that bestow – and deny – rights and privileges. As illustrated in the presentation by Davis of the problems associated with the CAF assuming it had adopted gender-neutral policies, and especially George's critique of the failure to recognize institutionalized whiteness, there are multiple aspects of military culture that award social privilege and power to some and deny status, recognition, power, or acceptance to others.

The military intentionally creates significant social power, hence social privilege, within the profession. The status associated with rank, officers' commissions, and formal appointment in the role of Commanding Officers are obvious illustrations. As with many other social institutions, these three convey meanings that the profession sees as enabling valid, functional purposes. The military relies on obedience to authority as a critical component of professional practice, particularly in control of lethal force; hence, the "chain of command" constructed through rank, commissions, and command appointments is required to fulfil the military's obligations to the state.[35] A challenge is that the symbolism of confirming obedience to authority by one member saluting to acknowledge the other's commission and, as relevant, higher rank, is an eighteenth-century adaptation of the medieval "tugging of the forelock," in which peasants acknowledged the other's higher social status and signalled their subservience to their "better."

The construction of a clear social hierarchy is also manifest in many other facets of the military. Beyond rank, the entire suite of accoutrements worn on the uniform, including colour, medals, insignia, badges, and often different types of clothing, convey important symbolic messages that produce and reproduce this hierarchy. Those who can decode the symbols quickly understand the social stratification created and their place in the pecking order. The construction of place and the social norms associated with military messes and, in particular, the notion that military members will socialize primarily with "their own kind," as by those reserved for officers vs senior non-commissioned vs junior non-commissioned ranks are obvious extensions of the British and French class structures from which these were derived. The best illustration is with messing onboard naval vessels with the additional differentiation that Captains of the ship have their own individual mess contained within their cabin, thus replicating the structure of monarchy, nobility, tradespeople, and serfs.

To extend on the critiques presented by Davis and by George, the key issue of social privilege is reflected in the phrase that those who are left-handed know they live in a right-handed world; those who are right-handed don't. Fundamentally, the extent of social privilege is most often much more obvious to those who do not enjoy such status than to those who do. By extension, the concept that those who have power learn to use it, while those who don't, learn how those who do have power are going to use it. Individuals who see themselves as lacking social power face strong pressures to conform to dominant group norms. This perspective helps explain the continued practices of gender assimilation, the failures of the military to understand the limitations placed by the dominant group on accommodating "others," and the inability of many to name whiteness or acknowledge racialization within. Of importance, and as argued elsewhere,[36] while the CAF has developed policies to accommodate differences due to factors such as religious practices, spiritual belief systems, or family circumstances, the processes used to access such accommodations results in institutionalized outing: individuals must publicly declare the basis on which they are entitled to these accommodations and hence must identify for others the ways in which they differ from the dominant group. As with all social privilege, those who are part of the majority group automatically receive special considerations, such as Christians having time off from work for important annual observances, and hence neither must declare their identity nor acknowledge that they are receiving specific benefits.

As highlighted by Davis in this volume and presented elsewhere,[37] the starting point for the military to appreciate the creation and consequences of social privilege within is to critically analyse the construction of the "warrior" and the practices of militarized masculinities. When combined with the reality that the military "primacy of operations" becomes translated to the "primacy of operators,"[38] it is reasonable to speculate that core issues underlying inappropriate and harmful sexualized behaviours are unlikely to be fully addressed until the military understands and confronts the social privilege and power awarded to some but denied to others. As an extension, the application of institutional analysis presented by McLean clearly illustrates the pattern of the military over many years in changing the regulative domain to comply with external pressures but without amending the normative or cognitive domains, hence appearing to update policies yet not reforming key aspects of the operant culture.[39] Scott's institutional analysis framework provides an informative lens through which to examine CAF progress in implementing the new Diversity Strategy.[40]

From Social Privilege to a Diverse CAF

As an integration of the perspectives offered across all chapters in this volume, the clear conclusion is that in order to achieve the objectives of the CAF Diversity Strategy, the military must devote as much effort to understand the constructed and privileged "us" as to understand key variations across the Canadian population. To extend on the comment about primacy of operators, Pinch stated that the core issue becomes one of confronting the unconscious assumptions of the "operational imperatives model," for which he states, "The image of the entire institution is based on the requirements of the core combat segment, from whence flows an all-encompassing ideology of homogeneous norms, manifested in political and social conservatism (Huntington, 1957), a collective orientation and unlimited liability on the part of military members. In systems terms, the *ideal military* under this conception is a closed, ascriptive institution that sharply diverges in its norms and values from other institutions in its host society."[41]

Three observations are offered in considering this "closed, ascriptive institution." First, as also explored elsewhere,[42] it would be worth considering the differences between tight and loose cultures.[43] The former are characterized by homogeneity with clear boundaries; a strong single identity for all members; explicit social norms and standards of appropriate behaviour; clearly differentiated and stratified role requirements and role obligations; concern for clarity in language, rules, and social regulation with limits on the articulation of contrary viewpoints or acts of disobedience; and reliance on history, customs, and traditions to reinforce key themes and to ensure cultural continuity and stability. The latter is very much the opposite of pluralism/heterogeneity; acceptance that individuals may have multiple or polymorphic identities; flexible social norms and standards; few status distinctions or role-specific obligations; acceptance of social ambiguity and the likelihood of miscommunication and misunderstanding with the obligation of each to actively work to understand the other's perspective; and an expectation that societies and social norms will evolve, hence, an orientation towards the future as something to be created rather than a past to be preserved.

While seniors or traditionalists will likely see the characteristics of a loose culture as the recipe for confusion and disorder that would erode success in operations, this approach would not only accommodate individuals who do not share the same characteristics of the current culture, but would also enable military members to apply the different perspectives that the CAF now says are valued in operations. The result of a shift from tight to loose(r) culture is that the prototype "ideal" soldier can evolve to encompass a number of perspectives of "effective members," and the understandings of what is expected, right, or proper can become more nuanced with greater appreciation of context-specific or culturally relevant norms, behaviours, and assessments.

As part of reassessing the prototype ideal, the second recommendation is to expand on ideas presented above, and by George in this volume, to assess who has social privilege. This necessarily involves challenging the assumptions that the CAF is gender-neutral or that it fully accommodates cultural differences. In doing so, it is suggested that the military recognize that those who have been inculcated in the military culture and who enjoy social privilege not likely the ideal individuals to conduct such an assessment. It would also be helpful to recall that part of social construction involves myth-making, in which militaries engage rather effectively, but with the corollary reminder that those who have been constructing the myth will likely have difficulty recognizing when this does not reflect reality.

The third recommendation is to capitalize on a Canadian-led NATO research group, which from 2017 to 2020 will be working to develop a "Culture and Gender Inclusive Model of Military Professionalism."[44] This project has the potential to provide valuable updates to the conceptualization of the military as a profession as well as comparisons across nations in how they address diversity within.

From a Diverse CAF to an Inclusive Military

As presented in the CAF Diversity Strategy, the military is moving from a minimally compliant approach to meet the legal obligations of the Employment Equity Act, to a values-based model that harnesses the power of diversity within. As Leuprecht highlighted, the net result is that CAF will need to shift from seeing diversity as a problem to be managed to a strength to be developed. The implications, however, are more extensive. The intent is to ensure that the differing values, world views, and cultural perspectives of those from many backgrounds can actually inform how the CAF conducts operations, so the military must engage in deep internal analyses and create an inclusive culture.

There are important conceptual and practical differences between a diverse workplace and an inclusive one. In providing recommendations for the U.S. Department of Defense, and noting that a key component of diversity discourse in the United States is race, the Lim et al. RAND report cites Thomas: "*Diversity* refers to the differences, similarities, and related tensions that exist in any mixture. Note especially that the term includes differences and similarities. Diversity is not limited to issues of race and gender, nor is it confined to the workforce."[45] Conversely, Mor Barak and

Cherin define *inclusion* as "the extent to which individuals can access information and resources, are involved in work groups, and have the ability to influence decision-making processes."[46] Thus, inclusion involves individual participation and empowerment, with the obverse of not creating exclusion from networks of information and career opportunities. In her review of the differences between diversity and inclusion, Robertson states, "Rather than emphasizing difference as an organizational commodity that has exchange value in terms of economic performance, inclusion is focused on the degree to which individuals feel a part of critical organizational processes."[47]

The central conclusion offered is that the focus must shift from the organization's interest in fostering and promoting different perspectives amongst the workforce, to understanding how different individuals perceive their own status, sense of worth, and value within the work team. As Thomas indicated above, a key for the military is that inclusion cannot be seen solely as a workplace issue, for it extends across all facets of each individual's experiences in and around that member's military service. Several chapters in this volume provide insights into this issue, with the most direct commentary being in George's presentation of Shannon's observation: *"So while you can sit here by yourself and have no friends or you can get in there and throw a rock down the ice and have a beer and just try to like it because that's what the dominant crowd is doing."*

It will be important for the CAF to attend to the ways in which some who perceive they are being marginalized choose to disrupt the status quo. An example is offered from the author's recent observations at Canadian Forces College. Every year, the Majors and Colonels attending their year-long course are encouraged to join the college rugby team with the rationale that this promotes fitness, team building, and esprit de corps. One year, a group who were not interested in rugby formed a yoga group, which very pointedly practised yoga on the lawn next to where the rugby team practised their drills. While a small minority on the rugby team were women (two) and a small minority doing yoga were men (one), the juxtaposition of two forms of fitness, team building, and esprit de corps was clear: what would be seen by many as a very masculine way of performing these acts versus what many would see as a feminine way of doing the same. The challenge was that neither the members of the rugby team nor the college as a whole were able to see the direct test of the status quo.

It is in this context of ethno-cultural blindness that significant work will be needed to conduct the research, analyses, and policy development required to create an inclusive military. Achieving that level of cultural awareness to understand the ways in which marginalized individuals experience military service and, from there, to detect the small acts of rebellion to challenge the dominant culture would be a valuable first step. The chapters in this volume provide several perspectives that can inform this work. A key will be to recognize and address intersectionality. To return to the opening comments by Mangat, while different chapters speak to issues related to women, francophones, racialized soldiers, or Muslim youth, they do not provide an understanding of the experiences or perspectives of the francophone woman of colour of the Islamic faith. It is only when the CAF examines the multiple factors that explain individual identity and places them in the context of military policies, doctrine, socialization, and culture that the appropriate measures can be taken to create the type of inclusive military that can harness the strengths of the diversity of Canadian society.

Notes

1. Unpacking Diversity and Inclusion

1 Department of National Defence, "Canadian Armed Forces Diversity Strategy" (Ottawa: Department of National Defence, 2016), 1.
2 Wiebren S. Jansen, Sabine Otten, and Karen I. van der Zee, "Being Part of Diversity: The Effects of an All-Inclusive Multicultural Diversity Approach on Majority Members' Perceived Inclusion and Support for Organizational Diversity Efforts," *Group Processes & Intergroup Relations* 18, no. 6 (November 2015): 817–32, https://doi.org/10.1177/1368430214566892.
3 Alan Okros, "Rethinking Diversity and Security," *Commonwealth & Comparative Politics* 47, no. 4 (November 2009): 348, https://doi.org/10.1080/14662040903362990.
4 Felicity Ogilvie, "Identical Twins the Same, but Different," ABC News, 12 October 2011, http://www.abc.net.au/news/2011-10-12/study-finds-identical-twins-not-the-same/3554332.
5 J.P. Clark, "Organizational Change and Adaptation in the US Army," *Parameters* 46, no. 3 (2016): 25.
6 Karen D. Davis, "Sex, Gender and Cultural Intelligence in the Canadian Forces," *Commonwealth & Comparative Politics* 47, no. 4 (November 2009): 431, https://doi.org/10.1080/14662040903375091.
7 Mike Vernon, *Desert Lions: Canadian Forces Mentors in Kandahar*, documentary (Canadian Army, 2011), https://www.youtube.com/watch?v=p5LUhmfSxMw.
8 Vernon, *Desert Lions*.
9 Jan van der Meulen and Joseph Soeters, "Introduction," in *Cultural Diversity in the Armed Forces: An International Comparison*, ed. Joseph

Soeters and Jan van der Meulen, Cass Military Studies, 4–7 (London, UK: Routledge, 2007).

10 Statistics Canada, "The Daily – Study: A Look at Immigration, Ethnocultural Diversity and Languages in Canada up to 2036, 2011 to 2036," 25 January 2017, http://www.statcan.gc.ca/daily-quoti-dien/170125/dq170125b-eng.htm.

11 Remi M. Hajjar, "A New Angle on the U.S. Military's Emphasis on Developing Cross-Cultural Competence: Connecting In-Ranks' Cultural Diversity to Cross-Cultural Competence," *Armed Forces & Society* 36, no. 2 (January 2010): 248, https://doi.org/10.1177/0095327X09339898.

12 Hajjar, "New Angle."

13 Hajjar, "New Angle."

14 Zoe Todd, "Canadian Troops Deploy to Latvia for NATO Defence Mission," CBC News, 10 June 2017, http://www.cbc.ca/news/canada/edmonton/edmonton-soldiers-deploy-latvia-nato-military-russia-1.4154973.

15 Lynn M. Shore, Amy E. Randel, Beth G. Chung, Michelle A. Dean, Karen Holcombe Ehrhart, and Gangaram Singh, "Inclusion and Diversity in Work Groups: A Review and Model for Future Research," *Journal of Management* 37, no. 4 (July 2011): 1262–89, https://doi.org/10.1177/0149206310385943.

16 Michàl E. Mor Barak, "Beyond Affirmative Action: Toward a Model of Diversity and Organizational Inclusion," *Administration in Social Work* 23, no. 3–4 (September 1999): 52, https://doi.org/10.1300/J147v23n03_04.

17 Mor Barak, "Beyond Affirmative Action."

18 Hajjar, "New Angle on the U.S. Military's Emphasis," 248.

19 Patricia Hill Collins, "Intersectionality's Definitional Dilemmas," *Annual Review of Sociology* 41, no. 1 (14 August 2015): 2, https://doi.org/10.1146/annurev-soc-073014-112142.

20 Michael K. Jeffery, *Inside Canadian Forces Transformation: Institutional Leadership as a Catalyst for Change / Michael K. Jeffery* (Kingston, ON: Canadian Defence Academy, 2009), 17.

21 Florence A. Heffron, *Organization Theory and Public Organizations: The Political Connection* (Englewood Cliffs, NJ: Prentice Hall, 1989), 155.

22 Heffron, *Organization Theory and Public Organizations*, 54.

23 Franklin C. Pinch, "An Introduction to Challenge and Change in the Military: Gender and Diversity Issues," in *Challenge and Change in the Military: Gender and Diversity Issues*, ed. Franklin C. Pinch, Allister T. MacIntyre, Phyllis Browne, and Alan C. Okros (Winnipeg: Canadian Forces Leadership Institute, Canadian Defence Academy, 2004), 3.

24 Pinch, "Introduction to Challenge and Change," 3.
25 Murray Brewster, "New Defence Minister Harjit Singh Sajjan Proved Mettle in Afghanistan," *Globe and Mail*, 5 November 2015, sec. Politics, https://www.theglobeandmail.com/news/politics/new-defence-minister-harjit-singh-sajjan-proved-mettle-in-afghanistan/article27114750/.
26 Meagan Campbell, "Meet the World's First Female Combat General," *Maclean's*, 3 June 2016, http://www.macleans.ca/news/canada/jennie-carignan-will-be-the-first-female-general-from-the-combat-arms-trades.
27 David Pugliese, "New Judge Advocate General Named: DND Says First Female JAG Appointed," *Ottawa Citizen*, 20 June 2017, http://ottawacitizen.com/news/national/defence-watch/new-judge-advocate-general-named-dnd-says-first-female-jag-appointed.
28 Edgar H. Schein, "The Learning Leader as Culture Manager," in *Classic Readings in Organizational Behavior*, ed. J. Steven Ott, Sandra J. Parkes, and Richard B. Simpson, 3rd ed., 87–96 (Belmont, CA: Thomson/Wadsworth, 2003).
29 Warren G. Bennis, "Why Leaders Can't Lead," *Training and Development Journal* 43, no. 4 (1989): 35–9.
30 Joerg Wombacher and Joerg Felfe, "United We Are Strong: An Investigation into Sense of Community among Navy Crews," *Armed Forces & Society* 38, no. 4 (October 2012): 565.
31 Okros, "Rethinking Diversity and Security," 369–70.
32 Maja Apelt, Cristina Besio, Giancarlo Corsi, Victoria von Groddeck, Michael Grothe-Hammer, and Veronika Tacke, "Resurrecting Organization without Renouncing Society: A Response to Ahrne, Brunsson and Seidl," *European Management Journal* 35, no. 1 (February 2017): 10, https://doi.org/10.1016/j.emj.2017.01.002.
33 Karen D. Davis, "Sex, Gender and Cultural Intelligence in the Canadian Forces," *Commonwealth & Comparative Politics* 47, no. 4 (November 2009): 430–55, https://doi.org/10.1080/14662040903375091.
34 Department of National Defence, "Canadian Armed Forces Diversity Strategy" (Ottawa: Department of National Defence, 2016), 1.

2. Demographic Imperatives for Diversity and Inclusion

1 This chapter draws in part on Christian Leuprecht, "Diversity as Strategy: Democracy's Ultimate Litmus Test," in special issue, "Accommodating Diversity in the Security Sector," ed. Christian Leuprecht, *Commonwealth and Comparative Politics* 47, no. 4 (2009):

559–79; Leuprecht, "Socially Representative Armed Forces: A Demographic Imperative," in *Europe without Soldiers? Recruitment and Retention among Europe's Armed Forces,* ed. T. Szvircsev Tresch and C. Leuprecht, 35–54 (Montreal and Kingston: McGill-Queen's University Press, 2010); Leuprecht, "Political Demography of Canada-US Co-dependence in Defence and Security," *Canadian Foreign Policy Journal* 20, no. 3 (2014): 291–304; Leuprecht, "Political Demography of the New Security Environment," in *The Encyclopaedia of Public Administration and Public Policy,* 3rd ed., ed. Melvin Dubnick and Domonic Bearfield, 2983–92 (New York: Taylor and Francis, (2015); and Leuprecht, "The Demographics of Inclusion: Recruitment, Attrition, and Retention of Citizen Soldiers," in *Canadian Defence: Theory & Policy,* ed. S. Vucetic, P. Lagassé, and T. Juneau (Basingstoke: Palgrave Macmillan, 2019).

2 Anne Irwin, "Diversity in the Canadian Forces: Lessons from Afghanistan," in special issue, "Accommodating Diversity in the Security Sector," in special issue, "Accommodating Diversity in the Security Sector," ed. Christian Leuprecht, *Commonwealth and Comparative Politics* 47, no. 4 (2009): 494–505.

3 Jelle van den Berg and Rudy Richardson, "Ethnic Cultural Minorities and Their Interest in a Job in the Royal Dutch Army," in special issue, "Accommodating Diversity in the Security Sector," ed. Christian Leuprecht, *Commonwealth and Comparative Politics* 47, no. 4 (2009): 456–75.

4 Philippe Manigart, "Risks and Recruitment in Postmodern Armed Forces: The Case of Belgium," *Armed Forces and Society* 31, no. 4 (2005): 559–82.

5 Tibor Szvircsev Tresch, "Challenges in the Recruitment of Professional Soldiers in Europe," *Strategic Impact* 3, no. 28 (2008): 76–86.

6 David Mason and Christopher Dandeker, "Evolving UK Policy on Diversity in the Armed Services: Multiculturalism and Its Discontents," in special issue, "Accommodating Diversity in the Security Sector," ed. Christian Leuprecht, *Commonwealth and Comparative Politics* 47, no. 4 (2009): 393–410.

7 Giuseppe Caforio and Marina Nuciari, "Military Profession in the View of European Officers," in *The Present and Future of Military Profession: Views of European Officers,* ed. J. Kuhlmann, 131–81 (Strausberg: Sozialwissenschaftliches Institut der Bundeswehr, 1996); Stefan Sarvas and Jin Hodny, "The Motivation to Become an Officer," in *The European Cadet: Professional Socialisation in Military Academies: A Crossnational Study,* ed. G. Caforio, 17–29 (Baden-Baden: Nomos, 1998); see also Frédéric Merand, *European Defence Policy: Beyond the Nation State* (Oxford: Oxford University Press, 2008).

8 Thomas Bulmahn, "Berufswunsch Soldat: Interessen und Motive," in *Handbuch Militär und Sozialwissenschaften*, ed. S. Gareis and P. Klein, 451–63 (Wiesbaden: VS Verlag für Sozialwissenschaften, 2004).

9 Christoph Jackwerth, "Ökonomische Aspekte eines Vergleiches unterschiedlicher Wehrsysteme," *Österreichische Militärische Zeitschrift, OEMZ* 36, no. 4 (1998): 378. See also Morris Janowitz and Charles C. Moskos, "Five Years of the All-Volunteer Force, 1973–1978," *Armed Forces & Society* 5, no. 2 (1979): 171–218.

10 Harley L. Browning, Sally C. Lopreato, and Dudley L. Poston Jr, "Income and Veteran Status: Variations among Mexican Americans, Blacks and Anglos," *American Sociological Review* 38, no. 1 (1973): 74–85.

11 Paul A. Gade, Hyder Lakhani, and Melvin Kimmel, "Military Service: A Good Place to Start?" *Military Psychology* 3, no. 4 (1991): 251–67.

12 Karen Davis, "Sex, Gender and Cultural Intelligence in the Canadian Armed Forces," *Commonwealth and Comparative Politics* 47, no. 4 (2009): 430–55; David Mason and Christopher Dandeker, "Evolving UK in Accommodating Diversity in the Security Sector," ed. Christian Leuprecht, special issue, "Policy on Diversity in the Armed Services: Multiculturalism and its Discontents," *Commonwealth and Comparative Politics* 47, no. 4 (2009): 393–410. Also see Davis in this volume.

13 Victoria Marie Basham, "Harnessing Social Diversity in the British Armed Forces: The Limitations of 'Management' Approaches," in "Accommodating Diversity in the Security Sector," ed. Christian Leuprecht, special issue, *Commonwealth and Comparative Politics* 47, no. 4 (2009): 411–29.

14 Charles Moskos, John Allen Williams, and David R. Segal, eds, *The Post-Modern Military: Armed Forces after the Cold War* (Oxford: Oxford University Press, 1999), chapter 1.

15 Morris Janowitz, *The Professional Soldier: A Social and Political Portrait* (Glencoe, IL: Free Press, 1960).

16 Charles Moskos, "From Institution to Occupation: Trends in Military Organization," *Armed Forces and Society* 4, no. 1 (1977): 41–50.

17 David Bell, *The Coming of the Post-Industrial Society: A Venture in Social Forecasting* (New York: Basic Books, 1973).

18 Christian Leuprecht, "Demographics and Ethno-Cultural Diversity in Canadian Military Participation," in *Challenge and Change in the Military: Gender and Diversity Issues*, ed. Franklin C. Pinch, Allister T. MacIntyre, Phyllis Browne, and Alan C. Okros (Kingston: Canadian Forces Leadership Institute, 2005), 122–45. See Romagnoli (this volume) on the challenges of adding diversity to the CAF chaplaincy.

19 Michael S. Teitelbaum, "Political Demography: Powerful Forces between Disciplinary Stools," *International Area Studies Review* 17, no. 2 (2014): 99–119; Jay Winter and Michael S. Teitelbaum, *The Global Spread of Fertility Decline: Population, Fear and Uncertainty* (New Haven, CT: Yale University Press, 2013); Jennifer Dabbs Sciubba, *The Future of War: Population and National Security* (Santa Barbara, CA: Praeger International Security/ABC-CLIO, 2011).

20 Massimo Livi-Bacci, *A Concise History of World Population*, 4th ed. (Oxford: Blackwell, 2007); Michael Anderson, *British Population History: From the Black Death to the Present Day* (Cambridge: Cambridge University Press, 1996).

21 Thomas L. Friedman "Don't Just Do Something. Sit There." *New York Times*, 26 February 2014, http://www.nytimes.com/2014/02/26/opinion/friedman-dont-just-do-something-sit-there.html?_r=0; David E. Bloom, David Canning, and Günther Fink, "Implications of Population Aging for Economic Growth," Harvard Program and the Global Demography of Aging working paper no. 64 (2011), https://www.nber.org/papers/w16705/.

22 Statistics Canada, *Immigration and Diversity: Population Projections for Canada and Its Regions*, 2006 to 2031, tables 7, https://www150.statcan.gc.ca/n1/pub/91-551-x/2010001/tbl/tbl007-eng.htm, 9 https://www150.statcan.gc.ca/n1/pub/91-551-x/2010001/tbl/tbl009-eng.htm, and 11 https://www150.statcan.gc.ca/n1/pub/91-551-x/2010001/tbl/tbl011-eng.htm. Publication 91-551-X (Ottawa, 2017).

23 Canadian Bilingualism outside of Quebec, 2006 Census + CAF 2002 Characteristics of Military Personnel.

24 Office of the Auditor General, *Report 5: Canadian Armed Forces Recruiting and Retention: National Defence* (2016), http://www.oag-bvg.gc.ca/internet/English/parl_oag_201611_05_e_41834.html#p108.

25 Irina Goldenberg, Brenda Sharpe, and Keith Neuman, *The Interest and Propensity of Designated Groups to Join the Canadian Forces*. Ottawa: Defence Research and Development Canada, report 2007-04 (2007), http://docplayer.net/49634456-The-interest-and-propensity-of-designated-groups-to-join-the-canadian-forces.html.

26 CAF Employment Equity Schedules 3–15, 2016.

27 Julie Coulthard and Leesa Tanner, *A Gap Analysis of Employment Equity and Diversity Research in the Canadian Armed Forces* (Ottawa: Defence Research and Development Canada, DGMPRA Technical Memorandum 2009-009 [2009]), http://cradpdf.drdc.gc.ca/PDFS/unc87/p531814.pdf.

28 Goldenberg, Sharpe, and Neuman, *Interest and Propensity of Designated Groups to Join the Canadian Forces*.

29 Morris Janowicz, *The Professional Soldier: A Social and Political Portrait* (Glencoe, IL: Free Press, 1960).

30 European Defence Agency, *An Initial Long-term Vision for European Defence Capability and Capacity Needs* (Brussels: European Defence Agency, 2006).

31 Walter A. Oechsler, *Personal und Arbeit: Grundlagen des Human Resource Management und der Arbeitgeber-Arbeinehmer-Beziehungen* (Munich: R. Oldenburg, 2000), 238.

32 Oechsler, *Personal und Arbeit*, 239.

3. Negotiating Gender Inclusion

1 Suzanne Simpson, Doris Toole, and Cindy Player, "Women in the Canadian Forces: Past, Present and Future," *Atlantis* 4, no. 3 (1979): 271; Sheila Hellstrom, "Women in the Canadian Forces: A Work in Progress," in *The Canadian Strategic Forecast 1996: The Military in Modern Democratic Society*, ed. Jim Hanson and Susan McNish (Toronto: Canadian Institute of Strategic Studies, 1996), 92.

2 In accordance with the National Defence Act, "The Canadian Forces are the armed forces of Her Majesty raised by Canada and consist of one Service called the Canadian Armed Forces." Although referred to as the Canadian Forces for several decades following unification in 1968, in recent years it has been referred to as the Canadian Armed Forces. As such, identified throughout this chapter as CF or CAF as relevant to the time period under discussion.

3 Representing 2.4 per cent of officers and non-commissioned members serving in the Regular component combat engineering, infantry, armour, and artillery occupations; see Canada, *Canadian Armed Forces Employment Equity Report, 2016/2017* (2017).

4 See Karen D. Davis, "Sex, Gender and Cultural Intelligence in the Canadian Forces," *Commonwealth & Comparative Politics* 47, no. 4 (2009): 430–55.

5 Helena Carreiras, *Gender and the Military: Women in the Armed Forces of Western Democracies* (London: Routledge, 2006), 87.

6 Carreiras, *Gender and the Military*.

7 See, for example, discussion of United States Heritage Foundation questions challenging the role of women in combat, in Karen D. Davis and Brian McKee, "Women in the Military: Facing the Warrior Framework," in *Challenge and Change in the Military: Gender and Diversity Issues*, ed. F.C.

Pinch, A.T. MacIntyre, P. Browne, and A.C. Okros, 52–75 (Kingston, ON: Canadian Defence Academy Press, 2004).

8 See, for example, Linda Grant de Pauw, *Battle Cries and Lullabies: Women in War, from Prehistory to the Present* (Norman: University of Oklahoma Press, 1998).

9 Judith Youngman, "The Warrior Ethic," in *Women in Uniform: Perceptions and Pathways*, ed. Kathryn Spurling and Elizabeth Greenhalgh (Canberra: School of History, Australian Defence Force Academy, 2000), 43–4.

10 Contemporary usage of the term *gender* as a socially constructed concept can be traced to the second-wave feminist movement and its rejection of biological determinism that is implicit in the use of terms such as *sex* or *sexual difference* (see, for example, Joan W. Scott, "Gender: A Useful Category of Historical Analysis," *American Historical Review* 91, no. 5 [1986]: 1053–75), and is also currently reflected in Canadian government approaches to gender-based analysis (see Status of Women Canada, "Introduction to GBA+, 2018," http://www.swc-cfc.gc.ca/gba-acs/course-cours-2017/eng/mod01/mod01_02_04.html).

11 See National Defence, *Canadian Armed Forces Employment Equity Report 2015–2017* (2017).

12 See Status of Women Canada, "GBA+ Research Guide," 2017, http://www.swc-cfc.gc.ca/gba-acs/guide-en.html.

13 See Canada, Bill C-16: An Act to Amend the Canadian Human Rights Act and the Criminal Code, First Reading 17 May 2016.

14 Adapted from Global Affairs Canada, "Mainstreaming of a Gender Perspective," https://international.gc.ca/world-monde/funding-financement/mainstream-integration.aspx?lang=eng.

15 Analysis of the Canadian media response to Captain Goddard's death is presented in Karen D. Davis, "Media, War and Gender: Considering Canadian Casualties in Afghanistan," in *Security and the Military between Reality and Perception*, ed. Marjan Malešič and Gerhard Kümmel, 63–78 (Baden-Baden, Germany: Nomos Verlagsgesellschaft, 2011).

16 Addressing the public on behalf of National Defence, Lieutenant Morgan Bailey stated that it cannot be stressed enough "that we view all of our fallen comrades, who pay the ultimate sacrifice in support of their nation, equally and regardless of gender." Scott Simmie, "Deaths Hit Home Regardless of Gender; All Deserve Same Respect, but Few Women in Combat Roles," *Toronto Star*, 18 May 2006.

17 Davis, "Media, War and Gender."

18 *Toronto Star*, "More Than Just a Female Soldier," 18 May 2006.

19 Gallagher cited in C. Blatchford, *Fifteen Days: Stories of Bravery, Friendship, Life and Death from inside the New Canadian Army* (Toronto: Doubleday Canada, 2007), 167–8. Gallagher was Goddard's Battery Commander in Afghanistan.

20 Canada, *Report of the Royal Commission on the Status of Women in Canada* (1970), 136–8.

21 Hellstrom, "Women in the Canadian Forces," 94.

22 Simpson, Toole, and Player, "Women in the Canadian Forces," 272.

23 Canada, Department of National Defence, Directorate of Personnel Information System Job #2146, 1993.

24 Leesa M. Tanner, *Status of Trained Women in the Canadian Forces*, Project Report 581 (Ottawa: National Defence, Operational Research and Analysis Establishment, Directorate of Manpower Analysis, 1992).

25 Canada, Department of National Defence, NDHQ Action Directive D2/79 Employment of Servicewomen in Non-Traditional Areas, 1243-23-2 5320-6 (CDS), 14 February 1979.

26 Rosemary E. Park (Major), *Final Report of the Social/Behavioural Science Evaluation of the SWINTER Sea Trial* (Willowdale, ON: Canadian Forces Personnel Applied Research Unit, 1984).

27 Karen D. Davis, "Negotiating Gender in the Canadian Forces, 1970–1999" (PhD diss., Royal Military College of Canada, 2013).

28 See National Defence, "Combat Related Employment of Women (CREW) Update," draft CANFORGEN, 5324-1 (DG CREW), June 1987, AI 2009-00385, RG 24, Library and Archives Canada.

29 National Defence Headquarters, "Director General Combat Related Employment of Women (DG CREW)," SITREP – CREW TRIALS, 21 February 1989.

30 Canadian Human Rights Commission, Tribunal Decision 3/89, 1989.

31 Canada Department of National Defence Headquarters, Canadian Human Rights Tribunal Decision: Women in Combat. Ottawa, Chief of the Defence Staff, Canadian Forces General Message, CANFORGEN CLS 014, 1 March 1989.

32 Davis, "Negotiating Gender in the Canadian Forces."

33 National Defence Headquarters, Combat Related Employment of Women – Liability to Serve and Occupation Transfer. Canadian Forces General Message, CANFORGEN 034 ADM (PER) 052, 261200Z, July 1989.

34 Davis, "Negotiating Gender in the Canadian Forces."

35 Colonel (Retired) Franklin Pinch, personal interview, 8 July 2010; Colonel Pinch was the Director Conditions of Service (DC Svc) from 1990 to 1992.

36 Rosemary E. Park, *"Corporate" Activity Following the 1989 Canadian Human Rights Tribunal Decision Ordering Full Integration of Servicewomen in the Canadian Forces* (Richmond Hill, ON, 31 March 1996).

37 In 1993, the MAB changed its name to Minister's Advisory Board on Gender Integration to better reflect its mandate to monitor gender integration, rather than act as a status of women "watchdog"; see National Defence, *The MND Advisory Board on Gender Integration in the Canadian Forces,* [Third] *Annual Report 1992–1993,* Ottawa, 1993.

38 Association for Women's Equity in the Canadian Forces, news release, 5 February 1990, cited in the newsletter of the *Association for Women's Equity in the Canadian Forces* 2, no. 2 (April 1990): 3–4.

39 Davis, "Negotiating Gender in the Canadian Forces."

40 National Defence, Minutes of the Mid-Term Review of the Minister's Advisory Board on Gender Integration in the Canadian Forces – 1 February 1995, Ottawa, internal memorandum, 1150-110/A203 (D Pers Pol 5-3), 31 May 1995, 15.

41 Brigadier-General (retired) Sheila Hellstrom, interview, 30 June 2010.

42 Leesa Tanner, *Gender Integration in the Canadian Forces: A Qualitative and Quantitative Analysis,* ORD Report PR9901 (Ottawa: Department of National Defence, Operational Research Division, 1999).

43 Park, *"Corporate" Activity,* cited in Davis, "Sex, Gender and Cultural Intelligence."

44 Davis, "Negotiating Gender in the Canadian Forces," 174.

45 Rosemary E. Park, "Opening the Canadian Forces to Gays and Lesbians," in *Gays and Lesbians in the Military: Issues, Concerns, and Contrasts,* ed. Wilbur J. Scott and Sandra Carson Stanley (New York: Aldine de Bruyter, 1994), 174.

46 Although established in 1986, it was not until 1996 that amendments to the *Employment Equity Act* resulted in the inclusion of the Canadian Forces and the Royal Canadian Mounted Police as federal organizations subject to the act.

47 National Defence, "Minister Creates Advisory Board on Canadian Forces Gender Integration and Employment Equity," DND/CF news release, 16 November 1998.

48 Michele Falardeau-Ramsay, Chief Commissioner Canadian Human Rights Commission, to General Maurice Baril, Chief of the Defence Staff, 8 February 1999.

49 National Defence, Minister's Advisory Board on Canadian Forces Gender Integration and Employment Equity, *2000 Annual Report* (Ottawa, 2000).

50 Canada, *Cultural Diversity and Gender Integration: CDS Guidance to Commanding Officers* (Ottawa: National Defence, 1999), 3.
51 Nicola J. Holden and Karen D. Davis. "Harassment in the Military: Cross-National Comparisons," in *Challenge and Change in the Military: Gender and Diversity Issues*, ed. Franklin C. Pinch, Allister T. MacIntyre, Phyllis Browne, and Alan C. Okros, 97–121 (Kingston: Canadian Defence Academy, 2004).
52 Julie Coulthard and François Larochelle. The Canadian Forces (CF) Workplace Harassment Survey: Topline Results. Letter Report, Department of National Defence, Director General Military Personnel Research and Analysis, 2013.
53 Noémi Mercier and Alec Castonguay, "Crimes sexuels: le cancer qui ronge l'armée canadienne," *L'Actualité*, 24 April 2014; and Noémi Mercier and Alec Castonguay, "Our Military's Disgrace," *Maclean's*, 5 May 2014.
54 Marie Deschamps, *Report of the External Review Authority on Sexual Harassment and Sexual Misconduct in the Canadian Armed Forces*, 27 March 2015.
55 Deschamps, *Report*, 14.
56 Canadian Armed Forces, CDS OP Order – Operation Honour, August 2015.
57 General Jonathan Vance, "The Chief of the Defence Staff, General Jonathan Vance, Addresses Sexual Misconduct in the Canadian Armed Forces," *Canadian Military Journal* 16, no. 4 (2016): 6–15.
58 Adam Cotter, *Sexual Misconduct in the Canadian Armed Forces, 2016*, Statistics Canada, 2016, 5.
59 Cotter, *Sexual Misconduct*, 34.
60 Similar arguments put forward by others include Zillah Eisenstein, *Sexual Decoys: Gender, Race and War in Imperial Democracy* (London: Zed Books, 2007), 20–1; and in Canadian context, see Sandra Whitworth, *Men, Militarism & UN Peacekeeping: A Gendered Analysis* (Boulder, CO: Lynne Rienner Publishers, 2007), 153.
61 For example, in 2010, Major Eleanor Taylor (Infantry, now Lieutenant-Colonel) served as Company Commander (Charles Company, 1 Royal Canadian Regiment Battlegroup), and from 2009 to 2010, Lieutenant-Colonel Jennie Carignan (now Major-General) served as the Commanding Officer, Task Force Kandahar Engineer Regiment.
62 National Defence, Canadian Armed Forces Diversity Strategy, Office of the Chief of the Defence Staff, 2016.
63 Canada, National Defence, *Strong, Secure, Engaged: Canada's Defence Policy* (Ottawa: National Defence, 2017).

64 See, for example, Vance, "Chief of the Defence Staff."
65 Canada, Chief of the Defence Staff, CDS Directive for Integrating UNSCR 1325 and Related Resolutions into CAF Operations and Planning. Ottawa, ON: National Defence Headquarters, 29 January 2016; and Canada, National Defence, *Strong, Secure, Engaged.*

4. Coming Out in Uniform: A Personal Reflection

1 The authors wish to acknowledge the etymological limitations of current labels (i.e., LGBTQ) to define sexual minorities, and the conflation of gender and sexual identity challenges and experiences.
2 Tim Sweijs, "LGBT Military Index," The Hague Centre for Strategic Studies (February 2014), http://www.hcss.nl/news/lgbt_military_index_1.
3 U.S. General Accounting Office (GAO), *Homosexuals in the Military: The Policies and Practices of Other Countries.* Report B-25359 (Washington, DC, 1993), http://www.gao.gov/assets/220/218039.pdf; Nathaniel Frank, "What Does the Empirical Research Say about the Impact of Openly Gay Service on the Military? A Research Memo," Palm Center – Blueprints for Sound Public Policy (2010); Suzanne Goldberg, "Open Service and Our Allies: A Report on the Inclusion of Openly Gay and Lesbian Service Members in U.S. Allies' Armed Forces," *William & Mary Journal of Women and the Law* 17, no. 3 (2011), 547–90, http://scholarship.law.wm.edu/cgi/viewcontent.cgi?article=1317&context=wmjowl; RAND, *Sexual Orientation and U.S. Military Personnel Policy: Options and Assessment* (Santa Monica: RAND Corporation, 1993), http://www.rand.org/content/dam/rand/pubs/monograph_reports/2009/RAND_MR323.pdf.
4 Cass R. Sunstein, "Social Norms and Social Roles," *Columbia Law Review* 96, no. 4 (1996): 903–68.
5 Marie Deschamps, "External Review into Sexual Misconduct and Sexual Harassment in the Canadian Armed Forces," *Canadian Armed Forces: External Review Authority*, 30 April 2015, https://www.canada.ca/en/department-national-defence/corporate/reports-publications/sexual-misbehaviour/external-review-2015.html.
6 Deschamps, "External Review."
7 Deschamps, "External Review."
8 Gary Kinsman, "'Character Weaknesses' and 'Fruit Machines': Towards an Analysis of the Anti-Homosexual Security Campaign in the Canadian Civil Service," *Labour / Le Travail* 35 (1995): 133–16,

https://doi.org/10.2307/25143914; Carmen Poulin, Lynne Gouliquer, and Jennifer Moore, "Discharged for Homosexuality from the Canadian Military: Health Implications for Lesbians," *Feminism & Psychology* 19, no. 4 (2009): 496–516, https://doi.org/10.1177/0959353509342772.

9 Carmen Poulin and Lynne Gouliquer, "Clandestine Existences and Secret Research: Eliminating Official Discrimination in the Canadian Military and Going Public in Academia," *Journal of Lesbian Studies* 16, no. 1 (2012): 54–64, https://doi.org/10.1080/10894160.2011.557643.

10 See, for example, Aaron Belkin and Jason McNichol, "Homosexual Personnel Policy in the Canadian Forces: Did Lifting the Gay Ban Undermine Military Performance?" *International Journal* 56, no. 1 (2000): 73–88; Frank, "What Does the Empirical Research Say?"; GAO, *Homosexuals in the Military*; Goldberg, "Open Service and Our Allies"; RAND, *Sexual Orientation and US Military Personnel Policy*.

11 See Morgan Brigg and Roland Bleiker, "Autoethnographic International Relations: Exploring the Self as a Source of Knowledge," *Review of International Studies* 36, no. 3 (2010): 779–98.

12 See Department of National Defence (DND), "Homosexuality: Sexual Abnormality, Investigation, Medical Investigation and Disposal," Canadian Forces Administrative Order 19-20 (1967), https://fr.scribd.com/document/319471670/CFAO-19-20#download&from_embed; Belkin and McNichol, "Homosexual Personnel Policy in the Canadian Forces."

13 Kinsman, "'Character Weaknesses' and 'Fruit Machines.'"

14 Gouliquer and Moore, "Discharged for Homosexuality in the Canadian Military."

15 Murray Brewster, "Ottawa Faces Class-Action Lawsuit over Fired LGBT Civil Servants," CBC News, 1 November 2016, http://www.cbc.ca/news/politics/lgbtq-class-action-lawsuit-1.3830310; Poulin, Gouliquer, and Moore, "Discharged for Homosexuality"; Michael Tutton, "Lawsuit Alleges Military Aggressively Interrogated Gay Members from 1969 to 1995," *Star*, 8 December 2016, https://www.thestar.com/news/canada/2016/12/08/lawsuit-alleges-military-aggressively-interrogated-gay-members-from-1969-to-1995.html.

16 Poulin, Gouliquer, and Moore, "Discharged for Homosexuality"; Tutton, "Lawsuit Alleges."

17 Poulin, Gouliquer, and Moore, "Discharged for Homosexuality."

18 Brewster, "Ottawa Faces Class-Action Lawsuit"; Poulin, Gouliquer, and Moore, "Discharged for Homosexuality"; Tutton, "Lawsuit Alleges."

19 Poulin, Gouliquer, and Moore, "Discharged for Homosexuality."

20 Poulin and Gouliquer, "Clandestine Existences and Secret Research";
Jim Bronskill, "Canadian Military May Need to Search Archives to Find
Extent of Gay Purge," *Toronto Star*, 4 June 2017.

21 Zoe Chong, "Alumni Profile: Military Woman Turned Activist Michelle
Douglas on Her Life and Time at Carleton," *Charlatan*, 5 January 2016,
http://charlatan.ca/2016/01/alumni-profile-military-woman-turned-
activist-michelle-douglas-on-her-life-and-time-at-carleton/.

22 Aaron Belkin and Jason McNichol, "Homosexual Personnel Policy
in the Canadian Forces: Did Lifting the Gay Ban Undermine Military
Performance?" *International Journal: Canada's Journal of Global
Policy Analysis* 56, no. 1 (2001): 73–88, https://doi.org/10.1177/
002070200105600105.

23 John de Chastelain, "Subject: Homosexual Conduct," Canadian Forces
memo 0104271550 Z (October 1992), http://lgbtpurge.com/wp-content/
uploads/2018/02/CFAO-19-20-English-and-French.pdf.

24 De Chastelain, "Subject: Homosexual Conduct."

25 Belkin and McNichol, "Homosexual Personnel Policy"; Kinsman,
"'Character Weaknesses' and 'Fruit Machines'"; Poulin Gouliquer, and
Moore, "Discharged for Homosexuality."

26 Belkin and McNichol, "Homosexual Personnel Policy."

27 Belkin and McNichol, "Homosexual Personnel Policy."

28 Belkin and McNichol, "Homosexual Personnel Policy."

29 Belkin and McNichol, "Homosexual Personnel Policy."

30 Belkin and McNichol, "Homosexual Personnel Policy."

31 Belkin and McNichol, "Homosexual Personnel Policy."

32 Goldberg, "Open Service and Our Allies."

33 Belkin and McNichol, "Homosexual Personnel Policy."

34 Jonathan H. Vance, "Chief of the Defence Staff LGBTQ2 Message,"
28 November 2017, National Defence and the Canadian Armed Forces,
http://www.forces.gc.ca/en/news/article.page?doc=chief-of-the-
defence-staff-lgbtq2-message/jafhg8an.

35 Justin Trudeau, "Remarks by Prime Minister Justin Trudeau to Apologize
to LGBTQ2 Canadians," 28 November 2017, https://pm.gc.ca/eng/
news/2017/11/28/remarks-prime-minister-justin-trudeau-apologize-
lgbtq2-canadians.

36 RBC, "What Is Diversity & Inclusion?" (2006), http://www.rbc.com/
diversity/what-is-diversity.html.

37 The White House, "Remarks by the President and Vice President at
Signing of the Don't Ask, Don't Tell Repeal Act of 2010," Office of the
Press Secretary, 22 December 2010, https://obamawhitehouse.archives.

gov/the-press-office/2010/12/22/remarks-president-and-vice-president-signing-dont-ask-dont-tell-repeal-a.

38 Lee Berthiaume, "Canadian Armed Forces Aims to Fix Its Recruitment System to Foster Diversity," *Toronto Star,* 25 June 2017, https://www.thestar.com/news/canada/2017/06/25/canadian-forces-aims-to-fix-its-recruitment-system-to-foster-diversity.html.

39 Katie Zezima, "Ted Cruz: The Military Shouldn't Be a 'Cauldron for Social Experiments,'" *Washington Post,* 12 October 2015, https://www.washingtonpost.com/news/post-politics/wp/2015/10/12/ted-cruz-the-military-shouldnt-be-a-cauldron-for-social-experiments/?utm_term=.3e03b42af259.

40 Deloitte, "Inclusion | Deloitte US," 13 June 2017, https://www2.deloitte.com/us/en/pages/about-deloitte/articles/deloitte-inclusion.html.

5. The North's Canadian Rangers

1 Canadian Army, "Canadian Rangers," 2009, http://www.army-armee.forces.gc.ca/en/canadian-rangers/index.page.

2 National Defence and the Canadian Armed Forces, "Backgrounder: Canada's Reserve Forces," 2018, http://www.forces.gc.ca/en/news/article.page?doc=canada-s-reserve-force/hnmx18w6.

3 Department of National Defence, *Strong, Secure, Engaged: Canada's Defence Policy* (Ottawa: DND, 2017), 79, http://dgpaapp.forces.gc.ca/en/canada-defence-policy/docs/canada-defence-policy-report.pdf.

4 Only 25.6 per cent of Rangers in 1 CRPG had completed a cultural self-identification survey by July 2016, with nearly all returns appearing to come from Yukon. Accordingly, the statistics are not representative. By contrast, 81.7 per cent of Rangers in 2 CRPG completed the survey, with 56.9 per cent self-identifying as Aboriginal peoples, 2.5 per cent as visible minorities, and 1.1 per cent as persons with disabilities. Statistics provided by the Office of the Chief of Staff Army Reserve.

5 DND, *Strong, Secure, Engaged,* 6.

6 This chapter adopts a mixed qualitative methodology based on several decades of archival research, field research with the Rangers, and my regular visits and conversations with Rangers as the Honorary Lieutenant Colonel of the 1st Canadian Ranger Patrol Group (1 CRPG) since 2014. This chapter expresses my personal views and assessments and in no way should be misconstrued as the official position of the government of Canada or the Canadian Armed Forces.

7 As of 15 June 2017. See Canadian Army, "1st Canadian Ranger Patrol Group," 2019, http://www.army-armee.forces.gc.ca/en/1-crpg/index.page.

8 For more on this theme, see P. Whitney Lackenbauer, *Vigilans: The 1st Canadian Ranger Patrol Group* (Yellowknife: 1 CRPG, 2015).

9 National Defence and the Canadian Armed Forces, "Backgrounder."

10 The following section is derived from P. Whitney Lackenbauer, *The Canadian Rangers: A Living History* (Vancouver: UBC Press, 2013). See this source for detailed referencing to primary source material.

11 Robert Taylor, "Eyes and Ears of the North," *Star Weekly Magazine,* 22 December 1956, 2–3.

12 Larry Dignum, "Shadow Army of the North," *Beaver* 39, no. 2 (Autumn 1959): 22–4.

13 John Kirton and Don Munton, "Manhattan Voyages," in *Politics of the Northwest Passage*, ed. F. Griffiths (Montreal and Kingston: McGill-Queen's University Press, 1987), 73–5; R.J. Orange, House of Commons, *Debates*, 21 May 1971, 6065.

14 Major S.J. Joudry, "Study Report: Northern Region Canadian Rangers," 27 May 1986, DND file NR 5323-2 (SSO R&C), 8.

15 See Yale Belanger and P. Whitney Lackenbauer, eds, *Blockades or Breakthroughs? Aboriginal Peoples Confront the Canadian State* (Montreal and Kingston: McGill-Queen's University Press, 2014).

16 See P. Whitney Lackenbauer, ed., *Canada's Rangers: Selected Stories, 1942–2012* (Kingston: Canadian Defence Academy, 2013).

17 See, for example, Franklyn Griffiths, Rob Huebert, and P. Whitney Lackenbauer, *Canada and the Changing Arctic: Sovereignty, Security and Stewardship* (Waterloo, ON: Wilfrid Laurier University Press, 2011).

18 Prime Minister's Office, "Prime Minister Announces Expansion of Canadian Forces Facilities and Operations in the Arctic," 10 August 2007, https://www.canada.ca/en/news/archive/2007/08/prime-minister-announces-expansion-canadian-forces-facilities-operations-arctic.html.

19 Lieutenant-General M.J. Dumais, "Commander Canada Command Recommendation for the Expansion of Canadian Ranger Patrols," March 2008, DND, Canada Command, file 3440-2 (J3 Plans 7), referencing "VCDS Report on Plans and Priorities 07/08." On the achievement of this benchmark, see Bryn Weese, "Harper Welcomes 5000th Ranger, Becomes Honorary Member," *Sarnia Observer*, 21 August 2013.

20 Tim Querengesser, "Embedded with the Canadian Rangers," *Up Here* 26, no. 7 (October–November 2010): 24.

21 DND, *Strong, Secure, Engaged*, 80. On the Trudeau government's Indigenous emphasis in its emerging Arctic Policy Framework, see P. Whitney Lackenbauer, "Arctic Defence and Security: Transitioning to the Trudeau Government," in *Whole of Government through an Arctic Lens,* ed. P. Whitney Lackenbauer and Heather Nicol, 308–40 (Antigonish: Mulroney Institute on Government, 2017).

22 Brigadier-General Kelly Woiden testimony, House of Commons Standing Committee on National Defence, 18 February 2015, 3.

23 Commander Canadian Army, Master Implementation Directive (MID) – Canadian Ranger Organization, 25 April 2015, DND file 1901-1 (CRNA).

24 Canadian Army Order (CAO) 11–99: Canadian Rangers, 1 November 2013.

25 On this topic, see Daniel McDonald and Kizzy Parks, *Managing Diversity in the Military: The Value of Inclusion in a Culture of Uniformity* (New York: Routledge, 2012).

26 See, for example, Kristen Everson, "'Significant Number' of Canadian Ranger Deaths flagged by Military Chaplain," CBC News, 20 April 2015, http://www.cbc.ca/news/politics/significant-number-of-canadian-ranger-deaths-flagged-by-military-chaplain-1.3035683.

27 Bob Weber, "Canadian Ranger Dies on Arctic Military Exercise," Canadian Press, 19 February 2013.

28 Ian Stewart, "Alex van Bibber, an Incredible Yukon Trapper, Just May Have Been the Toughest Man in Canada," *National Post*, 28 November 2014.

29 Statistics provided by 1 CRPG, November 2017.

30 Anne Duggan, "The Work of Canadian Ranger Dollie Simon Is Never Done," Canadian Army, 21 March 2016, http://www.army-armee. forces.gc.ca/en/news-publications/national-news-details-no-menu. page?doc=the-work-of-canadian-ranger-dollie-simon-is-never-done/ im0s9xag.

31 See, for example, Lackenbauer, *Canadian Rangers.*

32 See, for example, "Canada's 'Arctic Soldiers' Shouldn't Be Our Only Line of Defence in the North," *Ottawa Citizen*, 11 August 2017.

33 See Canadian Army, "Canadian Rangers," 2019, http://www.army-armee.forces.gc.ca/en/canadian-rangers/index.page; and Defence Administration Order and Directive (DAOD) 2020-2, Canadian Rangers, 21 May 2015, http://www.forces.gc.ca/en/about-policies-standards-defence-admin-orders-directives-2000/2020-2.page.

34 Lieutenant-General A.B. Leslie, "CLS Planning Guidance: Arctic Response," July 2009, draft, DND file 3000-1 (A/DLFD).

35 DND, *Northern Approaches: The Army Arctic Concept 2021* (Kingston: Canadian Army Land Warfare Centre, 2013), 23.
36 Our analysis here focuses on Chief of Force Development (CFD), *Arctic Integrating Concept* (2010); *Chief of the Defence Staff (CDS)/Deputy Minister (DM) Directive for DND/CF in the North* (12 April 2011); *Canadian Forces Northern Employment and Support Plan (CFNESP)* (November 2012); and Canadian Joint Operations Command (CJOC), *CJOC Plan for the North*, 28 January 2014.
37 Chief of Land Staff, "Army Support Plan Immediate Reaction Unit: Northern Contingency Plan," 14 December 2011, DND file 3350-1 (Army G35).
38 See Chief of Force Development, *Arctic Integrating Concept*, 23. Alan Okros notes that the need for comprehensive or whole-of-government approaches to address large-scale disasters has heightened the emphasis on cooperating across a range of first responders. Alan Okros, "Rethinking Diversity and Security," in *Defending Democracy and Security Diversity*, ed. Christian Leuprecht, 4–31 (New York: Routledge, 2011). See also P. Whitney Lackenbauer and Heather Nicol, eds, *Whole of Government through an Arctic Lens* (Kingston: Canadian Defence Academy Press, 2017).
39 See, for example, Paul Kaludjak, "Use the Inuit," *Ottawa Citizen*, 18 July 2007; and Mary Simon, "A New Shared Arctic Leadership Model," March 2017, http://publications.gc.ca/collections/collection_2017/aanc-inac/R74-38-2017-eng.pdf.
40 See, for example, Frances Abele, "Confronting 'Harsh and Inescapable Facts': Indigenous Peoples and the Militarization of the Circumpolar Region," in *Sovereignty and Security in the Arctic*, ed. Edgar Dosman (London: Routledge, 1989), 189; and Mary Simon, "Militarization and the Aboriginal Peoples," in *Arctic Alternatives: Civility or Militarism in the Circumpolar North*, ed. Franklyn Griffiths (Toronto: Samuel Stevens, 1992), 60.
41 P. Whitney Lackenbauer, *If It Ain't Broke, Don't Break It: Expanding and Enhancing the Canadian Rangers*, Working Papers on Arctic Security No. 6 (Toronto: Walter and Duncan Gordon Foundation and ArcticNet Arctic Security Projects, 2013). On inflated threats to Canadian Arctic sovereignty and security, see, for example, Lackenbauer, "Polar Race or Polar Saga? Canada and the Circumpolar World," in *Arctic Security in an Age of Climate Change*, ed. James Kraska, 218–43 (Cambridge: Cambridge University Press, 2011); and Lackenbauer and Adam Lajeunesse, "The Canadian Armed Forces in the Arctic: Building Appropriate

Capabilities," *Journal of Military and Strategic Studies* 16, no. 4 (March 2016): 7–66.

42 DND, *Strong, Secure, Engaged*, 108.

43 Justin Trudeau, Minister of National Defence mandate letter, 12 November 2015, http://pm.gc.ca/eng/minister-national-defence-mandate-letter.

44 National Defence and Canadian Forces Ombudsman, "Ombudsman Message: Progress Update on the Canadian Army's Review of the Canadian Rangers Organization," 20 September 2017, http://www.ombudsman.forces.gc.ca/en/ombudsman-news-events-messages/omb-message-update-on-rangers-review.page; Ombudsman, "Ranger Health Care Entitlements," n.d., http://www.ombudsman.forces.gc.ca/en/ombudsman-questions-complaints-helpful-information/healthcare-for-canadian-rangers.page; P. Whitney Lackenbauer, "Arctic Defence and Security: International and Domestic Dimensions," submission to Defence Policy Review consultation meeting, Yellowknife, 24 May 2016, http://dgpaapp.forces.gc.ca/en/defence-policy-review/docs/yellow-knife/lackenbauer-yellowknife-submission.pdf.

45 McDonald and Parks, *Managing Diversity in the Military*, 14.

46 CJOC Plan for the North, 28 January 2014, DND file 3350-1 (J5), 3.

47 See Christian Leuprecht, "Diversity as Strategy," in *Defending Democracy and Security Diversity*, ed. Leuprecht, 217–37 (New York: Routledge, 2011).

6. Diversifying the Canadian Armed Forces' Chaplaincy

1 When the branch was first established it was called the Chaplain Branch, and subsequently changed to the Royal Canadian Chaplain Service in 2014.

2 Department of National Defence, *Religions in Canada* (Ottawa: Directorate of Human Rights and Diversity, 2008).

3 Joanne Rennick, *Religion in the Ranks: Belief and Religious Experience in the Canadian Forces* (Toronto: University of Toronto Press, 2011), 19.

4 Rennick, *Religion in the Ranks*, 20.

5 While there were Chaplains from African-Canadian and Indigenous communities, they only served alongside non-white or Indigenous battalions and were sent back to Canada if the units were disbanded. See Rennick, *Religion in the Ranks*.

6 Robert Ogle, "The Faculties of Canadian Military Chaplains: A Commentary on the Faculty Sheet of December, 1955, and the Directives for Holy Week Promulgated March 14, 1956," 1956, 7.

7 Rennick, *Religion in the Ranks*, 19.
8 Rennick, *Religion in the Ranks*.
9 Ogle, "Faculties of Canadian Military Chaplains," 22.
10 Rennick, *Religion in the Ranks*, 21. The branch was separated into Catholic and Protestant branches. This division continues to today where the Catholic Chaplains are regulated under the Catholic branch, while the Protestant side is used to represent all other faiths, including the imams and rabbis who have joined in the last few years.
11 National Defence and the Canadian Arms Forces, "The Canadian Forces Chaplaincy," 12 March 2007, http://www.forces.gc.ca/en/news/article.page?doc=the-canadian-forces-Chaplaincy/hnps1tlr.
12 Anne Irwin, "Diversity in the Canadian Forces: Lessons from Afghanistan," *Commonwealth & Comparative Politics* 47, no. 4 (2009): 450; Rennick, *Religion in the Ranks*, 6.
13 Irwin, "Diversity in the Canadian Forces."
14 Rennick, *Religion in the Ranks*, 11.
15 Sikata Bannerjee and Harold Coward, "Hindus in Canada: Negotiating Identity in a 'Different Homeland,'" in *Religion and Ethnicity in Canada*, ed. P. Bramadat and D. Seljak, 30–1 (Toronto: Pearson Longman, 2005); Harold Jantz, "Canadian Mennonites and a Widening World," in *Religion and Public Life in Canada*, ed. M. Van Die, 329–45 (Toronto: University of Toronto Press, 2001); Paul Bramadat and David Seljak, eds, *Religion and Ethnicity in Canada* (Toronto: Pearson Longman, 2005); Paul Bramadat and David Seljak, *Christianity and Ethnicity in Canada* (Toronto: University of Toronto Press, 2008).
16 See Emilie Durkheim, *The Elementary Forms of Religious Life* [1912] 2008; Clifford Geertz, *The Interpretation of Cultures* (New York: Basic Books, 1973); and Talal Asad, *Genealogies of Religion: Discipline and Reasons of power in Christianity and Islam* (Baltimore: Johns Hopkins Univeristy Press, 1993), for a history on the definition of religion.
17 Rennick, *Religion in the Ranks*, 99.
18 Rennick, *Religion in the Ranks*, 99.
19 Rennick, *Religion in the Ranks*, 98.
20 Rennick, *Religion in the Ranks*, 98.
21 While the Chaplain handbook states that Chaplains should remove specific religious terminology (*God, Jesus*, etc.) from their ceremonies, many soldiers believe that it is impossible to remove religious bias completely.
22 Rev. Dr Michael Peterson, *The Reinvention of the Canadian Armed Forces Chaplaincy and the Limits of Religious Pluralism: Theses and Dissertations*

(Comprehensive) (Waterloo, ON: Wilfrid Laurier University Press, 2015), 1–208.

23 Chaplains are prohibited from handling firearms and therefore, while they undergo basic training, they are exempted from this portion.

24 Being recruited "green" refers to being compatible with the physical and psychological requirements of soldiering, while purple – the colour of the Chaplaincy, to pay homage to the purple stoles worn by Catholic priests – requires the recruit to be accepted as a padre.

25 While rare, it is possible for a non-commissioned member to be commissioned without an undergraduate degree upon reaching the rank of sergeant.

26 DND, *Canadian Forces Chaplain Branch Manual* (Ottawa: DND, 2003); Diana Swift, "Canadian Council of Churches: Still Vital at 70?" *Anglican Journal* 140, no. 9 (2014): 2. The ICCMC's focus is to support the Chaplain Branch in the unique context of the Canadian Armed Forces. ICCMC is an affiliation of the Canadian Council of Churches, which represents twenty-five churches, including Orthodox, Protestant, and Roman Catholic.

27 Guy Chapdelaine, "Working towards Greater Diversity: A Blessing or a Curse? The Experience of the Canadian Military Chaplaincy," *Canadian Military Journal* 15, no. 1 (2014): 39.

28 Rennick, *Religion in the Ranks*, 38; 90 Roman Catholic; 127 Protestant; 47 Anglican; 28 United with 2 imams and 2 rabbis.

29 Statistics Canada, "National Household Survey: Religion," 2011, http://www12.statcan.gc.ca/nhs-enm/2011/dp-pd/prof/details/page.cfm?Lang=E&Geo1=PR&Code1=01&Data=Count&SearchText=Canada&SearchType=Begins&SearchPR=01&A1=Religion&B1=All&Custom=&TABID=1.

30 Peterson, *Reinvention of the Canadian Armed Forces Chaplaincy*, 105–22. When the Chaplain corps was first founded, all padres wore a Maltese cross. This insignia was broadened to allow for badges with the image of the crescent moon for Islam and stone tablets of the Torah and the Star of David for Judaism. However, there has been no move to add insignias for Buddhism, Hinduism, Sikhs, Pagans, or Indigenous (all of which are recognized traditions within the CAF). These changes were also accompanied by a 2005 decision to change the branch motto from the traditional Christian "In Hoc Signo Vince" (In this sign you shall conquer), to the less controversial "Vocatio Ad Servitium" (Called to serve). Similarly, the Chaplaincy hymn was changed from "Onward Christian Soldiers" to "Joyful We Adore Thee." However, while the original hymn affirmed a

Christian hierarchy that created a bias for Christian denominations, the change continues to represent only Abrahamic faiths.

31 Pastoral associates are lay members of the Chaplain Branch who perform the duties of Chaplains but without ordination, and therefore their position is somewhat limited. Having pastoral associates in the CAF allows for individuals who cannot (or do not want to be) ordained to serve in the branch. For example, women who cannot be ordained as priests in the Roman Catholic Church can serve as lay pastoral associates.

32 CBC News, "Military Welcomes Its First Muslim Chaplain," 6 January 2004, http://www.cbc.ca/news/canada/military-welcomes-its-first-muslim-Chaplain-1.479726.

33 CBC News, "Military Welcomes Its First Muslim Chaplain."

34 National Defence and the Canadian Armed Forces, "Canadian Forces Welcomes Jewish Chaplain," 13 March 2007, http://www.forces.gc.ca/en/news/article.page?doc=canadian-forces-welcomes-jewish-chaplain/hnps1tt3.

35 Ron E. Hassner, *Religion on the Battlefield* (Ithaca, NY: Cornell University Press, 2016).

36 Kim Philip Hansen, *Military Chaplains & Religious Diversity* (New York: Palgrave Macmillan, 2012), 42.

37 Jennifer H. Wortman, Crystal L. Park, and Donald Edmondson, "Trauma and PTSD Symptoms: Does Spiritual Struggle Mediate the Link?" *Psychological Trauma* 3, no. 4 (2011): 442–52; Justin Orton, "Can Religious Coping, Religious Involvement, Spirituality and Social Support Predict Trauma Symptoms at Six Months after Combat?" (PhD diss., George Fox University, 2011).

38 For an analysis of the positive impact of diversity on organizational capacity, see B.M. Cole and Manjula S. Salimath, "Diversity Identity Management: An Organizational Perspective," *Journal of Business Ethics* 116, no. 1 (2013): 151–61.

39 Rennick, *Religion in the Ranks*, 55.

40 Rennick, *Religion in the Ranks*, 57. Traditions such as Indigenous, Muslim, Hindu, and Wiccan, to name a few, have so many variations and subgroups that it would be impossible for the CAF to provide each group with their own Chaplain.

7. Francophone Inclusion and Bilingualism in the Canadian Armed Forces

1 A. van Dijk and J.L. Soeters, "Language Matters in the Military," in *Armed Forces and Conflict Resolution: Sociological Perspectives*, vol. 7, *Contributions*

to Conflict Management, Peace Economics and Development, ed. G. Caforio, G. Kummel, and B. Purkayastha, 303–25 (Bingley, UK: Emerald Group Publishing, 2008).

2 Luc Gaudet, "Canadian Forces Leadership Effectiveness: Competing Values. Perspectives on Bilingualism" (MA thesis, University of Calgary, 2011), https://prism.ucalgary.ca/bitstream/handle/1880/49326/2011_Gaudet_MA.pdf;jsessionid=408551FEFAF86B6972361D19CE96151B?sequence=1.

3 Captain Hans Jung, "Can the Canadian Forces Reflect Canadian Society?," *Canadian Military Journal* 8, no. 3 (2007): 27.

4 Linda Cardinal and Selma Sonntag, eds, *State Traditions and Language Regimes* (Montreal and Kingston: McGill-Queen's University Press, 2015), 3.

5 The author wishes to emphasize that she does not discredit the participation of the First Nations to the foundation of Canada. The myth of the "two founding nations" is, however, one that is historically representative of the discussions leading to Confederation.

6 Marcel Martel and Martin Pâquet, *Langue et politique au Canada et au Québec: Une synthèse historique* (Montreal: Éditions du Boréal, 2010), 16.

7 At the time of its entry into Confederation in 1870, Manitoba had provisions for legislative and judiciary bilingualism. However, in 1890, the provincial legislature passed an Official Language Act – an unconstitutional document stating that all laws would be adopted in English only, and that English was the sole language of the provincial courts. This act was deemed inoperative by the Supreme Court of Canada in 1979 in the *Forest* decision (*Attorney General of Manitoba v Forest*, [1979] 2 SCR 1032).

8 In the late 1800s and early 1900s, a number of provincial governments (Nova Scotia, New Brunswick, Manitoba, then Ontario) forbade the teaching of French in schools, resulting in a major crisis in all of French Canada. The adoption of Regulation 17 by Ontario's Queen's Park in 1912 particularly marked this era, and it is now understood to be a major reason for French Canadians' refusal to enrol in the CAF during the First World War. Martel and Pâquet, *Langue et politique*, 79.

9 Richard A. Preston, "Bilingualism and Multiculturalism in the Armed Forces," in *Ethnic Armies: Polyethnic Armed Forces from the Time of the Habsburgs to the Age of the Superpowers*, ed. N.F. Dreisziger (Waterloo, ON: Wilfrid Laurier University Press, 1990), 159.

10 Veterans Affairs Canada, "La force francophone: The Military," 2014, http://www.veterans.gc.ca/eng/remembrance/history/second-world-war/la-force-francophone/military.

11 Jean Pariseau and Serge Bernier, *French Canadians and Bilingualism in the Armed Forces* (Ottawa: Department of Supply and Services, 1986), 144.

12 Preston, "Bilingualism and Multiculturalism," 163.

13 Royal Commission on Bilingualism and Biculturalism, *Rapport préliminaire de la Commission royale d'enquête sur le bilinguisme et le multiculturalisme* (Ottawa: Queen's Printer, 1965), 67.

14 Julien Labrosse, "'I didn't have the time to find the English words': The Korean War's Role in the Evolution of Bilingualism in the Canadian Armed Forces" (MA thesis, University of Ottawa, 2016), 52.

15 Martel and Pâquet, *Langue et politique*, 95 (personal translation).

16 Royal Commission, *Rapport préliminaire*, 5 (personal translation).

17 Royal Commission, *Rapport préliminaire*, 14–15.

18 Labrosse, "'I didn't have the time,'" 55.

19 van Dijk and Soeters, "Language Matters," 313.

20 Pariseau and Bernier, *French Canadians and Bilingualism*, 160.

21 Gaudet, "Canadian Forces Leadership Effectiveness," 22.

22 Pariseau and Bernier, *French Canadians and Bilingualism in the Armed Forces*, 211.

23 Canada, Official Languages Act (1988).

24 Department of National Defence, "Defence in the 70s: White Paper on Defence," 1971, http://publications.gc.ca/collections/collection_2012/dn-nd/D3-6-1971-eng.pdf.

25 DND, "Defence in the 70s," 46; Gaudet, "Canadian Forces Leadership Effectiveness," 23.

26 Gaudet, "Canadian Forces Leadership Effectiveness," 23.

27 Gaudet, "Canadian Forces Leadership Effectiveness," 23.

28 DND, as cited in Gaudet, "Canadian Forces Leadership Effectiveness," 25.

29 Gaudet, "Canadian Forces Leadership Effectiveness," 25.

30 Graham Fraser, "Notes for an Address to the Officer Cadets of the Royal Military College of Canada," 16 September 2016, http://www.ocol-clo.gc.ca/en/news/speeches/2016/2016-09-16.

31 Gaudet, "Canadian Forces Leadership Effectiveness," 28.

32 Gaudet, "Canadian Forces Leadership Effectiveness," 28.

33 Graham Fraser, "Appearance before the House of Commons Standing Committee on Official Languages," last modified 8 August 2017, http://www.ocol-clo.gc.ca/html/speeches_discours_01032007_e.php.

34 Gaudet, "Canadian Forces Leadership Effectiveness," 29.

35 "The bilingual regions for language of work purposes are defined by Treasury Board and include: the National Capital Region (NCR); the

province of New Brunswick; the bilingual region of Montreal; the bilingual regions of 'other parts of Quebec,' and the bilingual regions of Eastern and Northern Ontario." Department of National Defence, Memo 1211-69 (DOL) *Official Languages Action Plan 2017–2022 / Plan d'action sur les langues officielles 2017–2022*, 2017, 4.

36 DND, *Official Languages Action Plan 2017–2022*, 5.

37 Statistics Canada, "2011 Census of Canada: First Official Language Spoken," catalogue no. 98-314-XCB2011056, http://www12.statcan. gc.ca/census-recensement/2011/dp-pd/tbt-tt/Rp-eng.cfm?TABID=2&L ANG=E&A=R&APATH=3&DETAIL=0&DIM=0&FL=A&FREE=0&GC=0 1&GL=-1&GID=1159230&GK=1&GRP=1&O=D&PID=108264&PRID=10 &PTYPE=101955&S=0&SHOWALL=0&SUB=0&Temporal=2011&THEM E=90&VID=0&VNAMEE=&VNAMEF=&D1=0&D2=0&D3=0&D4=0&D5 =0&D6=0, 11; Statistics Canada, "French and the *francophonie* in Canada," catalogue no. 98-314-X2011003 (2015), 1, https://www12.statcan.gc.ca/ census-recensement/2011/as-sa/98-314-x/98-314-x2011003_1-eng.cfm.

38 These statistics were provided by DND's Directorate of Official Languages for 2017. They did not provide the number of bilingual members at the time.

39 Jungwee Park, *A Profile of the Canadian Forces* (Ottawa: Statistics Canada, 2008), http://www.statcan.gc.ca/pub/75-001-x/2008107/pdf/10657-eng.pdf, 18.

40 Statistics Canada, "French and the *francophonie* in Canada," 9.

41 Eve Haque, *Multiculturalism within a Bilingual Framework: Language, Race, and Belonging in Canada* (Toronto: University of Toronto Press, 2012).

42 Commissioner of Official Languages, *What New Canadians Can Tell Us about the Canada of Tomorrow* (Ottawa: Government of Canada, 2014), 1.

43 Luc Turgeon, Antoine Bilodeau, Alain-G. Gagnon, and Ailsa Henderson, "Attitudes toward Official Bilingualism in Multilingual States: The Canadian Case," International Political Science Association, Montreal, 24 July 2014, 3.

44 Commissioner of Official Languages, *What New Canadians Can Tell Us*.

45 Turgeon et al., "Attitudes toward Official Bilingualism," 5.

46 Turgeon et al., "Attitudes toward Official Bilingualism," 5.

47 Turgeon et al., "Attitudes toward Official Bilingualism," 6.

48 Turgeon et al., "Attitudes toward Official Bilingualism," 8.

49 Unsurprisingly, there is overwhelming support for bilingualism among Canadian francophones, with 94 per cent of French-speaking respondents strongly in favour or somewhat in favour of bilingualism. Turgeon et al., "Attitudes toward Official Bilingualism," 3.

50 Jean-François Lepage and Jean-Pierre Corbeil, *The Evolution of French-English Bilingualism from 1961 to 2011* (Ottawa: Statistics Canada, 2013), 2; see also Turgeon et al., "Attitudes toward Official Bilingualism," 5.
51 Lepage and Corbeil, *Evolution of French-English Bilingualism*, 5.
52 Ellen Bialystok, Fergus I.M. Craik, Raymond Klein, and Mythili Viswanathan, "Bilingualism, Aging, and Cognitive Control: Evidence from the Simon Task," *Psychology and Aging* 19, no. 2 (2004), 290–303; Olof Sandgren and Ketty Holmström, "Executive Functions in Mono- and Bilingual Children with Language Impairment: Issues for Speech-Language Pathology," *Frontiers in Psychology* 6 (2015): 1074. See also Rebecca Callahan and Patricia Gandara, eds, *The Bilingual Advantage: Language, Literacy and the US Labor Market* (Bristol: Multilingual Matters, 2014), for a perspective on the benefits of bilingualism in the U.S. labour market.

8. Race and Belonging

1 There is a small but expanding body of work on the subject of minority Canadian participation in the world wars: Markland Stuart Hunt, *Nova Scotia's Part in the Great War* (Halifax: Nova Scotia Veteran Publishing, 1920), 148–53; Barbara M. Wilson, *Ontario and the First World War, 1914–1918: A Collection of Documents* (Toronto: Champlain Society, 1977), cviii–cxiv; Roy Ito, *We Went to War: The Story of Japanese Canadians Who Served during the First and Second World Wars* (Toronto: University of Toronto Press, 1984); Patricia Roy, "The Soldiers Canada Didn't Want: Her Chinese and Japanese Citizens," *Canadian Historical Review* 59 (1978): 341–58; James Walker, "Race and Recruitment in World War I: Enlistment of Visible Minorities in the Canadian Expeditionary Force," *Canadian Historical Review* 70 (1989): 1–26. Recently, a few scholars have begun to engage with the racialized subjectivities of soldiers transnationally, mainly in the United States and United Kingdom: Victoria Basham, *War, Identity and the Liberal State: Everyday Experiences of the Geopolitical in the Armed Forces* (New York: Routledge, 2013); Vron Ware, *Military Migrants: Fighting for YOUR Country* (London: Palgrave Macmillan, 2012).
2 Gada Mahrouse, "Deploying White/Western Privilege in Accompaniment, Observer, and Human Shield Transnational Solidarity Activism: A Critical Race, Feminist Analysis" (PhD diss., University of Toronto, 2007), 39.
3 Basham, *War, Identity and the Liberal State*, 154.
4 B. Erickson, "'A Phantasy in White in a World That Is Dead': Grey Owl and the Whiteness of Surrogacy," in *Rethinking the Great White*

North: Race, Nature and the Historical Geographies of Whiteness in Canada, ed. A. Baldwin, L. Cameron, and A. Kobayashi, 19–38 (Vancouver: UBC Press, 2012).

5 Yasmeen Abu-Laban and Christina Gabriel, *Selling Diversity: Immigration, Multiculturalism and Employment Equity, and Globalization* (Peterborough, ON: Broadview, 2002); Himani Bannerji, *The Dark Side of the Nation: Essays on Multiculturalism, Nationalism and Gender* (Toronto: Canadian Scholars' Press, 2000); C.T. Mohanty, *Feminism without Borders: Decolonizing Theory, Practicing Solidarity* (Durham, NC: Duke University Press, 2003); Nirmal Puwar, *Space Invaders: Race, Gender, and Bodies out of Place* (Oxford: Berg, 2004); J.M. Alexander, *Pedagogies of Crossing: Meditations on Feminism, Sexual Politics, Memory and the Sacred* (Durham, NC: Duke University Press, 2005); Sherene Razack, *Looking White People in the Eye: Gender, Race, and Culture in Courtrooms and Classrooms* (Toronto: University of Toronto Press, 1998).

6 Mohanty, *Feminism without Borders*, 193.

7 Alexander, *Pedagogies of Crossing*, 135, as cited in Sara Ahmed, *On Being Included: Racism and Institutional Life* (Durham, NC: Duke University Press, 2012), 14.

8 Puwar, *Space Invaders*, 1.

9 Emphasis in original. Ahmed, *On Being Included*, 34.

10 Deborah Cowen, *Military Workfare: The Soldier and Social Citizenship in Canada* (Toronto: University of Toronto Press, 2008), 160.

11 Cowen, *Military Workfare*, 162.

12 Cowen, *Military Workfare*.

13 Cowen, *Military Workfare*, 178.

14 Cowen, *Military Workfare*; Glen Sean Coulthard, *Red Skin, White Masks: Rejecting the Colonial Politics of Recognition* (Minneapolis: University of Minnesota Press, 2014).

15 V. Edwards, "Don't Mention It! The Oka Crisis and the Recruitment of Aboriginal Peoples," Conference of Defence Associations Institute, Student Conference Proceedings, Ottawa, 2002; Yale Belanger and P. Whitney Lackenbauer, eds, *Blockades or Breakthroughs? Aboriginal Peoples Confront the Canadian State* (Montreal and Kingston: McGill-Queen's University Press, 2014).

16 Grazia Scoppio, "Diversity Best Practices in Military Organizations in Canada, Australia, the United Kingdom, and the United States," *Canadian Military Journal* 9, no. 3 (2010): 17–30. According to Scoppio, several programs enhance the participation of Indigenous members in the CAF.

17 Cowen, *Military Workfare*, 170.

18 Cowen, *Military Workfare*.
19 CFPARU, 1975, as cited in Cowen, *Military Workfare*, 170.
20 The Somalia Affair was an important event for the Canadian Forces. See Sherene Razack, *Dark Threats White Knights: The Somalia Affair, Peacekeeping, and the New Imperialism* (Toronto: University of Toronto Press, 2004).
21 Cowen, *Military Workfare*, 188.
22 Cowen, *Military Workfare*, 161.
23 Rick Baldoz, *The Third Asiatic Invasion: Migration and Empire in Filipino America, 1898–1946* (New York: NYU Press, 2011), 8.
24 Peter S. Li, "Deconstructing Canada's Discourse of Immigrant Integration," *Journal of International Migration and Integration / Revue de l'intégration et de la migration internationale* 4, no. 3 (2003): 315–33.
25 Neil Bissoondath, *Selling Illusions: The Cult of Multiculturalism in Canada*, rev. ed. (Toronto: Penguin, 2002), 94.
26 Miles, *Racism*, 79.
27 Bannerji, *Dark Side of the Nation*; Grace-Edward Galabuzi, *Canada's Economic Apartheid: The Social Exclusion of Racialized Groups in the New Century* (Toronto: Canadian Scholars' Press, 2006); Sherene H. Razack, *Race, Space and the Law: Unmapping a White Settler Society* (Toronto: Between the Lines, 2002); Sunera Thobani, *Exalted Subjects: Studies in the Making of Race and Nation in Canada* (Toronto: University of Toronto Press, 2007).
28 Patricia Price, "At the Crossroads: Critical Race Theory and Critical Geographies of Race," *Progress in Human Geography* 34, no. 2 (2010): 147–74.
29 Vijay Agnew, ed., *Interrogating Race and Racism* (Toronto: University of Toronto Press, 2007); Bannerji, *Dark Side of the Nation*; J. Mensah, *Black Canadians Second Edition: History, Experience, Social Conditions*, rev. ed. (Halifax, NS: Fernwood Publishing, 2010); Razack, *Race, Space and Law*; Thobani, *Exalted Subjects*.
30 Bannerji, *Dark Side of the Nation*.
31 Bannerji, *Dark Side of the Nation*, 64.
32 Razack, *Looking White People in the Eye*.
33 David Theo Goldberg, *The Threat of Race: Racial Neoliberalism* (Malden, MA: Blackwell Publishing, 2009).
34 Razack, *Race, Space and Law*.
35 Audrey Kobayashi and Linda Peake, "Racism Out of Place: Thoughts on Whiteness and an Antiracist Geography in the New Millennium," *Annals of the Association of American Geographers* 90, no. 2 (2000): 392–403.

36 Cowen, *Military Workfare*, 20.
37 Homi K. Bhabha, *The Location of Culture* (London: Routledge, 1994); bell hooks, *Outlaw Culture: Resisting Representations* (New York: Routledge, 1994); Trinh T. Minh-ha, "Writing Postcoloniality and Feminism," in *The Postcolonial Studies Reader*, ed. Bill Ashcroft, Gareth Griffiths, and Helen Tiffin, 264–69 (New York: Routledge, 1995); Gayatri Chakravorty Spivak, "Can the Subaltern Speak?," in Ashcroft, Griffiths, and Tiffin, *Post-Colonial Studies Reader*, 24–8; Chris Weedon, *Feminist Practice and Poststructuralist Theory* (London: Blackwell, 1997).
38 Georgina Tsolidis, "Difference and Identity: A Feminist Debate Indicating Directions for the Development of Transformative Curriculum," *Melbourne Studies in Education* 34, no. 1 (1993): 52–3.
39 Robert Gilbert and Pam Gilbert, *Masculinity Goes to School* (Sydney: Allen & Unwin, 1998).
40 Michel Foucault, *The Birth of the Clinic* (London: Tavistock, 1973).
41 Foucault, *Birth of the Clinic*.
42 Weedon, *Feminist Practice and Poststructuralist Theory*.
43 Preston Mulligan, "2 Former Forces Members Say Racism Forced Them out of the Military," CBC Online, 8 May 2018, https://www.cbc.ca/news/canada/nova-scotia/2-former-forces-members-say-racism-forced-them-out-of-the-military-1.4652129.
44 Interview with Ruben "Rocky" Coward, retired Canadian soldier.
45 Interview with Blaze, retired Canadian soldier.
46 Interview with George, Reserve Force, Canadian Forces.
47 Southern Poverty Law Centre, "Active Hate Groups in the United States 2014," *Intelligence Report*, 10 March 2015, https://www.splcenter.org/fighting-hate/intelligence-report/2015/active-hate-groups-united-states-2014.
48 Joe Friesen, "The Data behind Trump's Win," *Globe and Mail*, 10 November 2016, http://www.theglobeandmail.com/news/world/us-politics/white-voters-education-swing-states-the-data-behind-trumpswin/article32784716/. See also Rich Morin, "Behind Trump's Win in Rural White America: Women Joined Men Backing Him," Pew Research Center, 17 November 2016, http://www.pewresearch.org/fact-tank/2016/11/17/behind-trumps-win-in-rural-white-america-women-joined-men-in-backing-him/.
49 Goldberg, *Threat of Race*, 90.
50 Goldberg, *Threat of Race*.
51 Racial microaggressions are defined as "brief, everyday exchanges that send denigrating messages to people of colour because they belong to

a racial minority group." Derald Wing Sue and David Rivera, "Racial Microaggressions in Everyday Life: Implications for Clinical Practice," *American Psychologist* 62, no. 4 (2007): 273. See also Derald Wing Sue, *Microaggressions in Everyday Life: Race, Gender, and Sexual Orientation* (Hoboken, NJ: Wiley, 2010).

52 Interview with Coward.

53 Linda Williams examines how the "playing the race card" emerged historically. She argues that it first got much attention during the 1995 O.J. Simpson trial, where the defence decided to shed light on how the issue of race was essential to this particular case. O.J. Simpson and his defence team were accused by the prosecution of "playing the race card" in a case that until that point was not focused on the racist practices of the Los Angeles Police Department. The prosecution accused the O.J. Simpson's defence team of making "the case a race case" from that point on. For further details of its emergence, see Williams, *Play the Race Card: Melodramas of Black and White from Uncle Tom to O.J. Simpson* (Princeton, NJ: Princeton University Press, 2001).

54 Williams, *Play the Race Card.*

55 Anne A. Chen, *The Melancholy of Race: Psychoanalysis, Assimilation and Hidden Grief* (New York: Oxford University Press, 2000).

56 Daniel Burdsey, "That Joke Isn't Funny Anymore: Racial Microaggressions, Color-Blind Ideology and the Mitigation of Racism in English Men's First-Class Cricket," *Sociology of Sport Journal* 28 (2011): 268.

57 A. Doane, "What Is Racism? Racial Discourse and Racial Politics," *Critical Sociology* 32, no. 2/3 (2006): 255–74.

9. Canadian Muslim Youth and Military Service

1 R. Evans, "A History of the Service of Ethnic Minorities in the U.S. Armed Forces," Center for the Study of Sexual Minorities in the Military (Santa Barbara: University of California at Santa Barbara, 2003).

2 Donna J. Winslow, Lindy Heinecken, and Joseph L. Soeters, "Diversity in the Armed Forces," in *Handbook of the Sociology of the Military*, ed. Giuseppe Caforio, 299–310 (New York: Springer-Verlag, 2006).

3 Evans, "History of the Service"; Winslow, Heinecken. and Soeters, "Diversity in the Armed Forces."

4 Rudy Richardson, Tessa op den Buijs, and Karen van der Zee, "Changes in Multicultural, Muslim, and Acculturation Attitudes in the Netherlands Armed Forces," *International Journal of Intercultural Relations*

34 (2011): 580–91; Winslow, Heinecken, and Soeters, "Diversity in the Armed Forces."

5 Brenda L. Moore, "Reflections of Society: The Intersection of Race and Gender in the U.S. Army in World War II," in *Beyond Zero Tolerance: Discrimination in Military Culture,* ed. Mary Katzenstein and Judith Reppy (Lanham, MD: Rowman and Littlefield Publishers, 1999), 131–2; Maggi Morehouse, *Fighting in the Jim Crow Army: Black Men and Women Remember World War II* (Lanham, MD: Rowman and Littlefield Publishers, 2000).

6 Evans, "History of the Service."

7 Richardson, op den Buijs, and van der Zee, "Changes in Multicultural." See also Laura L. Miller and Charles C. Moskos, "Humanitarians or Warriors? Race, Gender, and Combat Status in Operation 'Restore Hope,'" *Armed Forces and Society* 21, no. 4 (1995): 615–37; and Jan van der Meulen and Joseph Soeter, "Introduction," in *Cultural Diversity in the Armed Forces: An International Comparison,* ed. J. Soeters and J. Van der Meulen, 1–14 (London: Routledge).

8 Richardson, op den Buijs, and van der Zee, "Changes in Multicultural," 581.

9 Cameron Pruitt, "U.S. Government Offers Citizenship through Military Service," *US Army,* 7 August 2009, https://www.army.mil/article/25610/us-government-offers-citizenship-through-military-service.

10 Joseph T. Glatthaar, "African Americans and the Mobilization for Civil War," in *On the Road to Total War: The American Civil War and the German Wars of Unification: 1861–1871,* ed. Stig Forster and Jorg Nagler (Washington, DC: German Historical Institute and Cambridge University, 1997), 202; Evans, "History of the Service."

11 Evans, "History of the Service."

12 L. Berthiaume, "Canadian Military Losing Soldiers at Increasing Rate as Headcount Drops to Level Not Seen in Years," *National Post,* 27 January 2016, http://news.nationalpost.com/news/canada/canadian-military-losing-soldiers-at-increasing-rate-headcount-drops-to-level-not-seen-in-years.

13 John Eighmey, "Why Do Youth Enlist?," *Armed Forces and Society* 32, no. 2 (2006): 307.

14 Eighmey, "Why Do Youth Enlist?," 308.

15 David Segal, Jerald Bachman, Peter Freedman-Doan, and Patrick O'Malley, "Propensity to Serve in the U.S. Military: Temporal Trends and Subgroup Differences," *Armed Forces and Society* 25, no. 3 (1999): 407–27.

16 Segal et al., "Propensity to Serve."

17 Eighmey, "Why Do Youth Enlist?"
18 Eighmey, "Why Do Youth Enlist?," 308.
19 Statistics Canada, "2011 National Household Survey: Data Tables (Religion 108)," http://www12.statcan.gc.ca/nhs-enm/2011/dp-pd/dt-td/Rp-eng.cfm?LANG=E&APATH=3&DETAIL=0&DIM=0&FL=A&FREE=0&GC=0&GID=0&GK=0&GRP=0&PID=105399&PRID=0&PTYPE=105277&S=0&SHOWALL=0&SUB=0&Temporal=2013&THEME=95&VID=0.
20 "Survey Shows Muslim Population Is Fastest Growing Religion in Canada," *National Post*, 8 May 2013, http://nationalpost.com/news/canada/survey-shows-muslim-population-is-fastest-growing-religion-in-canada/wcm/9f900421-b4bc-47c7-bfa0-f737ca997225.
21 Daood Hamdani, "Canadian Muslims: A Statistical Review" (Toronto: Canadian Dawn Foundation, 2015). According to the 2011 National Household Survey, these Canadian cities had a Muslim population of 15,000 or more: Toronto, Vancouver, Calgary, Montreal, Ottawa-Gatineau, Kitchener-Waterloo, London, Hamilton, Windsor, and Edmonton.
22 Young Muslims are self-identified Muslims whose age ranges from eighteen to thirty-four years.
23 Environics Institute, *Focus Canada: Survey of Muslims in Canada 2016*, Detailed Surveys Table (Toronto: Environics Institute, 2016), 2.
24 Inspirit Foundation, "Young Muslims in Canada," 5; Environics Institute, *Focus Canada*.
25 The authors were constrained by research ethics on what we could ask during our focus group session. On an anonymous cue card, participants could answer the question of whether they would join CAF, but were not permitted to provide identifying information. We are unable, therefore, to comment on or clarify differences in gender or ethnicity vis-à-vis the answers provided.
26 Environics Institute, *Focus Canada*, 15.
27 Uri Ben-Eliezer, "Post-Modern Armies and the Question of Peace and War: The Israeli Defence Force in the 'New Times,'" *International Journal of Middle East Studies* 36 (2004): 49–70.
28 Environics Institute, *Focus Canada*, 15.
29 Male and high school–level educated Muslims eighteen to thirty-four years of age were more likely to dislike Canada's foreign policy than other categories of the Muslim population in Canada. Environics Institute, *Focus Canada*, 15.
30 Matthew Rech, "Recruitment, Counter-Recruitment and Critical Military Studies," *Global Discourse: An Interdisciplinary Journal of Current Affairs and Applied Contemporary Thought* 4 (2014): 244–62.

31 Rech, "Recruitment."
32 Joanne Rennick, *Religion in the Ranks: Belief and Religious Experience in the Canadian Forces* (Toronto: University of Toronto Press, 2011). See also Romagnoli, this volume.
33 Department of National Defence, *Strong, Secure and Engaged: Canada's Defence Policy* (Ottawa: DND, 2017), 23.
34 Hamdani, "Canadian Muslims," 26.
35 Eighmey, "Why Do Youth Enlist?"

10. Introspection on Diversity in the Canadian Armed Forces

1 See Chief of Defence Staff, *Duty with Honour* (Kingston: Canadian Forces Leadership Institute, 2009).
2 See in particular, Office of the Auditor General, *Canadian Armed Forces Recruitment and Retention: National Defence (Report Five)* (Ottawa: OAG, 2016).
3 Chief of Defence Staff, *Canadian Armed Forces Diversity Strategy* (Ottawa: Directorate of Human Rights and Diversity, 2016).
4 The negotiations involved establishing the appropriate objectives for representation of women, visible minorities, and Aboriginal People in the CAF.
5 Noting that the Canadian government has published specific Canadian Forces Employment Equity Regulations (SOR/2002-421), which take into account unique aspects of military operational effectiveness. Although commonly assumed by many in uniform, these regulations do not exempt the CAF from reporting data on persons with disabilities (see SOR/2002-421 paragraphs 10.1 and 23); however, the CAF is not required to establish goals to achieve a specified representation of persons with disabilities across the organization.
6 Canadian Armed Forces, *Canadian Armed Forces Diversity Strategy*, 4.
7 Canadian Armed Forces, *Canadian Armed Forces Diversity Strategy*, foreword.
8 Canadian Armed Forces, *Canadian Armed Forces Diversity Strategy*, foreword.
9 Gauthier et al. and *Canadian Armed Forces*; T.D. 3/89; 20 February 1989.
10 For an evaluation of CAF policies related to sexual orientation, see A.C. Okros and D. Scott, "An Update on Canadian Forces Approaches to Gays and Lesbians in Uniform" (Santa Barbara, CA: Palm Center, 2009), and for CAF policies related to gendered identities, see A.C. Okros and D. Scott, "Gender Identity in the Military: Perspectives on Trans Members of the Canadian Forces" (Santa Barbara, CA: Palm Center, 2014).

11 For a summary of the Royal Proclamation and recommended additional readings, see *Royal Proclamation, 1763*, http://indigenousfoundations. arts.ubc.ca/royal_proclamation_1763/.

12 J. Pariseau and S. Bernier, *French Canadians and Bilingualism in the Canadian Forces*, vol. 1, *1763–1969: The Fear of a Parallel Army* (Ottawa: Supply and Services Canada, 1986).

13 Canada, Commissioner of Official Languages, "Linguistic Audit of the Individual Training and Education System Canadian Forces," Department of National Defence Ottawa (Office of the Commissioner of Official Languages, June 2013).

14 M. Deschamps, "External Review on Sexual Misconduct and Sexual Harassment in the Canadian Armed Forces" (report released by the Chief of Defence Staff, March 2015).

15 *Robichaud v Canada (Treasury Board)*, [1987] 2 SCC (2 SCR 84).

16 A.C. Okros, "Rethinking 'Diversity' and 'Security,'" *Commonwealth & Comparative Politics* 47, no. 4 (2009): 346–73.

17 K.J. Gergen and M. Gergen, "Social Constructionism," in *The Sage Encyclopedia of Qualitative Research Methods*, ed. L.M. Givens, 2:171–89 (Thousand Oaks, CA: Sage, 2008).

18 In particular, see the seminal work by Peter Berger and Thomas Luckmann, *The Social Construction of Reality* (New York: Penguin Books, 1966).

19 Brian Selmeski also highlights how Indigenous people across a range of countries have engaged in social construction of the "Indigenous soldier," with examples ranging from Navajo code-talkers through members of ascribed "martial races" (Scottish Highland clans, Gurkha warriors, etc.) to those deemed to possess valuable survival skills (Kalahari "bushmen," Nepalese Sherpas, Inuit peoples). Brian R. Selmeski, "Multicultural Citizens, Monocultural Men: Indigeneity, Masculinity, and Conscription in Ecuador" (PhD diss., Syracuse University, 2007), http://surface.syr.edu/ant_etd/23/.

20 Canadian Armed Forces, "Diversity Strategy," 1.

21 This critique applies to all federal government organizations, as it emanates from the technical details in the Employment Equity Act, including, by omission, section 9.2, which does not require women to self-identify.

22 For a summary of the work conducted, see A.C Okros, "Slide to Unlock: Implication from the Harnessing 21st Century Competencies Project" (Report submitted to Director General Military Personnel Research and Analysis, September 2015).

23 See "The Gender-Fluid Generation: Young People on Being Male, Female or Non-Binary," *Guardian*, 23 March 2016, https://www.theguardian.

com/commentisfree/2016/mar/23/gender-fluid-generation-young-people-male-female-trans; Lauren Booker, "What It Means to Be Gender-Fluid," CNN, 13 April 2016, http://www.cnn.com/2016/04/13/living/gender-fluid-feat/; and Vivian Giang, "Trans-Gender Is Yesterday's News: How Companies Are Grappling with the 'No Gender' Society," *Fortune*, 29 June 2015, http://fortune.com/2015/06/29/gender-fluid-binary-companies/.

24 Curtis M. Wong, "50 Percent of Millenials Believe Gender Is a Spectrum, Fusion's Massive Millenial Poll Finds," Huffpost, 2 February 2016.

25 Chief of Defence Staff, "Leadership in the Canadian Forces: Conceptual Foundations" (Kingston, ON: Canadian Forces Leadership Institute, 2005).

26 F.C. Pinch, L.W. Bentley, and P.P. Browne, *Research Program on the Military Profession: Background Considerations* (Kingston, ON: Canadian Forces Leadership Institute, 2003).

27 Pinch, Bentley, and Browne, *Research Program*.

28 E. Goffman, *Asylums: Essays on the Social Situation of Mental Patients and Other Inmates* (New York: Doubleday/Anchor, 1961).

29 N. Lim, M. Cho, and K. Curry, *Planning for Diversity: Options and Recommendations for DoD Leaders* (Arlington, VA: RAND, 2008).

30 See Okros, "Rethinking 'Diversity'"; K. Davis, "Sex, Gender and Cultural Intelligence in the Canadian Armed Forces," *Commonwealth & Comparative Politics* 47, no. 4 (2009): 430–55.

31 In addition to the chapter by Davis, the assessment of practising assimilation rather than integration is presented in Okros, "Rethinking 'Diversity'"; the theoretical work in this area is presented in J.W. Berry and D.L. Sam, "Acculturation and Adaptation," in *Handbook of Cross-cultural Psychology*, vol. 31, *Social Behaviour and Application*, ed. J.W. Berry, M.H. Segall, and C. Kagicibaci, 291–326 (Boston: Allyn & Bacon, 1997).

32 See the Chief of Defence Staff, "CDS Operation Order: Op HONOUR," August 2015, http://www.forces.gc.ca/en/caf-community-support-services/cds-operation-order-op-honour.page.

33 See Chief of Military Personnel, *Canadian Armed Forces: Progress Report Addressing Inappropriate Sexual Behaviour*, 30 August 2016, http://publications.gc.ca/site/archivee-archived.html?url=http://publications.gc.ca/collections/collection_2016/mdn-dnd/D12-23-2016-1-eng.pdf.

34 This presentation of performance is informed by Judith Butler's *Gender Trouble: Feminism and the Subversion of Identity* (New York: Routledge, 2006).

35 For the rationale presented, see Chief of Defence Staff, *Duty with Honour*; for a critique of the "boss texts" embedded in this document,

see N. Taber, "The Profession of Arms: Ideological Codes and Dominant Narratives of Gender in the Canadian Military," *Atlantis* 34, no. 1 (2009): 27–36.

36 Okros, "Rethinking 'Diversity.'"
37 V.A. Brown and A.C. Okros, "Culture and the Soldier: How Identities, Values, and Norms Intersect in Military Engagements," in *Force & Tool*, ed. H.C Breede, 52–80 (Vancouver: University of British Columbia Press, 2019).
38 Meaning that those in the occupations deemed to be operational or primarily combat trades are awarded the highest social status.
39 R. McLean, "Equal but Unfair: The Failure of Gender Integration in the Canadian Armed Forces " (Master's of Defence Studies paper, 2017).
40 W. Richard Scott, *Institutions and Organizations: Ideas, Interests, and Identities*, 4th ed. (London: Sage, 2014).
41 F.C. Pinch, *Perspectives on Organizational Change in the Canadian Forces* (Alexandria, VA: U.S. Army Research Institute, 1993), 3.
42 Okros, "Rethinking 'Diversity.'"
43 This discussion draws on P.J. Pelto, "The Differences between 'Tight' and 'Loose' Societies," *Trans-actions* 5, no. 5 (1968): 37–40.
44 As developed, updates to this research project and final reports should be accessible at North Atlantic Treaty Organization / Science and Technology Organization, https://www.sto.nato.int/Pages/activitieslisting.aspx.
45 R. Roosevelt Thomas Jr, *Building on the Promise of Diversity* (New York: AMACOM, 2006), xi.
46 M.E. Mor Barak and D. Cherin, "A Tool to Expand Organizational Understanding of Workforce Diversity," *Administration in Social Work* 22 (1998): 51.
47 Q.M. Robertson, "Disentangling the Meanings of Diversity and Inclusion," Working Paper 04-05 (Ithaca, NY: Center for Advanced Human Resource Studies, 2004), 6–7.

Contributors

Stéphanie Chouinard is assistant professor in the Department of Political Science and Economics at Royal Military College (Kingston). She is cross-appointed to the Department of Political Studies at Queen's University. She earned her PhD in political science at the University of Ottawa, for which she was awarded a Vanier Scholarship and a fellowship from the Baxter & Alma Ricard Foundation. Her research interests focus on the relationship between courts and minorities in democratic systems, and particularly the Supreme Court of Canada's impact on the evolution of official-language rights and Aboriginal self-determination rights. She is also interested in territorial and non-territorial autonomy arrangements for linguistic minorities in the world.

Karen D. Davis is a defence scientist with Defence Research and Development Canada, Director General Military Personnel Research and Analysis. Karen holds a master of arts in sociology from McGill University and a PhD in war studies from the Royal Military College of Canada. Karen has published numerous research papers, book chapters, and journal articles related to the negotiation of gender in the Canadian military. Her current research engages a range of themes across the domains of leadership, culture, and gender in military context.

Nick Deshpande, CD, Captain (ret'd), a 2009 graduate in political science from the Royal Military College of Canada, was an officer with the Canadian Forces (Army). He has been published in the journals *Studies in Conflict and Terrorism* (January 2009) and *Risk, Hazards, & Crisis in Public Policy* (February 2011) as well as the *Canadian Military Journal*.

Alistair Edgar is the former executive director of the Academic Council on the United Nations System, faculty associate and Advisory Board member at the Laurier Centre for Military Strategic and Disarmament Studies, and is associate professor of political science at Wilfrid Laurier University. Outside of the university, Dr Edgar is president of the New Delhi–based International Jurist Organization; sits on the Board of the Canadian Land Mine Foundation; and is a former National Board member of the United Nations Association in Canada. He is active on the editorial boards of the Center for Governance and Sustainability (University of Massachusetts Boston) *Issue Briefs* series, and the *Journal of International Peacekeeping*.

Melissa Finn is lecturer in the Department of Political Science and the Department of Global Studies at Wilfrid Laurier University in Waterloo, Canada. Her post-doctoral research at the Balsillie School of International Affairs, University of Waterloo, focuses on citizenship mobilization, political agency, and refusal among ethnic minorities and other marginalized communities in Canada, the Middle East, and North Africa and East Africa.

Tammy George is assistant professor in the Department of Health Science, School of Kinesiology in the area of Critical Sociocultural and Policy Studies in Sport and Physical Activity at York University in Toronto. She completed her PhD at the Ontario Institute for Studies in Education at the University of Toronto, and has previously worked for the Canadian Association for the Advancement of Women in Sport and Physical Activity, the Office of the Auditor General of Canada, and Status of Women Canada.

P. Whitney Lackenbauer is Canada Research Chair (Tier 1) in the Study of the Canadian North and professor in the School for the Study of Canada at Trent University, Peterborough. He is honorary lieutenant-colonel of 1st Canadian Ranger Patrol Group headquartered in Yellowknife with sixty patrols spanning Yukon, Northwest Territories, and Nunavut.

Christian Leuprecht (PhD, Queen's) is Class of 1965 Professor in Leadership, Department of Political Science and Economics, Royal Military College, and Eisenhower Fellow at the NATO Defence College in Rome. He is cross-appointed, Department of Political Studies and the School of Policy Studies, Queen's University, where he is affiliated with both the Queen's Centre for International and Defence Policy and the Institute of Intergovernmental Relations, and adjunct research professor, Australian Graduate School of Policing and Security, Charles Sturt University, as well as the Centre for Crime Policy and Research, Flinders University. A recipient of RMC's Cowan Prize for Excellence in Research and an elected member of the College of New Scholars of the Royal Society of Canada, he is also Munk Senior Fellow in Security and Defence at the Macdonald Laurier Institute. An expert in security and defence, political demography, and comparative federalism and multilevel governance, he has held visiting positions in North America (Bicentennial Visiting Professor in Canadian Studies, Yale University), Europe (Eisenhower Fellow NATO Defence College, Hanse-Wissenschaftskolleg, University of Augsburg), and Australia (Matthew Flinders Fellow, Flinders University), and is regularly called as an expert witness to testify before committees of Parliament. He holds appointments to the board of the German Institute for Defence and Strategic Studies and the Police Services Board of the City of Kingston.

Jacqueline Lopour spent ten years at the Central Intelligence Agency, specializing in South Asia and the Middle East. She was a senior research associate with the Centre for International Governance Innovation, an independent, non-partisan think tank focused on international governance, and currently works at Alphabet's Google in Washington.

Rupinder Mangat is a recent graduate of the PhD Global Governance program at the Balsillie School of International Affairs. Her dissertation focused on the military's use of social media as a strategic communication tool to promote the strategic narratives of the state. She is also interested in climate change movements and has published articles on the fossil fuel divestment movement's use of strategic narratives to get traction on climate action. She has also presented research on the Canadian military's role in domestic disaster management and its implications for public-military relations.

Bessma Momani is professor of political science at the University of Waterloo and senior fellow at the Centre for International Governance and Innovation. She was a non-resident senior fellow at both the

Brookings Institution and Stimson Center in Washington, DC, a consultant to the International Monetary Fund, and a visiting scholar at Georgetown University's Mortara Center. She was a 2015 fellow of the Pierre Elliott Trudeau Foundation and now sits on its board of directors. She is also a Fulbright Scholar. She has authored and co-edited ten books and over eighty scholarly, peer-reviewed journal articles and book chapters that have examined international affairs, diversity and inclusion, Middle East affairs, and the global economy. She is the recipient of research grants from the Social Sciences and Humanities Research Council, International Development Research Council, and the Department of National Defence. Dr Momani is a regular contributor to national and international media on global security and economic policy. She has written editorials for the *New York Times*, the *Economist*, the *Globe and Mail*, the *Toronto Star*, *Newsweek*, and *Time*.

Alan Okros holds a bachelor of commerce from the University of Manitoba and a master of applied science and PhD in industrial and organizational psychology from the University of Waterloo. He is a full professor in the Department of Defence Studies at the Canadian Forces College, Toronto, and academic advisor to the Centre for National Security Studies located at CFC. As a Canadian Armed Forces officer and defence academic, Dr Okros has conducted research and policy development on diversity in the Canadian military for over thirty years. He is the chair of IUS Canada, the Inter-University Seminar on the Armed Forces and Society – Canada.

Bianca Romagnoli is an MA student at the Department for the Study of Religion, University of Toronto. Her research explores the use of the category of religion in the Canadian Armed Forces and how terminology surrounding religion is used in relation to minority traditions and its effects on current service members.

Index